Changing the Guard

Private Prisons and the Control of Crime

Edited by
Alexander Tabarrok

The INDEPENDENT
INSTITUTE

Oakland, California

The Independent Institute
100 Swan Way, Oakland, CA 94621-1428
Telephone: 510-632-1366 • Fax 510-568-6040
E-mail: info@independent.org
Website: www.independent.org

Library of Congress Catalog Number: 2002113328
ISBN: 0-945-999-87-9

Published by The Independent Institute, a nonprofit, nonpartisan, scholarly research and educational organization that sponsors comprehensive studies on the political economy of critical social and economic issues. Nothing herein should be construed as necessarily reflecting the views of the Institute or as an attempt to aid or hinder the passage of any bill before Congress.

10 9 8 7 6 5 4 3 2

Changing the Guard
Private Prisons and
the Control of Crime

Contents

Foreword

CHARLES H. LOGAN

One seldom reads anything but bad news about prisons—there are too many of them, they cost too much, they are crowded, dirty, dangerous, inhumane—and privately operated prisons seem to come in for a lot more than their due share of this bad press. This book brings refreshing relief from the widespread cant and negativity about prisons in general and privately operated prisons in particular.

Kenneth Avio, an expert on law and economics, explores some economic fundamentals of imprisonment and offers a model for calculating costs and benefits, along with a theoretical rationale for predicting increased efficiencies from privatization. Charles Thomas, without doubt the foremost authority on private prisons today, reviews the track record of this industry since its inception in the mid-1980s. He notes that dire predictions of unconstitutionality, strikes, riots, fiscal irresponsibility, and legal unaccountability in private operations have all been wide of the mark. Jan Brakel, who has monitored the performance of both public and private prisons, reviews an extensive literature comparing prisons of each type on cost and quality; he finds a persistent pattern of outcomes favoring the private sector. Finally, Bruce Benson, who has elsewhere built the most theoretically sophisticated and thoroughly documented scholarly case for privatization of every aspect of the legal system, including police, courts, and corrections, has begun to have some second thoughts about contracting out. . . . He's afraid it may be too successful! As an advocate of small government who sees the war on drugs being used as an excuse to expand the power and scope of the state, Benson fears that private prisons may pose an indirect threat to liberty precisely because of the efficiencies the private sector can bring to this aspect of what he has famously entitled the "enterprise of law." So, okay, maybe this book isn't all positive, but it's still refreshing, given that so much written about private prisons is tendentious and ideological, in contrast to the carefully researched contributions here.

Some people are deeply suspicious of the very idea of privately operated prisons. They commonly voice their concern with phrases like "punishment for profit," or "dungeons for dollars." They fear that private companies, because they respond to economic incentives, will somehow be less accountable than "public servants," who supposedly have unselfish motives. This suspicion toward the private operators is an example of having the right attitude for the wrong reason. It is because they exercise authority and power over our fellow citizens that we must be ever vigilant over those who run our prisons—not because they get paid, one way or another, to do so. It makes no difference in this regard whether they are paid with a fee (determined by competition among private companies) or with a budget (determined by negotiations with unionized public employees).

However, while the method of payment makes no difference to the need for accountability, it makes a big difference in the form that accountability will take. Precisely because they must make a profit to survive, and even more precisely because they must compete in order to do so, private prison companies are subject to forms of market discipline that are unknown to monopolistic government agencies with relatively secure budgets, such as departments of corrections. Commercial prisons, unlike the state, cannot indefinitely absorb or pass along to taxpayers the costs of riots, high insurance rates, extensive litigation by maltreated prisoners, cancellations of poorly performed or controversial contracts, or even a wave of adverse publicity. Indeed, some private corrections firms have gone out of business and been replaced by superior performers, but no local, state, or federal correctional agency has ever experienced any equivalent fate. The worst that happens to them is when they are placed under court order, an event that invariably increases their budgets. Thus, while private competitors are rewarded for success and punished for failure, governmental monopolies often face a perverse incentive structure that actually rewards them for failure.

In the final analysis, what counts is how prisons are run, not by whom. Whether they are operated by private companies or by public employees, we want our prisons to be as humane, effective, and efficient as possible. The best way to measure and ensure such performance is through comparison and competition. For the latter to exist, there must be at least some participation by the private sector. This, I think, is the strongest argument for privatization. Comparison of public versus private performance will sometimes favor one, sometimes the other, but continuously making the comparison will always benefit the public.

1

Introduction

ALEXANDER TABARROK

We now have several decades of experience with prison privatization. Judging from the continued controversy, we have learned little from this experience. Yet if we look behind the controversy and evaluate the accumulated evidence, it becomes clear that we have learned a great deal.

We now know that private prisons can be built more quickly, operated at lower cost, and maintained at a quality level at least as high as government-run prisons. To be sure, some private prisons are better than others, and the worst-run private prisons are not as good as the best-run government prisons. But as Samuel Jan Brakel and Kimberly Gaylord demonstrate in chapter 4, we now have ample evidence to say that on average private prisons offer substantial cost savings with no loss in quality. (All the authors in this volume discuss the cost issue but, in particular, see chapters 2 [Avio], 3 [Thomas], and 4 [Brakel and Gaylord].)

You Get What You Contract For

What we have learned from prison and other types of privatization is that you get what you contract for. The early critics of prison privatization were correct that if governments were to write prison contracts solely based on price, then they would get cheap prisons of low quality. What the critics didn't understand, however, was that with experience it has become possible to write effective multi-dimensional contracts that include procedures for the careful monitoring of prison output. Such contracts provide incentives to produce high-quality prisons that are nevertheless considerably less expensive to run than their government counterparts.

The argument that privatization works when governments write multidimensional contracts with procedures for the careful monitoring of output does contain a hint of inconsistency. One of the arguments for privatization is that owing to a lack of incentives, government tends to be inefficient. But if government is inefficient at producing the output of prisons, why should we expect it to be any more efficient at producing prison contracts? This point surely has merit, which is one reason to maintain a distinction between the terms *contracting out* (in which the government remains as buyer of privately produced goods and services) and *privatization* (in which the government exits the industry as both buyer and seller).[1]

The inefficiency of government as a contract writer is a real problem. In his chapter, Charles Thomas points out that in many cases privatization has turned into "governmentalization" because contracts with private suppliers are made so detailed that the private suppliers in essence are required to duplicate public facilities down even to the prisoner meal plan (see also Benson's chapter). It is a tribute to private industry or perhaps an indictment of government production that some meaningful cost savings are possible even in this constrained setup. Nevertheless, "the same only somewhat cheaper" is not an inspiring slogan. The really significant gains from privatization will come when the private sector is given room to innovate and experiment.

It is not easy to write contracts that prevent private firms from taking advantage of government bureaus yet that allow them enough flexibility to innovate. Even for those of us who believe that government is terribly inefficient, contracting out might be worse than government provision precisely because it combines a buyer who has weak incentives to choose carefully with a seller who has strong incentives to cut costs. When a government bureau is the seller, you don't expect it to be very efficient, but that includes not being very efficient at taking advantage of the buyer. (See also Ken Avio's comments on this issue in chapter 2.) That is some comfort, but not much. Scandals involving public prisons are plentiful enough that it is surprising how little attention has been given to the monitoring and disciplining of public bureaus compared to the attention lavished on the problem of monitoring and disciplining private corrections firms.

In principle, contracts that discourage opportunism and allow innovation are easy enough to write *if* the buyer can measure and rate the firm's output; however, prison output is not easy to measure. Prison privatization, however, has encouraged better contract writing, and large strides have been made in accurately measuring output. In chapter 3, Thomas discusses a number of the best practices that have been established, including on-site monitoring, penalty and bonus clauses, and third-party quality assurance by organizations such as the American Correctional Association.

Another solution to the problem of opportunism and innovation is repeated dealings. Private firms' expectation of earning repeat business functions as a check on opportunism and gives government bureaus the confidence to write more open-ended contracts that allow for innovation. The gains from a given prison privatization thus will be larger the more secure privatization is as a staple of the correctional system. The process can work in reverse as well. When public-sector employee unions threaten to "take back" the private prisons through their political power, they threaten the entire enterprise because they make the industry less secure of its future and thus more amenable to opportunism.

The gains from privatization also will increase the more extensive privatization becomes. At present, private firms compete primarily with public bureaus—which is sort of like the repeated competition between the Harlem Globetrotters and the Washington Generals. But to raise the level of the industry truly, it is necessary that the best compete against the best. Competition works better when *all* the competitors have strong incentives to achieve, which means that privatization will be more successful when a large share of the prison industry is privatized, and competition between private firm and private firm is the norm.

Prison Privatization and Airport Security

It is unfortunate that the knowledge we have gained from prison privatization was not put to use in the debate over airline security following the terrorist attacks of 11 September 2001. After the attacks, many people immediately assumed that more government was necessary, and thus the Aviation Security Act, passed just two months after the attacks, federalized airport security.[2] But on 11 September 2001 airport security did not fail at its assigned task, which was to keep bombs and illegal weapons off the plane. It is difficult to see, therefore, how federal workers would have performed better.[3]

No country has more experience with terrorism than Israel, and Tel Aviv's Ben Gurion Airport uses private security firms to do major portions of its security work. In Europe, entire airports increasingly are run by private corporations. The main airports at Athens, Copenhagen, Frankfurt, London, Rome, Vienna, and Zurich, for example, are run by private for-profit firms (Poole and Butler 2001). Government is not absent in these airports, but, as with private prisons, it remains content with defining acceptable levels of output and creating procedures to measure and test the performance of the private companies. As a result, European airports typically are run more efficiently and more safely than their U.S. counterparts.

The Big Picture

The case for private prisons is best evaluated in the context of the case for prisons more generally. Thus, economist Ken Avio opens *Changing the Guard* with an analysis of the broader questions: Does prison pay? What do we know about punishment and recidivism? How large is the crime-deterrence effect? What is an optimal prison sentence? Are too many people in prison or too few? Who should go to prison?

Bruce Benson's chapter demonstrates the importance of these larger issues by questioning a central tenet of pro-privatization doctrine. When prison privatization first became an issue, a common argument was that private prisons would not reduce costs, but that if they did so, cost savings would come at the expense of quality. We now can say with assurance that the evidence rejects this argument. Does it follow that private prisons are therefore desirable? Not at all, argues Benson. The Roman Empire's private tax collectors raised revenue efficiently, but it is difficult to argue that such efficiency benefited the populace. Similarly, Benson argues that precisely because private prisons reduce costs, they should be avoided—so long as they are embedded within a criminal justice system that wastes lives and resources on imprisoning people for victimless crimes. Not everyone will accept Benson's conclusion, but his warning is well taken; private prisons and other innovations in crime control cannot be evaluated without also taking a hard look at who we imprison and why.

The Politics of Prisons

Even if we accept Benson's normative foundations, we may nevertheless favor private prisons over public prisons if the political pressure to expand public prisons is greater than the pressure to expand private prisons. Benson himself notes that public law enforcement bureaucracies have been among the most powerful interest groups lobbying in favor of prison-expanding policies such as the war on drugs. Like other groups, law enforcement lobbies for policies that increase the demand for its services. It is no accident, for example, that every year the California Correctional Peace Officers Association (CCPOA), one of the most powerful unions in California, sponsors the Victim's March on Sacramento. The prison union is also the main backer of such "grassroots" groups as Crime Victims United of California. Similarly, the union was one of the primary funders of the effort to pass California's three-strikes law and is today one of the primary opponents of limiting three strikes only to violent offenders. Not surprisingly, in a fact that reminds us that Benson's concerns are not restricted to private prisons, the union also works to restrict drug policies that promote treatment over imprisonment.[4]

Of course, it is true that the owners of private prisons also would have an incentive to lobby for more prisons, but there is a difference. The CCPOA has a virtual monopoly on prison workers, so any increase in prisons benefits its constituents. But even today there are multiple firms that run private prisons; thus, a firm that lobbies to expand prisons in general (as opposed to lobbying to expand *its* prisons) does more to benefit its competitors than it does to benefit itself. Indeed, as the private-prison industry grows larger, the incentive for any one firm to lobby for general prison-expanding policies declines.[5]

It is difficult to say whether the increase in the demand for prisons brought about by the lobbying of the prison guard union will exceed the increase in the quantity of prisons that would occur with the lower costs brought about by prison privatization. But, even if we accept Benson's concern for the victims of victimless crimes (i.e., those who are imprisoned for such crimes), it still might be the case that private prisons are favored.[6]

Rightly or wrongly, most interested observers of prisons are concerned about costs and quality, not about what an economist would call the general-equilibrium effects of prison privatization on how many people are imprisoned and for what crimes. On the cost score, as the chapters in *Changing the Guard* demonstrate, private prisons are superior to their public counterparts. Why then do we not see more privatization? Charles Thomas, who has plenty of experience in this area, points to politics and the power of special-interest groups, in particular the correctional agencies and the prison guard unions. Of course, he is correct. Prison populations skyrocketed in the 1980s and 1990s, and the pressures this escalation brought to bear allowed for some privatization. Now that prison populations appear to be leveling off, it will be more difficult to overcome the barriers to change. Yet I remain optimistic that the facts in favor of privatization have some weight—not as much as I would like, but enough so that *Changing the Guard* may make a difference in changing public policy toward prisons.

Notes

1. Alas, this book violates this dictum in its title (and elsewhere), but familiarity and alliteration unfortunately have made *prison privatization* the standard term.

2. The Aviation Security Act had a one-year timetable for federalization.

3. Indeed, the most serious failures of September 11 would seem to be attributable to federal workers. The Federal Bureau of Investigation, for example, failed to follow up on a July report from one of its own agents, warning that suspected terrorists might be enrolling in U.S. aviation schools and recommending that FBI agents canvass such schools for suspicious Middle Eastern students. Furthermore, despite ample warnings and precedent, the Central Intelligence Agency failed to consider that suicide attacks might be possible using hijacked airplanes. President Bush was briefed on the possibility of terrorism in the United States and warned of potential al-Qaida attacks just weeks before September 11 but failed to take any action. When civil society fails, the calls come for more government. When government fails, the calls come for still more government. See, "Special Report" 2002.

4. On the prison guard union and California prison politics, see Biewen 2002. The CCPOA's power has not gone unnoticed in the press; see, for example, Macallair and Schiraldi 2000 and "Prison Guard Clout" 2002.

5. Private firms might be able to join together to promote general prison-expanding policies, but absent government intervention (as occurs, for example, with milk-marketing boards), such efforts are rarely successful.

6. Of course, if we reject Benson's normative analysis (and believe, for example, that the drug war should be expanded), then we would have to conclude that the CCPOA's self-interested actions are nevertheless serving the public interest.

References

Biewen, John. 2002. Corrections Inc. *American Radio Works (NPR News)*. Available on-line at http://www.americanradioworks.org/features/corrections/index.html.

Macallair, Dan, and Vincent Schiraldi. 2000. If Your Job Depends on It, Throwing Non-violent Drug Users in Jail Makes Sense. *San Jose Mercury News,* 22 June.

Poole, Robert W., and Viggo Butler. 2001. Fixing Airport Security: 21st Century Strategies for 21st Century Threats: RPPI Rapid Response No. 106. Los Angeles: Reason Public Policy Institute. Available online at http://www.rppi.org/rr106.html.

Prison Guard Clout Endures (editorial). 2002. *Los Angeles Times,* 1 April. 1

Special Report: Did It Have to Happen? 2002. *Time Magazine* (27 March).

2

The Economics of Prisons

KENNETH L. AVIO[1]

Introduction

The number of prisoners in the United States quadrupled in the 1980s and 1990s, rising from 319,000 in 1980 to more than 1.33 million in 2001. The total number of persons in the correctional system—that is, in prison, in jail, or on probation or parole—has more than tripled, rising from 1.8 million to 6.3 million.[2] The correspondingly enormous increase in the direct and indirect costs of the criminal justice system raises the obvious question: Have the outlays been well spent? Does prison pay? Within this larger question lie a host of other questions. What are the alternatives to prison? How extensive should parole and probation be in an optimal prison system? How do prisons fit within the larger criminal justice system? Can and should prisons be privatized? What do we know about recidivism? Do rehabilitation programs or manpower programs work to reduce recidivism? What are the long-run costs of prison on former inmates? With the goal of shedding light on some of these questions, this paper surveys the English-language literature on prisons since Becker's 1968 seminal paper. Discussion is for the most part limited to research by economists or to authors taking a law and economics perspective.

For ease of use the paper is divided into eleven more or less independent sections: (1) Efficiency and Equity; (2) Prisons versus Fines; (3) Parole; (4) Organizational Design; (5) Privatization; (6) Statistical

Models of Recidivism; (7) In-prison Rehabilitation; (8) Manpower Programs for Former Prison Inmates; (9) Criminal and Legitimate Labor Market Opportunities for Former Prison Inmates; (10) Do Prisons Pay?, and (11) Additional Topics and Suggestions for Future Research.

Efficiency and Equity

Economists are typically consequentialists: they assume that consequences alone should be taken into account when making judgments about right (better) and wrong (worse). Adam Smith (1791 [1976], 79, 87–91) suggestively remarked, however, that the private demand for punishment is independent of any consideration of social advantage. (See also Shoup 1964, Thurow 1970, and D. Friedman 2000 on potential conflicts between efficiency and equity.) Ehrlich (1982) permits goals such as retribution to be reflected in the social-cost function, with the degree of retribution related to the number of unpunished offenders and to the severity of their crimes (also see Miceli 1991). However, such grafts rarely seem to capture the considerations that nonconsequentialists deem important. In contrast to economic models, Kantian inspired retributive ("just deserts") models and their cousins (e.g., the restorative theory of Cragg 1992; the Rawlsian-inspired rectification theory of Adler 1991; the restitutive theory of Barnett 1977 and 1998, chaps. 8, 10, 11) generally argue that punishment can and must be justified independent of the consequences as measured in a social-cost function (Duff 1986, 1996). Economic and retributive models have difficulty rationalizing certain policies that most modern penal systems have adopted or at least acknowledged: economic prescriptions appear inconsistent with constitutional constraints on cruel and unusual punishments, and classical retributive models specify punishments that may be insufficient for deterrence. Constitutional contractarian models applied to punishment can rationalize independent constraints on social-cost minimization (Avio 1993a) and will be implicitly assumed in what follows.

Prisons versus Fines

Prisons provide protection services to society by incarcerating criminals. In principle, incarceration might be replaced or supplemented by a cheaper system of fines or corporal punishments or both, which have been the sanctions of choice throughout most of human history. But constitutional constraints in modern democracies restrict corporal punishments, and the limited wealth of most offenders relative to the social value of the harm they create renders sole reliance on fines inefficient (Garoupa 1997; Polinsky and Shavell 1984; Shavell 1985, 1987a, 1987b). Moreover, Levitt (1997) notes that the authorities may not even know the wealth level of offenders and may be unable to distinguish between individuals with different subjective disutilities of prison terms. This latter fact is important because the threat of imprisonment must ultimately lie behind any fine. Because the typical criminal has a relatively low disutility of prison term, "the fine must be low relative to the jail sentence to be incentive compatible" (Levitt 1997, 181). But relatively low fines will induce other types of agents to become offenders. Nevertheless, a case can be made that fines are underutilized in Western societies, although less so in Europe than in the United States. Benson (1996) favors a system of fines as restitution for victims. He argues that the coerced supply of offender labor services may overcome the wealth constraint (at a cost), and the incentive for victims to cooperate in the prosecution of offenders increases the effectiveness of the police and courts. Conversely, the promise of fines as restitution may lead to overzealous prosecution by victims. David Friedman (1999) makes the case against efficient punishment succinctly. "In a world of efficient punishments, somebody gets most of what the convicted defendant loses. It is in that somebody's interest to convict defendants whether or not they are guilty" (S262). For the remainder of this essay, the relative efficiency of incarceration as a criminal sanction is assumed.

Modern prisons may be viewed as multiproduct firms providing incarceration days and rehabilitation opportunities (Avio 1973). The threat of incarceration has a putative general deterrent effect on prospective offenders (D. Lewis 1986), but (unlike fines) incarceration also prevents inmates from committing crimes against those outside the prison walls. This incapacitation effect may be in part offset by an increased number of "new" criminals if the returns to crime increase as incarcerated offenders are temporarily removed from the criminal market (Cook 1977; Ehrlich 1981). The rehabilitation effect acknowledges that a convicted offender's proclivity for crime may decrease as a result of the incarceration experience, as well as by virtue of the fact that age has an independent impact on criminality. The school-for-crime syndrome, criminal stigmatization, and the natural depreciation of human capital while offenders are incarcerated—all pull in the opposite direction. Thus, the rehabilitation effect may more properly be labeled a "training" effect, which from a social standpoint may be either positive or negative. Insofar as potential offenders forecast this effect, the actual discounted expected costs of engaging in current crime may increase or decrease. This result is tempered by the widely held belief that offenders as a whole tend to discount the future more heavily than nonoffenders (Gill 1994; Herrnstein 1983; Wilson 1983, 223–49; Wilson and Herrnstein 1985, 166–72, 416–22).

Parole

Parole (or probation or both) reduces the costs of crime to potential offenders and reduces the incapacitation effect. Parole can also reduce social costs by prompting prison inmates to behave and by decreasing the number of person-days of incarceration supplied. The efficient punishment balances these costs and benefits. In a model of the prison wherein a central authority chooses the optimal lengths of the incarceration and parole periods for individual offenders, Miceli (1994) finds that efficiency typically requires parole—that is, a period of imprisonment followed by supervised release—as opposed to either probation (immediate release) or unconditional release following incarceration.

Miceli also demonstrates that the socially optimal policy varies across individual offenders. Thus, he concludes that a grid-style sentencing scheme such as that promulgated by the U.S. Sentencing Commission, which leaves little room for consideration of the full range of offender-specific characteristics, increases the cost of providing a given level of deterrence. These costs are defined to exclude consideration of retribution and disparities in punishment, factors that in part motivate grid-type sentencing systems (Parker and Block 1989; Parker 1989; see Easterbrook 1983 for a market-analogy argument favoring discretion in sentencing). Garoupa (1996) generalizes Miceli's results somewhat and examines the effects of the U.K. Criminal Justice Act, 1991, which increased the proportion of the sentence that prisoners had to serve before being eligible for parole and also lengthened parole periods. Garoupa finds that the act could have lowered social welfare, although this conclusion is not certain.

Donald Lewis (1979, 1983), in an attempt to provide an empirically feasible guide to parole officials, seeks to establish the optimal parole period given exogenously determined conviction rates *and* original sentence lengths. The maximand consists of "the expected cost to society . . . during the period of the original sentence as a function of the number of months served prior to parole" (D. Lewis 1979, 382). The model is simulated under a range of assumptions concerning the impact of time served on the rate of recidivism.

Neither D. Lewis (1979, 1983) nor Miceli (1994) nor Garoupa (1996) account for the impact and effects of inmate training on the recidivism rate. This consideration requires abandoning Becker's (1968) static framework and including social investments in inmate training as a new choice variable (Avio 1975). Limited progress has been made with highly stylized two-period models of punishment (Burnovski and Safra 1994; Davis 1988; Nash 1991; Polinsky and Rubinfeld 1991; Rubenstein 1980). These papers explicitly or implicitly assume that punishment is by fine, and they ignore recidivistic behavior. The theme of dynamic efficiency and recidivism is taken up in Flinn 1986 and Leung 1995, but in-prison investments in human capital and their impact on recidivism remain unanalyzed. A dynamic general equilibrium model has yet to be developed.

Organizational Design

For organizational reasons, the current criminal justice system is unlikely to be efficient. Miceli's (1994) model, for example, assumes that one agent chooses both length of sentence and length of parole period, but in reality different agents with different mandates choose them independently. Insofar as different agents with different mandates choose decision variables such as overall prison budget, sentence lengths, rehabilitation opportunities, parole release, and so on, it is unlikely that the resulting product mix would be efficient. Because the incentives that motivate the legislature to set the overall prison budget are likely to be quite different than those that motivate judges to set sentence lengths and parole boards to grant parole, the decreed sentence lengths and consequent level of rehabilitation services would not in general be expected to be efficient for any given budget.

A system of indeterminate sentences alleviates the coordination and informational problems inherent in a decentralized penal system (Avio 1973). Decisions about confinement and rehabilitation opportunity become centralized, and maximum incentives for offenders to avail themselves of rehabilitation opportunities are provided. The general rejection of such programs for all but repeat violent offenders is based on several factors: the difficulties with protecting the civil rights of inmates under such a regime; the frustrations arising from several decades of inconclusive research on inmate rehabilitation; a perceived lack of success in predicting recidivism on an individual offender basis; and an increased emphasis on retribution as the primary goal of punishment.

Former Home Secretary Michael Howard (1996) of the United Kingdom proposed a hybrid determinate/indeterminate sentencing scheme reminiscent of "three strikes and you're out" regimes, but retaining the benefits of "marginal deterrence" (Stigler 1970). Under this scheme, repeat violent offenders would automatically receive life sentences with the option of parole. The trial judge would set a minimum period intended to satisfy the need for retribution and deterrence. Once that period is served, penal authorities would determine whether and when the inmate is released. Upon release, offenders would be subject to recall for the rest of their lives.

Tabasz (1974) proposes an earlier two-part penalty scheme. The first part of the sentence targets retribution. It would be determinate, independent of offender characteristics, of relatively short duration, and served in an environment devoid of amenities. The offender would then pass on to a different environment to serve out the second, indeterminate stage directed to the rehabilitation goal. Again, the purpose of the indeterminate sentence would be to align the incentives of the offender with society's goal of minimizing the overall time-discounted social costs of crime. Tabasz suggests that the condition for release be some readily visible sign of achievement on the part of the offender, such as the attainment of a definable educational or vocational training goal.

One difficulty with two-part penalty schemes is that the various penal functions (retribution, rehabilitation, deterrence) do not map separately into the determinate and indeterminate portions of the sentence. Any hardening of the inmate during the first stage would presumably have to be rectified during the second, and because loss of liberty represents an important component of incarceration, the retributive function is in play during both phases. If the first phase is thought to fulfill the offender's debt to society, then imposition of the second may be constitutionally impermissible. Of course, this latter objection might apply to any sentencing scheme that incorporates goals other than retribution, a term (like *debt to society*) of art.

Roper (1986) proposes a different solution to the decentralization-coordination problem. He conceptualizes prison output as the delivery of a crime-free offender over the period of the court-rendered sentence. Taking this period as a constraint, Roper's prison decides whether to keep the offender in custody over the entire sentence or to release him early. As Roper puts it, "the essence of the [prison's] role [is] to assess the risks uniquely associated with the probability of a given offender reoffending" (91). The author goes on to suggest that the prison enter into contracts with prospective parolees; the prisoner agrees to desist from criminal activities for the duration of the sentence, while the authorities provide financial support, rehabilitation services, employment assistance, and so on, and release the inmate on parole. If the released offender violates a contract term, then he or she is liable not only for the new criminal charge, if any, but also for a civil contracts suit. The argument is presented in terms of a private (for-profit) prison, but a state-operated prison might function in the same manner.

Although Roper's proposal represents an interesting attempt to correct the principal-agent problem between the state and the offender, as well as the decentralization problem, substantial difficulties remain. First, because most prisoners possess limited wealth, the scope for fines is limited. Hence, the contract remedy must stipulate a return to prison. This penalty would be independent of any sentence levied for the crime causing the contract violation. But it is unlikely that the courts would permit such a remedy. As an alternative, the contract might promise a financial reward subject to forfeit, which will avoid the dubious remedy of confinement, but may serve to entice prospective offenders into committing crime in the first place. Second, independent of remedy, the courts may not recognize the validity of such contracts; what economists define as a *voluntary* transaction may not fall within the range recognized by the courts, given that the offender is bargaining for his or her freedom and ipso facto is under duress.

Nardulli (1984) and Giertz and Nardulli (1985) take up another aspect of the decentralization problem: judges and prosecutors may treat prison space as a commons (see also Benson and Wollan 1989 and Benson 1990, 1994a, which identify the common pool/property rights nature of the decentralization problem). These authors view judges as rendering inefficiently severe sentences as the result of a free-rider problem emanating from a misalignment of incentives and cost bearing. Citizens of the local government derive benefits (protection and retribution) from longer sentences, which happen to be specified by local authorities. However, a senior level of government may in part shift the costs of providing prison services from one sentencing jurisdiction onto another via prison financing. Thus, the cost of delivery does not fully constrain the local demand for confinement. The tendency to prison overcrowding in the federal part of the system and to underbuilding in the local part follows directly.

The short-run solution Giertz and Nardulli (1985) propose is to allocate total available prison space to individual sentencing jurisdictions, while continuing with the current division of cost and sentencing responsibilities. This solution would to an extent defuse free-riding behavior, but one could imagine disagreeable (and constitutionally questionable) inequities in sentencing arising from the constraint. For example, suppose only shoplifters are predicted to appear before a court during some period, so that relatively harsh sentences are compatible with the given space allocation. Then if an armed robber unexpectedly appears in court, either he will receive a comparatively light sentence, or else one of the previously convicted shoplifters must be released earlier than expected. Unless judges accurately forecast the distribution of upcoming cases, a shortage or surplus of prison space would develop, leading to disparities in sentences actually served for offenders who have committed the same crime. This argument might apply to a senior administrative jurisdiction as well, but the greater number of cases reduces the risk of prediction errors. The *long-run* solution Giertz and Nardulli offer is to hold local jurisdictions responsible for their full share of the cost of incarceration. An alternative is for the senior fiscal authority to impose a mandatory grid sentencing scheme on all courts within its jurisdiction, thus to some extent negating the free-rider problem.

Gillespie (1983) proposes a market for prison space administered by a centralized correctional authority. This market would facilitate the efficient transfer of prison space from local jurisdictions with excess supply to those with excess demand. Jurisdictions comprised of citizens with relatively heavy demand for long-term sentences backed by a willingness to pay would purchase access to penal space from other jurisdictions. Not only would the pricing mechanism overcome the short-run deficits or surpluses, but the market-determined price would signal the social value of new prison space and hence rationalize the construction of new correctional facilities. Gillespie argues that equity concerns can be addressed by altering the initial allocation according to whatever equity criterion is adopted. With appropriately identified prices and initial allocations, this system appears similar to one that gives local authorities a portion of the state budget to spend as they desire: on penal space at the state institution, on space at the local level, or on some other public expenditure (Nardulli 1984).

Would the Gillespie proposal lead to the same results as a centralized sentencing and prison-supply agency? Probably not, simply because income distribution across the local political units would affect the demands for prison space. For given sentences, the various market-oriented systems should cost less than the standard "first-come, first-served," free-rider system. Regardless of the efficiency implications, introducing a market for prison space would predictably exacerbate inequities in sentencing across jurisdictions. Other things being equal, low-income subunits would presumably impose relatively short sentences and sell their space allocations to high-income subunits, which would impose relatively severe sentences. A general equilibrium formulation of Gillespie's model would also have to consider the possibility that offenders might change their geographical areas of operation in response to different expected punishments.

Privatization

A more fundamental argument for the inefficiency of publicly operated prisons stems directly from the theory of bureaucracy/public choice literature. Profit maximization and its concomitant for nonmarket production, cost minimization, may not be adopted as the operational goal of the public entity. Some models of bureaucratic behavior assume or imply cost efficiency, whereas other do not. Niskanen (1971) argues that bureaus seek to maximize bureau size and hence overproduce, but whatever output they provide will be at least cost if the bureau is budget constrained. Other models (e.g., Williamson 1964) posit that bureau heads will optimize with respect to private objectives, and therefore cost minimization cannot be expected. The debate over private prisons typically draws on the latter genre of models, deemphasizing decentralization and informational difficulties. Privatization and the profit motive, it is argued, remove the wedge between output and returns for public employees, thus reducing agency costs.

If a private-prison contract bases remuneration for the corporate prison on the number of person-days of confinement supplied (subject to the provision of some standard level of amenities), the corporate prison has no incentive to provide rehabilitation services, except insofar as the latter act to decrease the current cost of confinement (Schmidt and Witte 1984, 345–46). If rehabilitation works, then the per diem contract is inferior to one that pays the private prison in accordance with the recidivism success of its releasees (Avio 1993b). Indeed, the argument has been made that corporate prisons operating under the per diem contract might perversely seek to stimulate recidivism in order to generate future "customers" (Avio 1991; Gentry 1986). Of course, the incentive structure embedded in the public prison system may be similarly inimical to social welfare. If prison officials wish to maximize their budget, then a clear incentive exists to stimulate recidivism. Similarly, if slack budget constraints and loose monitoring allow prison officials to optimize with respect to private objectives, then few incentives may exist for public prisons to stem recidivism.

Lanza-Kaduce, Parker, and Thomas (1999) offer one of the few papers comparing recidivism rates across public and private prisons. They find in a matched study that recidivism rates are significantly lower in private prisons. Arrest and resentencing rates in the twelve months following prisoner releases, for example, were approximately 50 percent lower for prisoners who had been incarcerated in private rather than public prisons. An earlier study with less-extensive controls also found that recidivism was lower for private than for public prisons (Hatry, Brounstein, and Levinson 1993). Hatry and his colleagues also examined escape rates, statistics on the physical and mental health of inmates, counseling, recreation facilities, and a variety of other quality indicators. They conclude: "for a substantial majority of these performance indicators, the privately operated facilities had at least a small advantage" (1993, 198). The two studies noted above are limited, small-scale studies, which makes firm conclusions tenuous. Nevertheless, they suggest that the burden of proof should be shifted toward those who claim private prisons will always result in cuts in quality.

The debate over private versus public prisons exhibits a peculiar tension, because when some outputs are unobservable and contracts are thus necessarily incomplete, the profit motive can have negative implications. Suppose—following Hart, Shleifer, and Vishny (1997) —that social welfare depends on cost and various quality considerations such as rehabilitation services, respect for prisoners' civil rights, low levels of inmate and guard violence, and so forth. Let some aspects of quality be unobservable (noncontractible). A private, profit-maximizing firm has stronger incentives than a public bureaucracy to reduce costs, but it also has stronger incentive to reduce costs at the expense of unobservable quality. The virtues and defects of private provision thus walk hand in hand.

Some privatization advocates recognize this tension, but their attempts to explain it away are unsatisfactory and reveal the inconsistency: Logan (1987, 39) argues that rather than maximizing profits, private prisons really seek to maximize convenience subject to some minimal profit constraint; Brakel (1988, 34, n. 92) argues that line employees of the private prison, whose actions have the greatest potential to affect postrelease behavior, are too distant from profit centers to act in accordance with the profit motive. But, in the same breath, he gives adherence to the profit motive with the attendant efficiencies as the overarching rationale for prison privatization.

Nevertheless, the argument for public provision, although cogent, is in a precise sense weak. After all, it doesn't follow from weak incentives to cut costs that public prisons will actually invest in rehabilitation services or respect the rights of prisoners or reduce guard violence. Clearly, many public prisons fail on all of these grounds. Moreover, many aspects of quality are observable and contractible. The American Correctional Association (ACA), a private nonprofit group, issues standards for good prisons and accredits prisons that meet them. Standards cover administrative and fiscal controls, staff training and development, physical plant facilities, safety and emergency procedures, sanitation, food service, and rules and discipline. Accreditation involves audits and monitoring. (The ACA also issues standards and certifies correctional workers.) Although not all aspects of quality can be contracted for, ACA standards indicate that many aspects can be contracted. For example, contracts can and have been written that require the prison to be ACA accredited (Hart, Shleifer, and Vishny 1997). Interestingly, ACA standards and procedures are also used to judge and monitor public prisons; accreditation of some public prisons, for example, has been court ordered following prisoners' rights cases.

The increasing popularity of private prisons in policy circles is attributable to more than the general privatization fashion. The modern conceptualization of prisons as a benign warehouse has replaced the "corrections" model in professional circles. This follows the retrenchment on treatment-oriented programs in the 1980s. The prison-as-warehouse conceptualization is consistent with both the static neoclassical and the Kantian-inspired retributive models discussed earlier. In the former, prisons are simply the institutions a society employs to effect the restriction of liberty necessary to attain the efficient amount of crime through deterrence and incapacitation. In Kantian retributive models, justice requires punishment in a rights-respecting environment; the moral autonomy of the individual demands that no attempt be made to "force" rehabilitation. The underlying function of prisons remains the same, a function that might equally well be provided by an institution operating under market incentives.

Noneconomic arguments may ultimately decide the scope that private prisons are allowed to play. A feeling of unease accompanies the thought of government delegating to private individuals the authority to punish (DiIulio 1988). Regulations such as those included in the American Bar Association Model Code and Model Statute for Private Incarceration may be necessary to protect offenders' civil liberties (Robbins 1989). Benson (1990, 1994b, this volume) extends the argument. The potential for success with prison privatization in terms of technological efficiency is so great that once bureaucratic resistance and other obstacles to private prisons are overcome, society may increasingly come to rely on incarceration as a means of social control. For example, special-interest groups may press for the expanded imprisonment of undocumented immigrants to control labor supply (Benson 1994b, 66–72). Prison privatization then poses a threat both to overall allocative efficiency and to individual liberty.

To date, the empirical evidence comparing private and public management of adult secure facilities has been scant and somewhat unsatisfactory. The number of surveys of these studies (McDonald 1990; Sellers 1993, chap. 4; Sichor 1995, chap. 9; Thomas and Logan 1993; USGAO 1991, 1996) nearly equals the number of studies simultaneously reflecting the youthfulness of the private-prison industry (the first adult secure facility went under private management in 1983), the difficulty of the research, and interest in the topic. The studies typically consist of cost and quality comparisons of matched institutions (see, for example, Edwards 1996). Thomas (1996) notes that comparisons of similarly designed facilities will not necessarily account for the cost-saving innovations that private prisons should bring because design is itself a major source of efficiencies. Also, recidivism rates of the various institutions are typically ignored (with the two exceptions noted above, Lanza-Kaduce, Parker, and Thomas 1999 and Hatry, Brounstein, and Levinson 1993). Econometric work on private prisons has yet to be undertaken (see In-Prison Rehabilitation below). Given the growth of the industry (from fewer than 3,000 rated capacity beds under contract in 1983 to more than 145,000 in the United States, the United Kingdom, and Australia at the end of 1999), the time is ripe for sophisticated quantitative research.

Statistical Models of Recidivism

Serving time in prison as well as participating in various prison and postrelease programs may have either a positive or negative effect on released prison inmates and their activities. Nailing down the specifics of the relationships is clearly an important factor in evaluating overall social policies toward crime as well as in evaluating specific programs for incarcerated and paroled offenders. If, for example, predictions of future behavior of individual convicted offenders prove to be sufficiently reliable, then a program of "selective incapacitation" becomes feasible, if not ethically acceptable (Greenwood 1982; Greenwood and Turner 1987). The extensive literature addressing criminal recidivism has for the most part been the preserve of criminologists, sociologists, and psychologists. Here the contributions of economists Peter Schmidt and Anne Witte are significant (also see Myers 1980b, 1983).

In a series of articles (Sickles, Schmidt, and Witte 1979; Schmidt and Witte 1980, 1989; Witte and Schmidt 1977, 1979) and books (Schmidt and Witte 1984, 1988), Schmidt and Witte and their associates exhaustively analyze follow-up microdata on releasees from North Carolina prisons. Because the theoretically relevant dependent variables—time devoted to criminal activity and the intensity thereof—cannot be observed directly, a number of proxy recidivism variables are employed, including the traditional binary "success-failure" measure, categories of crimes leading to reconviction, seriousness of crimes leading to reconviction, total length of prison sentences received during the follow-up period, length of time from release to first arrest leading to conviction, and length of time from release to first return to prison. The authors use different statistical models (qualitative variable models, survival time models) as appropriate for the different dependent variables they studied.

Schmidt and Witte (1984, chap. 3) find that the probability of reconviction is significantly responsive to the number of previous convictions, the youth of the offender, and the offender's use or nonuse of alcohol or hard drugs (45). Surprisingly, none of these same variables is a significant predictor of the type and the seriousness of offenses for which reconvictions are obtained. On the other hand, the type and the seriousness of previous offenses are found to be related to the type and seriousness of subsequent convictions, respectively, but not to the overall probability of reconviction.

Using two samples, Schmidt and Witte (1984, chap. 5) also analyze a more refined indicator of the seriousness of new offenses, the total length of time sentenced for recidivist offenses. The samples are those used in the previously reported research and a cohort group consisting of all individuals released in North Carolina during the first six months of 1975 (twenty-five- to thirty-one-month follow-up). In both samples, the total length of time sentenced for recidivist offenses increases with the youthfulness of the offender, a history of alcohol abuse, the number of previous convictions, crimes against property, and unsupervised release (Schmidt and Witte 1984, 73).

The authors note that the significance of alcohol and drug abuse as a predictor of reconviction and of the length of reconviction suggests that programs to treat these problems would be very beneficial if they worked. Unfortunately, few such programs appear to work well (Schmidt and Witte 1984, 83). Parole and work-release programs also appear to reduce recidivism, but Schmidt and Witte provide few details on the work-release program or on the caseload of parole officers. How much supervision is necessary to reduce recidivism? Although it is difficult to obtain data through time, anecdotes suggest that supervisor caseload has failed to increase proportionately with incarceration rates (recall that Schmidt and Witte use data from the late 1960s and early 1970s). In 1994, some 11,500 line officers supervised 2.9 million adult probationers for an average case load of 258 adult offenders per direct supervisor (Petersilia 1997, 3). Given these high caseloads (Petersilia suggests that a caseload of 30 probationers per line officer may be closer to ideal), it is less surprising to learn that in recent years a full 10 percent of probationers cannot be accounted for by the system because they have "absconded."[3] Although theoretical models (see the discussion in section 3) indicate the usefulness of parole, further empirical work on the effectiveness and cost of parole is necessary to formulate sound public policy.

A second set of models employed by Schmidt and Witte treat survival time—the length of time from release to recidivism. Not only is this variable of interest in itself, but ignoring information on length of time to recidivism (however defined) is statistically inefficient. The authors' extensive analyses (the present discussion is limited to Schmidt and Witte 1988) utilize various formulations found in the increasingly sophisticated criminogenic literature (Carr-Hill and Carr-Hill [1972] apparently were the first authors to apply survival models in this context) as well as innovations of their own. The data consist of two cohorts of approximately 9,500 individuals each released from all state prisons in North Carolina in separate twelve-month periods, with follow-ups ranging from forty-six to eighty-one months. Data limitations, as well as the needs of the correctional authorities supplying the data, dictated the dependent variable: the length of time from release to return to prison. (The length of time from release to first rearrest leading to conviction is analyzed in Schmidt and Witte [1984, chap. 7]). Among the important results are that the length of the sample incarceration increases the probability of a return to crime and shortens the time spent outside of the prison system. These latter results appear consistent with the school-for-crime theory (see Myers 1980b for a qualitatively similar conclusion with a sample of parolee data), but it is difficult to say whether the criminals with longer sentences learned more in prison and thus returned to a life of crime, or whether the length of the previous sentence simply indicates that something about these individuals disposed them to a life of crime.

Although Schmidt and Witte's predictions (1988, 15) are generally superior to those elsewhere in the literature), the authors emphasize that their best models (false positive rates of 47 percent and false negatives of 28 percent) are unsatisfactory for implementing a policy of selective incapacitation. One can conclude that there is value in using sophisticated models in predicting recidivism for random samples of released offenders, but that the models are not yet sufficiently refined for application to individuals.

Schmidt and Witte (1988, 150) note that further statistical experimentation and refined technique might lead to better predictions. Another suggestion is to take more seriously the economic model of crime by including explanatory variables measuring the certainty and severity of punishment as well as environmental variables representing legitimate and illegitimate opportunities. Typically models of recidivism assume that police activity and other environmental stimulants of crime (such as the unemployment rate) are constant during the observation period. But suppose that during the follow-up period there is variation across the relevant geographic jurisdictions or over time in police activity or both. Further suppose that these differences lead to variation in the probability of arrest. The economic model suggests that the pattern of criminal behavior of released inmates as well as that of individuals with no previous criminal record will be affected. Prediction accuracy might be impaired (and the model misspecified) if the standard criminal justice control variables are excluded. Data limitations may intrude (Schmidt and Witte 1988, 85). But even if the communities of residence of released offenders are unknown to officials, risk and punishment variables can probably be constructed on an aggregated geographical basis for each period during the follow-up. Examples of survival-time recidivism research employing environmental variables are provided by Visher, Lattimore, and Linster (1991) in their study of paroled California youths and by Kim, Benson, Rasmussen, and Zuehlke (1993) in their examination of Florida drug offenders. On a more micro level, Schmidt and Witte note that some of their research results might be attributable in part to police and prosecutors targeting offenders with certain personal characteristics, as well as to the characteristics themselves affecting criminal activity (1988, 9–11). Sorting out what causes people to commit crimes and what causes them to be arrested for crimes, which are hardly the same things, remains an important part of the research agenda in the economics of prisons.

In-Prison Rehabilitation

Psychologists, criminologists, sociologists, and public policy commentators have contributed to the extensive literature on the rehabilitation of convicted offenders. This topic shades into a discussion of the overall causes of crime. No attempt is made here to address the larger question, nor should the discussion in this section be considered a survey of anything but a select subsample of the rehabilitation literature. The limited number of economists' contributions to the direct evaluation of rehabilitation programs is taken up in this section and the next.

On the important question of research design, laboratory-like experiments comparing outcomes for randomly selected program and control groups are generally not possible in the criminal justice context (some exceptions are discussed later in this section). Researchers typically are forced to resort to quasi-experimental designs, which designate "a group of individuals (the comparison group) that is as much like the group of program participants studied as possible" (Grizzle and Witte 1980, 259). Alternatively, one can employ a "predicted versus actual" method in which the results of previous studies are used to predict what the behavior of a group would have been had they not entered the program; comparing the predicted with the actual then allows for program evaluation. The difficulty in both cases is that to control properly for the relevant variables the researcher must have in mind an underlying model of criminal and recidivistic behavior. Unless the true model is known, it will always remain possible that the control group or the statistical model used to predict behavior differs in some important way from the treatment group.

As we turn from methodological to substantive issues, what kinds of in-prison rehabilitative programs work, if any? The "nothing works" doctrine initiated in Martinson's well-known paper (Martinson 1974, previewing Lipton, Martinson, and Wilks 1975) ushered in an era of pessimism in penology. After reviewing the results of 231 papers (the majority dealing with programs of a therapeutic nature) published between 1945 and 1967, Martinson concluded that there was little evidence that rehabilitation programs work. The Panel of Research on Rehabilitative Techniques of the National Research Council (U.S.) restated Martinson's conclusion in a similar sweeping generalization: "it appears that nothing works or at least that there have not been any consistent and persuasive demonstrations of anything that works" (Sechrest, White, and Brown 1979, 27). This conclusion has not gone unchallenged (e.g., Gendreau and Ross 1987; Halleck and Witte 1977; Mair 1991), but "nothing works" remains a part of penological lore.

One response follows the lead of the second report of the Panel of Research on Rehabilitative Techniques (Martin, Sechrest, and Redner 1981) in questioning whether the strength and degree of implementation of in-prison programs are sufficient for definitive tests. Lattimore and Witte (1985, responding to Englander 1983; also see Englander 1985) note that many vocational programs are poorly designed, rather weak in intervention (e.g., training programs of short duration), and poorly and incompletely implemented (e.g., inmates drop in and out of programs). Lattimore, Witte, and Baker (1990) attempt to evaluate a vocational rehabilitation program for young property offenders in which care is taken to address these difficulties. The program consisted of six integrated in-prison subprograms (table 1, 120), any or all of which may have been completed by members of the sample. The sample consisted of 591 selected North Carolina male inmates ages eighteen to twenty-two enrolled in the umbrella project sometime between June 1983 and May 1986. Prison officials randomly partitioned the subjects into an experimental group and a control group. The two groups differed in their exposure to the various parts of the umbrella project and in their completion records for the various component parts of the project. Only 16 percent of the experimental group began all of the program components—that is, the umbrella program was only weakly implemented. Nevertheless, some programmatic effects were still evident: an examination of survival times indicates that the program reduced postrelease arrests by approximately 10 percentage points for releasees who had been out more than approximately six hundred days (128, fig. 2). Moreover, the survival history of those who completed a vocational program was significantly better than for those who did not, a result the authors could not account for in terms of their sociodemographic and criminality measures. Unfortunately, one of the coauthors of the original paper recently cast doubts on these results: "unpublished longer-term follow-up results show no significant differences in criminal activities between the experimental and the control groups" (Witte 1997, 226).

In summary, some well-funded, carefully implemented programs may have some short-term and even some longer-term beneficial effects. Nevertheless, especially when we take into account the realities of program implementation, the empirical evidence indicates that if "nothing works" is too strong an assessment, then "nothing works well" is quite justifiable.

Manpower Programs for Former Prison Inmates

Perhaps in part in response to the "nothing works" dialogue, economists' attention has largely shifted from in-prison rehabilitation programs to assistance programs for released prisoners. Based on a review of various labor market studies of parolees as well as on his own study utilizing a data set (collected and analyzed by Evans 1968) consisting of 327 male parolees from Massachusetts penitentiaries in 1959, Cook (1975) notes that (1) "discrimination is not an important factor in the work experience of parolees" (18); (2) the quality of jobs, not the quantity, is crucial in determining released offenders' employment record; (3) success in the job market for released offenders leads to lower recidivism rates; and (4) in-prison therapeutic, educational, and job-skills programs have little effect on postrelease success (see also Hardin 1975; Marks and Vining 1986). Even though remedial education and vocational training programs "have demonstrated success in providing prisoners and parolees with measurably increased academic and vocational skill" (Cook 1975, 47–48), they have typically not been successful in reducing recidivism rates. (Witte and Reid [1980] obtain similarly pessimistic results in examining the labor market performance of a group of former inmates not limited to parolees.) Long and Witte's survey is unequivocal: "Evaluations of vocational training and remedial education programs in prison, parole, or probation settings have almost uniformly found that such programs have insignificant effects on both labor market performance and criminality" (128). The hypothesis is that the programs have not improved offenders' job opportunities, even though they have improved their skill levels. Released offenders either are unable to find the better jobs, or if they do find jobs, they cannot keep them because of inadequate preparation for the demands of such work. Cook (echoed in Witte and Reid 1980) concludes that the evidence suggests job search and on-the-job training programs should be given priority. Whether the prospect of improved legitimate job opportunities will act to reduce the initial deterrent effectiveness of punishment remains a concern. Cook notes that increasing the probability of punishment may be an appropriate offset. Such a substitution will not be costless, however, which again points to the need for an analysis stressing the dynamic and general equilibrium modeling of crime.

Borus, Hardin, and Terry (1976; also see Hardin 1975) utilize a quasi-experimental design to evaluate a Michigan job placement program for selected parolees. The authors find that program participants did not fair better in terms of various indicators of job market success, and in fact "fared worse, on the average . . . as to hours employed, gross earnings, and take-home pay" (1976, 394).

Apparently no attempt was made to compare directly the recidivism experience of program participants with that of nonparticipants. This aspect was addressed in Mallar and Thornton (1978), which yielded a similarly pessimistic conclusion.

Mallar and Thornton (1978) report on the Living Insurance for Ex-Offenders (LIFE) program, seeking to establish whether transitional aid programs and job placement assistance for former prisoners reduce recidivism for theft crimes (also see Myers, 1983). A nonrandom sample of 432 high-risk prisoners from Maryland's state prisons released into the Baltimore area in the early 1970s was randomly partitioned into four treatment groups: one receiving direct financial aid (sixty dollars per week for three months); one receiving job placement assistance (for up to one year); one receiving both; and a control group receiving no assistance of either type. The authors conclude: "The provision of financial aid led to a large and statistically significant reduction in theft rearrests, while the provision of job-placement services proved to be singularly ineffective in reducing recidivism" (1978, 224). Subjects in the financial aid group were less likely to be employed full-time, especially during the first quarter after release, and more likely to be enrolled in school or a training program. The authors speculate that this apparent investment in human capital may widen the differential in recidivism response over time. It also appears that the transitional aid group achieved higher-paying jobs, leading the authors to suggest that transitional aid permitted subjects to invest more in a job search. Finally, the authors demonstrate the benefit/cost viability of the direct aid program.

Broadly similar results with respect to the job placement component were obtained in an expanded version of the LIFE program: the Transitional Aid Research Project (TARP; see Rossi, Berk, and Lenihan 1980). This program applied a controlled experimental design to all released inmates (not just to parolees) from Georgia and Texas state prisons. The transitional aid component also appeared to be unsuccessful, but the authors attribute this failure to work disincentive effects not in place for the LIFE program (for additional comment, see Long and Witte 1981, 129–30, and Englander 1983, 28–29). Again, these studies do not address the

ospect of transitional financial aid might
l deterrent effectiveness of punishment.
rted Work Program (Couch 1992;
Hollister, Kemper, and Maynard 1984) placed subjects in a variety
of supportive and subsidized work environments commensurate
with their backgrounds. The emphasis was on developing work
habits in accordance with a graduated stress concept of job market
preparation. As one author describes it, "Stress within the working
environment increased gradually during the training period until it
simulated the workplace norms of the private sector. At that point,
not more than 18 months after entry, individuals who received the
services . . . had to attempt a transition to unsubsidized employment" (Couch 1992, 381). During the period from March 1975
to July 1977, some 2,276 ex-offenders, one of four subject groups,
were randomly assigned to either an experimental group or a control group, with regular nine-month follow-ups extending to three
years. All subjects had been incarcerated sometime during the six
months preceding enrollment in the program, and the average
length of time served was four years. Less than 10 percent of this
group exhausted the allowable time in the program. The results
indicate no reduction in recidivism among the ex-offender experimental group as a whole and no measurable labor market effects
(Piliavin and Gartner 1984). An eight-year follow-up (Couch 1992)
indicates no improvement in labor market success for disadvantaged
youths (the ex-offender group did not receive the long-term follow-up). Other large-scale studies (for example, the Mathematica
Policy Research, Inc. study of the Job Corps [Mallar et al. 1982]
and the Abt Associates review of the Job Training Partnership Act
[JTPA] programs [Orr et al. 1996]) do not identify a former inmate
subgroup for analysis.

As with in-house rehabilitation programs, the evidence on
postrelease programs for former inmates can be summarized as
"nothing works well." Certainly the evidence suggests that a magic
one-size-fits-all rehabilitation bullet does not exist. These programs
tend to be "successful" only when evaluated on the basis of limited
(and variable) outcome measures, and even then the magnitudes
involved are typically small. Finally, it bears noting that even if

"something works," in the limited sense of achieving a beneficial measured outcome, it may still be the case that such programs are too expensive to be worthwhile or that the resulting added incentives for individuals to enter the criminal market make the programs undesirable on net.

Criminal and Legitimate Labor Market Opportunities for Former Prison Inmates

Results obtained from specific in-prison rehabilitation programs and manpower programs for released offenders have been weak and inconsistent. Coupled with the substantial increase in the proportion of the U.S. population incarcerated during the 1980s and 1990s, these results make the wide-scale implementation of costly rehabilitation programs unlikely. Consequently, recent economic research focuses on the effects of incarceration on the subsequent criminal and legitimate labor market activities of released offenders independent of specific implemented prison programs. Various kinds of empirical information and estimation strategies are employed.

Grogger (1991) uses panel data on California arrestees to attempt to determine the effect of imprisonment on future criminality and to estimate the incapacitative effect of prison. Because estimates of the proportion of all young California males arrested at some point reach as high as one-third, the sample of arrestees offers a more representative picture than data on prison releasees alone (see Witte 1980 and Myers 1983). Grogger's empirical results suggest that imprisonment has a criminogenic effect ("each additional month spent in prison increases average arrests by about 2 percent" [1991, 304]), which may be attributed to either negative training or negative labor market signaling. Moreover, under the assumption that sanction expectations are formed entirely from one's own historical involvement with the justice system (that is, "specific" as opposed to "general" deterrence), "the criminogenic effect of imprisonment is nearly three times as great as the deterrent effect" (Grogger 1991, 304). Prison is also found to have an incapacitative effect—each month reduces the average individual's criminal activity roughly in proportion to the time spent in prison. As Grogger (1991, 299) notes, the interpretation of the results depends crucially on whether arrests are an appropriate measure of criminal activity. In addition, unobserved fixed characteristics might also bias the results. For example, a penchant for violence might be correlated both with longer sentences for any given crime category and with greater postincarceration criminality. The following studies address this type of complication.

Freeman (1992) employs the National Longitudinal Survey of Youth and other surveys to estimate the long-run impact of incarceration on future legitimate employment of young U.S. males. After standardizing for observed personal characteristics of individuals in the sample, he finds that incarceration in 1980 had a substantial negative impact on whether the individual was employed in any given subsequent year (to 1988) and on the total number of subsequent weeks worked. "For the entire eight-year period, incarceration in 1980 reduced subsequent work weeks by 27 percent for blacks and 22 percent of all youth" (1992, 217). Only one-third of the negative employment effect is attributed to the exclusionary impact of current incarceration on current employment. Freeman tests whether his results might be owing to some unobserved characteristic correlated with both criminality and labor market fitness (such as functional illiteracy) by utilizing data on individuals' pre- and postincarceration employment experience. Adapting an omitted variables regression model, Freeman finds that incarceration continues to have a substantial impact on subsequent employment and also earnings, although the impact is reduced by up to one-half (1992, 225). He cautions that these results do not imply that a random person assigned a criminal record would necessarily have the predicted subsequent employment experience. Rather, the statistics indicate what happened to those who *chose* crime. In other words, the data remain consistent with rational decision making by far-sighted individuals facing the risk of incarceration and the potential loss of legitimate income.

Freeman's results may be compared with those in Grogger 1995. The treatment sample consists of young California males first arrested prior to 1985, and the comparison sample consists of those first arrested after 1984. Quarterly data on earnings and employment for each individual from 1980 through 1984 are merged with his particular criminal justice history. Although arrestees have significantly lower earnings than nonarrestees, Grogger finds that most of this difference is caused by a correlation between criminality and labor market fitness (people who have poor opportunities in the labor market are more likely to be arrested). Grogger claims that when this effect is corrected for, arrests and short-term jail sentences per se have only a small impact on earnings, an effect that quickly dissipates. That is, an arrest or a short jail term does not greatly reduce postarrest or postjail labor market earnings relative to what they would have been without an arrest or jail term. (Recall that Freeman found quite significant and long-lasting effects on both employment and earnings.) The difference between the two studies may be owing to the differences in sentence length, which are longer in Freeman's sample. Long sentences may have long-lasting effects, whereas short sentences have relatively short-lasting effects. Long sentences may have longer effects because negative training received in prison increases the payoff to crime either by reducing noncriminal skills or by increasing criminal skills. Because Grogger focuses on short-term prison sentences, he cannot pick up the effect of negative training, which takes time. Taken together, Grogger's and Freeman's results suggest that the labor market is relatively forgiving of arrests and incarceration per se (but see later in this section on labor market stigma for white-collar crime), but long prison terms make prisoners less able or less willing to renter the job market upon release. An interesting implication of either of these findings is that, all else equal, it is more desirable to increase certainty of punishment than length of time punished because certainty of punishment can be increased without increasing negative training for a given offender. It should be noted that neither of these two studies constructs empirical measures of actual sentence lengths served or of the quality and quantity of rehabilitation opportunities available in prison.

Other papers dealing with the impact of incarceration on earnings and employment stress the independent deterrent effect of criminal stigmatization, a byproduct of contact with the criminal justice system. Rasmusen (1996) presents two models of criminal stigmatization. The moral-hazard model has employers unwilling to pay the market wage to ex-offenders because of the offenders' lower net productivity (contribution to product less thievery from the firm and other destructive behaviors), whereas in the adverse-selection model criminal records signal exogenously lower *gross* productivity (for example, lower intelligence). Applied to the economics of prisons, the moral-hazard effect reflects negative training: time spent in prison increases offenders' relative productivity as criminals. Any deterrent effect of stigmatization would be expected to be greater for those with the highest education and greatest job market prospects. Lott (1992b) finds for a sample of U.S. federal larceny and theft offenders (typically involving government property or postal offenses) that "a one-month increase in sentence length causes a 5.5 to 32 percent greater reduction in postconviction income" (597). Waldfogel (1994b) similarly employs a sample of white-collar criminals to demonstrate that the reduction in job market prospects from imprisonment is owing primarily to stigma and not to stalled experience growth or to job displacement. Waldfogel cautions that his results may not be generalizable to offenders whose preconviction jobs did not involve substantial trust and whose convictions were for crimes other than fraud and larceny. (For example, Lott [1992a] finds that longer sentences do not affect the postimprisonment legitimate income of drug offenders.) To the extent that crime becomes more concentrated in an underclass composed of individuals who have little in the way of job market aspirations and opportunities, the deterrent effect of any criminal stigma may become insignificant. As well, the stigma measured by the disapproval of one's friends and neighbors will probably fall as the proportion of the population that is incarcerated increases, thereby decreasing the deterrent effectiveness of punishment (Freeman 1996, 32–33). Other papers more relevant to the impact of conviction as opposed to incarceration include Lott (1990), Freeman (1986), Grogger (1992), Waldfogel (1994a), and Nagin and Waldfogel (1995).

Do Prisons Pay?

Whether or not prisons pay is perhaps the most important public policy issue concerning the economics of prisons. Tabasz (1975), one of the first to try to answer this question systematically, constructs a linear-programming model of the U.S. Federal Bureau of Prisons. Although unmodified linear programming imposes severe technology constraints, interesting questions can be addressed using this technique. The goal is to allocate different types of offenders to different types of institutions and to different sentence lengths in a manner that maximizes net social benefits subject to the capacity of the prison system and to the flow of convicted offenders. In all, 2,700 decision variables are specified. Only benefits to incapacitation and rehabilitation are imputed, and the capital costs of prisons are ignored. The results indicate that prison resources should be concentrated on relatively young and dangerous offenders: inmates older than forty-five years of age should be assigned to "probation" (immediate release). The model cannot directly indicate how many resources should be allocated to the prison system, but it does give an approximation to the benefit-cost ratio potentially generated by prisons (8.51 in the "standard" version of the model applying 1973 data [Tabasz 1975, 129]). This estimate, which at face value rationalizes the buildup in prison capacity that began in the United States in the 1970s (Blumstein 1995), should not be taken too seriously. The relatively primitive nature of the data available to Tabasz required strong assumptions, in particular those related to the rates of crime commission, the social costs of crime, and the rehabilitative effects of incarceration. The methodology also imposed an interpretive constraint: the results do not necessarily reflect actual net benefits attained, but rather the *potential* benefits if decision variables are chosen optimally. Nonetheless, this study anticipates later attempts to evaluate the prison system as a whole.

Piehl and DiIulio (1995) review more recent work on whether prisons pay (see also see DiIulio and Piehl 1991). The idea in much of the recent literature is to use self-reports of incarcerated offenders to estimate the amount of crime such offenders would have committed if not incarcerated and then, after pricing these crimes, compare the "saved" social costs attributable to incarceration with the direct costs (capital and operating) of incarceration. The self-reports come from surveys constructed to minimize biased and inaccurate reporting. (The earliest reliable surveys were completed by the Rand Corporation; see the discussion in Visher 1986.) The survey results leave little doubt that on average prison pays. The "on average" qualifier is important. The distribution of offender reports is heavily skewed. The median prisoner, for example, reports engaging in 12 crimes in the year before imprisonment, but the mean report is 141 crimes—thus a minority of criminals account for a large majority of crime (DiIulio and Piehl 1991) The benefit-cost ratio for imprisoning nondrug criminals is 64.02 at the mean, which means that the imprisonment of a criminal who commits 141 crimes a year saves society sixty-four dollars for every dollar it costs to imprison him. But the median criminal commits only 12 crimes a year, and the benefit-cost ratio for that criminal is only 2.8. By definition, 50 percent of criminals commit fewer crimes than the median criminal, so substantial numbers of criminals are being imprisoned even though the benefit-cost ratio for doing so is relatively low. For criminals at the twenty-fifth percentile (25 percent commit fewer crimes, 75 percent commit more crimes), the benefit-cost ratio is less than 1, and at the tenth percentile it is only 0.07, suggesting that society would save considerably more by paroling these criminals than by imprisoning them. The difficulty is in estimating which criminals are mean criminals and which are only median. Clearly, one cannot use self-reports to assign prison time! Nevertheless, given the large differences in the benefit-cost ratios for imprisoning mean and median criminals, even imperfect estimates of crime potentiality can usefully distinguish those criminals for whom parole would be a better option for society than imprisonment. We know, for example, that age markedly affects the proclivity for crime (Blumstein and Cohen 1987), so when prisons are at capacity, it pays to parole older men in order to imprison younger men.

A critical assumption underlies the calculated benefit-cost ratios noted above. It is assumed that if a prisoner would have committed 12 crimes if not in prison, then imprisoning that criminal reduces the number of crimes by 12. This "incapacitation assumption" is not always correct. Imprisoning a drug seller, for example, will not reduce the amount of drugs sold by that seller's sales because the imprisoned drug seller will be replaced on the street by others. Given that most people are willing to pay less to avert a drug sale than an assault or a robbery, the benefits of imprisoning drug sellers (and users) are low to begin with and become much lower once it is recognized that imprisoning drug offenders does not substantially reduce the number of drug crimes. Thus, Piehl and DiIulio (1995) write that "[P]rison pays. But prison does not pay for all prisoners. . . . Most emphatically, it does not pay for all convicted drug felons. The public and its purse could benefit if 10–25 percent of prisoners were under some other form of correctional supervision or released from custody altogether" (21).

For other crimes, the incapacitation assumption is probably close to the truth. Imprisoning a rapist, for example, is unlikely to result in a significant replacement effect. The incapacitation assumption becomes more problematic when the crime has a substantial monetary aspect such as burglary or auto theft. The question then becomes: what is the net deterrent from more imprisonment? The answer depends on numerous variables not accounted for in the analysis, such as legitimate labor market opportunities and police resources, thus making inferences based solely on prisoner surveys unreliable. Note that the net deterrent from imprisonment might be lower or higher than the pure incapacitation effect. In the drug example, it is lower because an imprisoned drug seller is probably replaced quite quickly on the streets. The public imprisonment of Michael Milken for violation of the insider trading laws, however, probably reduced insider trading by much more than the number of violations attributable to Milken himself. Similarly, rapists are unlikely to be replaced, but they can be deterred. Thus, benefit-cost ratios based on incapacitation can either understate or overstate the benefits of imprisonment. In addition to ignoring replacement and deterrence, incapacitation studies also do not typically account for the training effects (whether positive or negative) of imprisonment.[4] One exception to these remarks is the work of Spelman (1994), who, after attempting to control for some of the above factors, calculates a "best-guess" incarceration elasticity of aggregate crime at .16 (220): that is, a doubling of the prison population is predicted to reduce the level of crime by about 16 percent.

An alternative methodology more in keeping with the economic model is presented in Levitt 1996 (also see Marvell and Moody 1994). Levitt estimates the reduction in crime caused by an increase in [a proxy for] prison populations. Estimating the impact of prisons on crime presents the same problem as estimating the impact of police on crime. The problem in both cases is that increases in crime can lead to more prisons and police. Thus, even if more prisons and police lead to less crime, the data may show that more prisons and police are associated with more crime (Cameron 1989 and Hersch and Netter 1984 attempt to estimate the impact of crime on sentence lengths and prison populations). What is needed to deduce the impact of prisons on crime is an increase or decrease in the number of prisoners that is not at all the result of a change in the amount of crime. Levitt argues that court-imposed rulings on prison overcrowding are independent of crime (the imposition of such rulings decreases prison populations, and the lifting of these rulings increases prison populations). Using legislation on prison overcrowding as a proxy for changes in prison populations not caused by changes in crime, Levitt finds that "each additional prisoner leads to a reduction of between five and six reported crimes. Including unreported crimes raises the total to fifteen" (1996, 345). This number is very close to the median numbers obtained from self-report surveys, although only incapacitation effects are accounted for in the latter studies. Levitt demonstrates that his estimates lead to a benefit-cost ratio for the marginal prisoner that exceeds unity, and he suggests that the current level of imprisonment (in the United States) is "roughly efficient" (324).

In a review of the literature, Donohue and Siegelman (1998) employ both the incapacitation and aggregate offense–supply models to calculate cost-benefit ratios from imprisonment in the United States. The goal is to establish whether a continuation of the huge run-up in the proportion of the population incarcerated during the 1980s and 1990s is cost justified. After reviewing the applicable studies, the authors adopt offense elasticities of approximately .15 (also see Wilson 1994). Attaching cost figures to these estimates suggests that further increases in the proportion incarcerated are unjustified for the United States, but recent levels may be justified. These calculations do not take into account the possible criminogenic impact of current incarcerations. If imprisonment increases the criminality of released prisoners, then the United States may be incarcerating at excessive rates.

Even if prisons are worthwhile social investments, it doesn't follow that they are the best investments of a given budget. Donohue and Siegelman (1998) argue, for example, that certain preschool enrichment programs are even more cost efficient than prisons at reducing the level of crime.

Additional Topics and Suggestions for Future Research

This review has not attempted to canvass all topics that might be included in a survey of the economics of prisons. Notable exclusions are prison industries (Auerbach et al. 1988; Barnes 1921); industrial relations in prisons (Peterson 1981; Staudohar 1976; Wynne 1978; Zimmer and Jacobs 1981); litigation of prisoner suits (Brown 1992); racial disparities in the prison population and in recidivism (Cameron 1989; DiIulio 1994; Freeman 1986, 1988; Langan 1994; Myers 1980a, 1980b, 1992; Myers and Sabol 1988); class-based models of prison use (Andrews 1993); various alternatives to imprisonment and to standard methods of incarceration such as fines, community-based sanctions, electronic monitoring, boot camp, and corporal punishment (Avio 1995; Benson and Rasmussen 1995; Kan 1996; Langbein 1977; Polinsky and Shavell 1984; Waldfogel 1995); and economic factors in the origins of prison systems (Conley 1981; Langbein 1976; F. Lewis 1988, 1990; Nicholas 1990).

The economics of prisons has come a long way since Becker rekindled economists' interest in crime in 1968. In general, one could argue that the punishment theories developed by economists, and within which the economics of prisons is embedded, need to pay more heed to the stylized facts uncovered by longitudinal studies: (1) most crimes are committed by youths, (2) only a small number of these youths persist in criminal activity as they age, but (3) these same people are responsible for the bulk of serious crimes (for discussion, see Farrington, Ohlin, and Wilson 1986; Moffitt 1994). The theoretical models developed in economics do not appear to address these facts satisfactorily. One policy implication is that more attention is paid to influencing the lifetime profile of established criminals than to attending to the prevention of such careers in the first place. Similarly, the underlying legal and social institutions providing the background environment for criminal activity require careful examination (Witte 1993). Akerlof and Yellen (1994) provide an illustrative model that points in the right direction (also see Becker 1996), a model that implicates "community policing" (Campbell 1994). Another promising line of research is suggested by Grogger's (1997) work on the incarceration rates of sons of teenage mothers. Finally, given their comparative advantage, economists have quite naturally confined themselves to the impact of the law and its administration on the incentives implicit in fixed preferences— that is, to short-run "carrot-and-stick" approaches to modifying criminal behavior. Perhaps a more comprehensive understanding of human nature than that depicted in the economic model of crime is warranted. It may now be time to explore the long-run preference-shaping impact of the law (Dau-Schmidt 1990; L. Friedman 1993; Robinson 1994) and of education (Usher 1997; Witte 1996, 1997), along with the role of habituation in that process (DiIulio 1996; Wilson 1994). We know little about how and why a shared moral order is developed and maintained (Robinson 1994). This change in perspective, calling as it does for an examination of the relationship between socialization and individuation, suggests a return to a relatively neglected part of the research program Adam Smith laid out in 1791. Analysis of the social institutions that inculcate self-command and that otherwise function as civilizing forces in our society (Muller 1993; Wilson 1993) should be part and parcel of the research strategy social scientists adopt to help understand and control crime.

Notes

1. An earlier version of this paper was commissioned for publication in the *Encyclopedia of Law and Economics,* edited by B. Bouckaert and G. De Geest (Edward Elgar, 2000). A slightly altered version appeared in the *European Journal of Law and Economics* 6 (1998). The author wishes

to express his appreciation to Alex Tabarrok, who revised and updated the earlier versions and made many substantive contributions to the paper as well. Edward Elgar Publishing and Kluwer Academic Publishers kindly gave their permission to republish the earlier material.

2. Data are from the Bureau of Justice Statistics Correctional Surveys, available online at http://www.ojp.usdoj.gov/bjs/correct.htm.

3. Bureau of Justice Statistics (BJS), Probation and Parole Statistics, http://www.ojp.usdoj.gov/bjs/pandp.htm; or BJS, Probation and Parole in the United States, 1998, August 1999, NCJ 178234.

4. Measures of the willingness to pay for retribution are also typically ignored.

References

Adler, Jacob. 1991. *The Urgings of Conscience: A Theory of Punishment.* Philadelphia: Temple University Press.

Akerlof, George, and Janet L. Yellen. 1994. Gang Behavior, Law Enforcement, and Community Values. In *Values and Public Policy,* edited by Henry J. Aaron, Thomas Mann, and Timothy Taylor, 173–209. Washington, D.C.: Brookings Institution.

Andrews, Marcellus. 1993. Schools, Jails, and the Dynamics of an Educational Underclass: Some Dreadful Social Arithmetic. *Journal of Economic Behavior and Organization* 22: 121–32.

Auerbach, Barbara J., George E. Sexton, Franklin C. Farrow, and Robert H. Lawson. 1988. *Work in American Prisons: The Private Sector Gets Involved.* Washington, D.C.: U.S. Department of Justice, National Institute of Justice, Office of Communication and Research Utilization (prepared by Criminal Justice Associates under subcontract from Abt Associates, Inc.).

Avio, Kenneth L. 1973. An Economic Analysis of Criminal Corrections: The Canadian Case. *Canadian Journal of Economics* 6: 164–78.

———. 1975. Recidivism in the Economic Model of Crime. *Economic Inquiry* 13: 450–56.

———. 1991. On Private Prisons: An Economic Analysis of the Model Contract and Model Statute for Private Incarceration. *New England Journal on Criminal and Civil Confinement* 17: 265–300.

————. 1993a. Economic, Retributive, and Contractarian Conceptions of Punishment. *Law and Philosophy* 12: 249–86.

————. 1993b. Remuneration Regimes for Private Prisons. *International Review of Law and Economics* 13: 35–45.

————. 1995. Economic, Contractarian, and Discourse Arguments against Efficient Torture. In *Law, Justice, and the State,* edited by Alexsander Peczenik and Mikael M. Karlsson, 265–72. Beiheft 58, Archives for Philosophy of Law and Social Philosophy. Stuttgart: Franz Steiner.

Barnes, Harry Elmer. 1921. The Economics of American Penology as Illustrated by the Experience of the State of Pennsylvania. *Journal of Political Economy* 8: 617–42.

Barnett, Randy E. 1977. Restitution: A New Paradigm of Criminal Justice. *Ethics* 87: 279–301.

————. 1998. *The Structure of Liberty: Justice and the Rule of Law.* Oxford: Oxford University Press.

Becker, Gary S. 1968. Crime and Punishment: An Economic Approach. *Journal of Political Economy* 76: 169–217.

————. 1996. Norms and the Formation of Preferences. In *Accounting for Tastes,* edited by Gary S. Becker, 225–30. Cambridge, Mass.: Harvard University Press.

Benson, Bruce L. 1990. *The Enterprise of Law: Justice without the State.* San Francisco: Pacific Research Institute for Public Policy.

————. 1994a. Are Public Goods Really Common Pools? Considerations of the Evolution of Policing and Highways in England. *Economic Inquiry* 32: 249–71.

————. 1994b. Third Thoughts on Contracting Out. *Journal of Libertarian Studies* 11: 44–78.

————. 1996. Restitution in Theory and in Practice. *Journal of Libertarian Studies* 13: 75–98.

Benson, Bruce L., and David W. Rasmussen. 1995. Crime and Punishment. In *The Economy of Florida,* edited by J. F. Scoggins and Ann C. Pierce, 99–116. Gainesville: University of Florida Press.

Benson, Bruce L., and Laurin A. Wollan Jr. 1989. Prison Overcrowding and Judicial Incentives. *Madison Paper Series* 3: 1–22.

Blumstein, Alfred. 1995. Prisons. In *Crime,* edited by James Q. Wilson and Joan Petersilia, 387–419. San Francisco: ICS.

Blumstein, Alfred, and Jacqueline Cohen. 1987. Characterizing Criminal Careers. *Science* 237: 985–91.

Borus, Michael E., Einar Hardin, and Patterson A. Terry. 1976. Job-Placement Services for Ex-Offenders: An Evaluation of the Michigan Comprehensive Offender Manpower Program (COMP) Job-Placement Efforts. *Journal of Human Resources* 11: 391–401.

Brakel, Samuel J. 1988. "Privatization" in Corrections: Radical Prison Chic or Mainstream Americana? *New England Journal on Criminal and Civil Confinement* 14: 1–39.

Brown, Jennifer G. 1992. Posner, Prisoners, and Pragmatism. *Tulane Law Review* 66: 1117–178.

Burnovski, Moshe, and Zvi Safra. 1994. Deterrence Effects of Sequential Punishment Policies: Should Repeat Offenders Be More Severely Punished? *International Review of Law and Economics* 14: 341–50.

Cameron, Samuel. 1989. Determinants of the Prison Population: An Empirical Analysis. *International Journal of Social Economics* 16: 17–25.

Campbell, John. 1994. Policing Crime. *Federal Reserve Bank of Boston Regional Review* 4: 6–11.

Carr-Hill, G. A., and R. A. Carr-Hill. 1972. Reconviction as a Process. *British Journal of Criminology* 12: 35–43.

Conley, John A. 1981. Revising Conceptions about the Origin of Prisons: The Importance of Economic Considerations. *Social Science Quarterly* 62: 247–58.

Cook, Philip J. 1975. The Correctional Carrot: Better Jobs for Parolees. *Policy Analysis* 1: 11–54.

———. 1977. Punishment and Crime: A Critique of Current Findings concerning the Preventive Effects of Punishment. *Law and Contemporary Problems* 41: 164–204.

Couch, Kenneth A. 1992. New Evidence on the Long-Term Effects of Employment Training Programs. *Journal of Labor Economics* 10: 380–88.

Cragg, Wesley. 1992. *The Practice of Punishment: Towards a Theory of Restorative Justice.* London: Routledge.

Dau-Schmidt, Kenneth. 1990. An Economic Analysis of the Criminal Law as a Preference-Shaping Policy. *Duke Law Review* 1: 1–38.

Davis, Michael. 1988. Time and Punishment: An Intertemporal Model of Crime. *Journal of Political Economy* 96: 383–90.

DiIulio, John J., Jr. 1988. What's Wrong with Private Prisons? *Public Interest* 92: 66–83.

———. 1994. The Question of Black Crime. *The Public Interest* 117: 3–32.

———. 1996. Help Wanted: Economists, Crime, and Public Policy. *Journal of Economic Perspectives* 10: 3–24.

DiIulio, John J., Jr., and Anne Morrison Piehl. 1991. Does Prison Pay? *Brookings Review* 9: 28–35.

Donohue, John J., III, and Peter Siegelman. 1998. Allocating Resources among Prisons and Social Programs in the Battle against Crime. *Journal of Legal Studies* 27: 1–43.

Duff, R. A. 1986. *Trials and Punishment.* Cambridge, England: Cambridge University Press.

———. 1996. Penal Communications: Recent Work in the Philosophy of Punishment. *Crime and Justice: A Review of Research* 20: 1–97.

Easterbrook, Frank H. 1983. Criminal Procedure as a Market System. *Journal of Legal Studies* 12: 289–332.

Edwards, Glyn. 1996. Public Crime, Private Punishment: Prison Privatization in Queensland. *International Journal of Social Economics* 23: 391–408.

Ehrlich, Isaac. 1981. On the Usefulness of Controlling Individuals: An Economic Analysis of Rehabilitation, Incapacitation, and Deterrence. *American Economic Review* 71: 307–22.

———. 1982. The Optimum Enforcement of Laws and the Concept of Justice: A Positive Analysis. *International Review of Law and Economics* 2: 3–27.

Englander, Frederick. 1983. Helping Ex-offenders Enter the Labor Market. *Monthly Labor Review* 106: 25–30.

———. 1985. Reply. *Monthly Labor Review* 108A: 49–50.

Evans, Robert, Jr. 1968. The Labor Market and Parole Success. *Journal of Human Resources* 3: 201–12.

Farrington, David P., Lloyd E. Ohlin, and James Q. Wilson. 1986. *Understanding and Controlling Crime: Toward a New Research Strategy.* New York: Springer.

Flinn, Christopher. 1986. Dynamic Models of Criminal Careers. In *Criminal Careers and "Career Criminals,"* vol. 2, edited by Alfred Blumstein, Jacqueline Cohen, Jeffrey A. Roth, and Christy A. Visher, 356–79. Washington, D.C.: National Academy Press.

Freeman, Richard B. 1986. Who Escapes? The Relation between Churchgoing and Other Background Factors to the Socioeconomic Performance of Black Male Youths from Inner-City Tracts. In *The Black Youth Employment Crisis,* edited by R. B. Freeman and H. J. Holzer, 353–76. Chicago: University of Chicago Press.

————. 1988. The Relation of Criminal Activity to Black Youth Employment. In *The Economics of Race and Crime,* edited by Margaret C. Simms and Samuel L. Myers Jr., 99–107. New Brunswick, N.J.: Transaction.

————. 1992. Crime and the Employment of Disadvantaged Youths. In *Urban Labor Markets and Job Opportunity,* edited by George E. Peterson and Wayne Vronman, 201–37. Washington D.C.: Urban Institute Press.

————. 1996. Why Do So Many Young American Men Commit Crimes and What Might We Do about It? *Journal of Economic Perspectives* 10: 25–42.

Friedman, David D. 1999. Why Not Hang Them All: The Virtues of Inefficient Punishment. *Journal of Political Economy* 107, no. 6 (pt. 2): S259–S269.

————. 2000. *Law's Order.* Princeton, N.J.: Princeton University Press.

Friedman, Lawrence M. 1993. *Crime and Punishment in American History.* New York: Basic.

Garoupa, Nuno. 1996. Prison, Parole, and the Criminal Justice Act of 1991. In *Research in Law and Economics,* no. 18, edited by Richard O. Zerbe and William Kovacic, 125–47. Greenwich, Conn.: JAI.

————. 1997. A Survey of the Theory of Optimal Law Enforcement. *Journal of Economic Issues* 11: 267–95.

Gendreau, Paul, and Robert R. Ross. 1987. Revivification of Rehabilitation: Evidence from the 1980s. *Justice Quarterly* 4: 349–407.

Gentry, James Theodore. 1986. The Panopticon Revisited: The Problem of Monitoring Private Prisons. *Yale Law Journal* 96: 353–75.

Giertz, J. Fred, and Peter F. Nardulli. 1985. Prison Overcrowding. *Public Choice* 46: 71–78.

Gill, Richard T. 1994. The Importance of Deterrence. *Public Interest* 117: 51–56.

Gillespie, Robert F. 1983. Allocating Prison Space: An Economic Approach Incorporating Efficiency and Equity. *Illinois Business Review* 40: 3–11.

Greenwood, Peter. 1982. *Selective Incarceration*. Santa Monica, Calif.: Rand Corporation.

Greenwood, Peter, and Susan Turner. 1987. *Selective Incapacitation Revisited*. Santa Monica, Calif.: Rand Corporation.

Grizzle, Gloria A., and Ann D. Witte. 1980. Criminal Justice Evaluation Techniques: Methods Other than Random Assignment. In *Handbook of Criminal Justice Evaluation,* edited by Malcolm Kleenin and Katherine S. Teilmann, 259–302. Beverly Hills, Calif.: Sage.

Grogger, Jeffrey. 1991. Certainty vs. Severity of Punishment. *Economic Inquiry* 29: 297–309.

————. 1992. Arrests, Persistent Youth Joblessness, and Black/White Employment Differentials. *Review of Economics and Statistics* 74: 100–106.

————. 1995. The Effect of Arrests on the Employment and Earnings of Young Men. *Quarterly Journal of Economics* 110: 51–71.

————. 1997. Incarceration-Related Costs of Early Childbearing. In *Kids Having Kids: Economic Costs and Social Consequences of Teen Pregnancy,* edited by Rebecca A. Maynard. Washington, D.C.: Urban Institute Press.

Halleck, Seymour L., and Ann D. Witte. 1977. Is Rehabilitation Dead? *Crime and Delinquency* 23: 372–82.

Hardin, Einar. 1975. Human Capital and the Labor Market Success of New Parolees. In *1975 Proceedings of the Business and Economic Statistics Section, American Statistical Association,* 330–35.

Hart, O., A. Shleifer, and R. W. Vishny. 1997. The Proper Scope of Government: Theory and an Application to Prisons. *Quarterly Journal of Economics* 451: 1127–162.

Hatry, Harry P., Paul J. Brounstein, and Robert B. Levinson. 1993. Comparison of Privately and Publicly Operated Corrections Facilities in Kentucky and Massachusetts. In *Privatizing Correctional Institutions,* edited by G. Bowman, S. Hakim, and P. Seidenstat, 193–212. New Brunswick, N.J.: Transaction. Reporting on Hatry, Harry P. (principal investigator). 1989. *Comparison of Privately and Publicly Operated Corrections Facilities in Kentucky and Massachusetts.* Washington, D.C.: Urban Institute.

Herrnstein, Richard J. 1983. Some Criminogenic Traits in Offenders. In *Crime and Public Policy,* edited by James Q. Wilson, 31–49. San Francisco: Institute for Contemporary Studies.

Hersch, Philip L. and Jeffry M. Netter. 1984. The Effects of Crime Rates on Time Served in Prison: An Empirical Analysis. *Public Finance* 39: 314–20.

Hollister, Robinson G., Peter Kemper, and Rebecca A. Maynard. 1984. *The National Supported Work Demonstration.* Madison: University of Wisconsin Press.

Howard, Michael. 1996. In Defence of Prisons. *The Economist* (22 June): 56–57.

Kan, Steven S. 1996. Corporal Punishments and Optimal Incapacitation. *Journal of Legal Studies* 25: 121–30.

Kim, Il-Joong, Bruce L. Benson, David W. Rasmussen, and Thomas W. Zuehlke. 1993. An Economic Analysis of Recidivism among Drug Offenders. *Southern Economic Journal* 60: 169–83.

Langan, Patrick A. 1994. No Racism in the Justice System. *Public Interest* 117: 48–51.

Langbein, John H. 1976. The Historical Origins of the Sanction of Imprisonment for Serious Crime. *Journal of Legal Studies* 5: 35–60.
————. 1977. *Torture and the Law of Proof: Europe and England in the Ancien Régime.* Chicago: University of Chicago Press.

Lanza-Kaduce, Lonn, Karen F. Parker, and Charles W. Thomas. 1999. A Comparative Recidivism Analysis of Releasees from Private and Public Prisons. *Crime and Delinquency* 45: 28–47.

Lattimore, Pamela K., and Ann D. Witte. 1985. Programs to Aid Ex-offenders: We Don't Know "Nothing Works." *Monthly Labor Review* 108A: 46–50.

Lattimore, Pamela K., Ann Dryden Witte, and Joanna R. Baker. 1990. Experimental Assessment of the Effect of Vocational Training on Youthful Property Offenders. *Evaluation Review* 14: 115–33.

Leung, Siu Fai. 1995. Dynamic Deterrence Theory. *Economica* 62: 65–87.

Levitt, Steven D. 1996. The Effect of Prison Population Size on Crime Rates: Evidence from Prison Overcrowding Litigation. *Quarterly Journal of Economics* 107: 319–51.

———. 1997. Incentive Compatibility Constraints as an Explanation for the Use of Prison Sentences Instead of Fines. *International Review of Law and Economics* 17: 179–92.

Lewis, Donald E. 1979. The Optimal Parole Period. *Economics Letters* 2: 381–86.

———. 1983. Economic Aspects of the Parole Decision. *Australian Economic Papers* 22: 259–79.

———. 1986. The General Deterrent Effect of Longer Sentences. *British Journal of Criminology* 26: 47–62.

Lewis, Frank D. 1988. The Cost of Convict Transportation from Britain to Australia, 1796–1810. *Economic History Review*, second series, 41: 507–24.

———. 1990. Australia: An Economical Prison? A Reply. *Economic History Review*, second series, 43: 477–82.

Lipton, Douglas, Robert Martinson, and Judith Wilks. 1975. *The Effectiveness of Correctional Treatment: A Survey of Treatment Evaluation Studies.* New York: Praeger.

Logan, Charles H. 1987. The Propriety of Proprietary Prisons. *Federal Probation* 51: 35–40.

Long, Sharon K., and Ann D. Witte. 1981. Current Economic Trends: Implications for Crime and Criminal Justice. In *Crime and Criminal Justice in a Declining Economy,* edited by Kevin N. Wright, 69–143. Cambridge, Mass.: Oelgeschlager, Gunn and Hain.

Lott, John R., Jr. 1990. The Effect of Conviction on the Legitimate Income of Criminals. *Economics Letters* 34: 381–85.

———. 1992a. An Attempt at Measuring the Total Monetary Penalty from Drug Convictions: The Importance of an Individual's Reputation. *Journal of Legal Studies* 21: 159–87.

———. 1992b. Do We Punish High Income Criminals Too Heavily? *Economic Inquiry* 30: 583–608.

Mair, George. 1991. What Works—Nothing or Everything? Measuring the Effectiveness of Sentences. *Home Office Research Bulletin* 30: 3–8.

Mallar, Charles, Stuart Kerachsky, Craig Thornton, and David Long. 1982. *Evaluation of the Economic Impact of the Job Corps Program: Third Follow-up Report*. Princeton, N.J.: Mathematica Policy Research (Final Report).

Mallar, Charles D., and Craig V. D. Thornton. 1978. Transitional Aid for Released Prisoners: Evidence from the LIFE Experiment. *Journal of Human Resources* 13: 208–36.

Marks, Denton, and Aidan Vining. 1986. Prison Labor Markets: The Supply Issue. *Policy Sciences* 19: 83–111.

Martin, Susan E., Lee B. Sechrest, and Robin Redner, eds. 1981. *New Directions in the Rehabilitation of Criminal Offenders*. Washington, D.C.: National Research Council, National Academy Press.

Martinson, Robert. 1974. "What Works"—Questions and Answers about Prison Reform. *Public Interest* 25: 22–54.

Marvell, Thomas, and Carlisle Moody. 1994. Prison Population Growth and Crime Reduction. *Journal of Quantitative Criminology* 10: 109–40.

McDonald, Douglas C. 1990. The Costs of Operating Public and Private Correctional Facilities. In *Private Prisons and the Public Interest,* edited by Douglas McDonald. New Brunswick, N.J.: Rutgers University Press.

Miceli, Thomas J. 1991. Optimal Criminal Procedure: Fairness and Deterrence. *International Review of Law and Economics* 11: 3–10.

————. 1994. Prison and Parole: Minimizing the Cost of Non-monetary Sanctions as Deterrents. *Research in Law and Economics* 16: 197–211.

Moffitt, Terrie E. 1994. Natural Histories of Delinquency. In *Cross-National Longitudinal Research on Human Development and Criminal Behavior,* edited by Elmar G. Weitekamp and Hans-Jürgen Kerner, 3–61. Dordrecht: Kluwer Academic.

Muller, Jerry Z. 1993. *Adam Smith in His Time and Ours: Designing the Decent Society*. New York: Free Press.

Myers, Samuel L., Jr. 1980a. Black-White Differentials in Crime Rates. *Review of Black Political Economy* 10: 133–52.

————. 1980b. The Rehabilitation Effect of Punishment. *Economic Inquiry* 18: 353–66.

————. 1983. Estimating the Economic Model of Crime: Employment versus Punishment Effects. *Quarterly Journal of Economics* 97: 157–66.

————. 1992. Crime, Entrepreneurship, and Labor Force Withdrawal. *Contemporary Policy Issues* 10: 84–97.

Myers, Samuel L., Jr., and William J. Sabol. 1988. Unemployment and Racial Differences in Imprisonment. In *The Economics of Race and Crime,* edited by Margaret C. Simms and Samuel L. Myers Jr., 189–209. New Brunswick, N.J.: Transaction.

Nagin, Daniel, and Joel Waldfogel. 1995. The Effects of Criminality and Conviction on the Labor Market Status of Young British Offenders. *International Review of Law and Economics* 15: 109–126.

Nardulli, Peter F. 1984. The Misalignment of Penal Responsibilities and State Prison Crises: Costs, Consequences, and Corrective Actions. *University of Illinois Law Review* 1984: 365–87.

Nash, John. 1991. To Make the Punishment Fit the Crime: The Theory and Statistical Estimation of a Multi-period Optimal Deterrence Model. *International Review of Law and Economics* 11: 101–10.

Nicholas, Stephen. 1990. Australia: An Economical Prison? Comments. *Economic History Review,* second series, 43: 470–76.

Niskanen, William A. 1971. *Bureaucracy and Representative Government.* Chicago: Aldine-Atherton.

Orr, Larry L., Howard S. Bloom, Stephen H. Bell, Fred Doolittle, Winston Lin, and George Cave. 1996. *Does Training for the Disadvantaged Work? Evidence from the National JTPA Study.* An Abt Associates study. Washington, D.C.: Urban Institute Press.

Parker, Jeffrey S. 1989. Criminal Sentencing Policy for Organizations: The Unifying Approach of Optimal Penalties. *American Criminal Law Review* 26: 513–604.

Parker, Jeffrey S., and Michael K. Block. 1989. The Sentencing Commission, P.M. (Post-*Mistretta*): Sunshine or Sunset? *American Criminal Law Review* 27: 289–329.

Petersilia, Joan. 1997. Probation in the United States. *National Institute of Justice Journal* (Sept.): 2–8.

Peterson, Andrew A. 1981. Deterring Strikes by Public Employees: New York's Two for One Salary Penalty and the 1979 Prison Guard Strike. *Industrial and Labor Relations Review* 34: 545–62.

Piehl, Anne Morrison, and John J. DiIulio Jr. 1995. Does Prison Pay? Revisited. *Brookings Review* 13: 21–25.

Piliavin, Irving, and Rosemary Gartner. 1984. The Impacts of Supported Work on Ex-offenders. In *The National Supported Work Demonstration,* edited by Robinson G. Hollister Jr., Peter Kemper, and Rebecca A. Maynard. Madison: University of Wisconsin Press.

Polinsky, A. Mitchell, and Daniel Rubinfeld. 1991. A Model of Optimal Fines for Repeat Offenders. *Journal of Public Economics* 46: 291–306.

Polinsky, A. Mitchell, and Steven Shavell. 1984. The Optimal Use of Fines and Imprisonment. *Journal of Public Economics* 24: 89–99.

Pyle, D. J. 1995. The Economic Approach to Crime and Punishment. *Journal of Interdisciplinary Economics* 6: 1–22.

Rasmusen, Eric. 1996. Stigma and Self-Fulfilling Expectations of Criminality. *Journal of Law and Economics* 39: 519–43.

Robbins, Ira R. 1989. The Legal Dimensions of Private Incarceration. *American University Law Review* 38: 531–654.

Robinson, Paul H. 1994. A Failure of Moral Courage. *Public Interest* 117: 40–48.

Roper, Brian A. 1986. Market Forces, Privatisation, and Prisons: A Polar Case for Government Policy. *International Journal of Social Economics* 13: 77–92.

Rossi, Peter H., Richard A. Berk, and Kenneth J. Lenihan. 1980. *Money, Work, and Crime: Experimental Evidence.* New York: Academic.

Rubenstein, Ariel. 1980. On an Anomaly of the Deterrent Effect of Punishment. *Economics Letters* 6: 89–94.

Schmidt, Peter, and Ann D. Witte. 1980. Evaluating Correctional Programs: Models of Criminal Recidivism and an Illustration of Their Use. *Evaluation Review* 4: 585–600.

———. 1984. *An Economic Analysis of Crime and Justice: Theory, Methods, and Applications.* New York: Academic.

———. 1988. *Predicting Recidivism Using Survival Models.* New York: Springer.

———. 1989. Predicting Criminal Recidivism Using "Split Population" Survival Time Models. *Journal of Econometrics* 40: 141–59.

Sechrest, Lee, Susan D. White, and Elizabeth D. Brown, eds. 1979. *The Rehabilitation of Criminal Offenders: Problems and Prospects.* Washington, D.C.: National Academy of Sciences.

Sellers, Martin P. 1993. *The History and Politics of Private Prisons: A Comparative Analysis*. Rutherford, N.J.: Fairleigh Dickinson University Press.

Shavell, Steven. 1985. Criminal Law and the Optimal Use of Nonmonetary Sanctions as a Deterrent. *Columbia Law Review* 85: 1232–266.

—————. 1987a. A Model of Optimal Incapacitation. *American Economic Association Papers and Proceedings* 77: 107–110.

—————. 1987b. The Optimal Use of Nonmonetary Sanctions as a Deterrent. *American Economic Review* 77: 584–92.

Shoup, Carl S. 1964. Standards for Distributing a Free Governmental Service: Crime Prevention. *Public Finance* 19: 383–92.

Sichor, David. 1995. *Punishment for Profit: Private Prisons/Public Concerns*. Thousand Oaks, Calif.: Sage.

Sickles, Robin C., Peter Schmidt, and Ann D. Witte. 1979. An Application of the Simultaneous Tobit Model: A Study of the Determinants of Criminal Recidivism. *Journal of Economics and Business* 31: 166–71.

Smith, Adam. [1791] 1976. *The Theory of Moral Sentiments*. Vol. 1 of *The Glasgow Edition of the Works and Correspondence of Adam Smith*. Edited by D. D. Raphael and A. L. Macfie. Oxford: Oxford University Press.

Spelman, William. 1994. *Criminal Incapacitation*. New York: Plenum.

Staudohar, Paul D. 1976. Prison Guard Labor Relations in Ohio. *Industrial Relations* 15: 177–90.

Stigler, George J. 1970. The Optimum Enforcement of Laws. *Journal of Political Economy* 78: 526–36.

Tabasz, Thomas F. 1974. Penology, Economics, and the Public: Toward an Agreement. *Policy Sciences* 5: 47–55.

—————. 1975. *Toward an Economics of Prisons*. Lexington, Ky.: Heath.

Tauchen, Helen, Ann Dryden Witte, and Harriet Griesinger. 1994. Criminal Deterrence: Revisiting the Issue with a Birth Cohort. *Review of Economics and Statistics* 76: 399–412.

Thomas, Charles W. 1996. Letter to the Subcommittee on Crime, Committee on the Judiciary, House of Representatives, Washington, D.C. (September 1).

Thomas, Charles W., and Charles H. Logan. 1993. The Development, Present Status, and Future Potential of Correctional Privatization in

America. In *Privatizing Correctional Institutions,* edited by Gary W. Bowman, Simon Hakim, and Paul Seidenstat, 213–40. New Brunswick, N.J.: Transaction.

Thurow, Lester C. 1970. Equity Versus Efficiency in Law Enforcement. *Public Policy* 18: 451–62.

United States Government Accounting Office (USGAO). 1991. *Private Prisons: Cost Savings and BOP's Statutory Authority Need to Be Resolved.* Report to the Subcommittee on Crime, Committee on the Judiciary, House of Representatives, Letter Report, GAO/GDD-91-21. Washington, D.C.: USGAO.

—————. 1996. *Private and Public Prisons: Studies Comparing Operational Costs and/or Quality of Service.* Report to the Subcommittee on Crime, Committee on the Judiciary, House of Representatives, Letter Report, GAO/GGD-96-158. Washington, D.C.: USGAO.

Usher, Dan. 1997. Education as a Deterrent to Crime. *Canadian Journal of Economics* 30: 367–84.

Visher, Christy A. 1986. The Rand Inmate Survey: A Reanalysis. In *Career Criminals and "Criminal Careers,"* vol. 2, edited by Alfred Blumstein, Jacqueline Cohen, and Jeffrey A. Roth, 161–211. Washington, D.C.: National Academy Press.

Visher, Christy A., Pamela K. Lattimore, and Richard L. Linster. 1991. Predicting the Recidivism of Serious Youthful Offenders Using Survival Models. *Criminology* 29: 329–366.

Waldfogel, Joel. 1994a. Does Conviction Have a Persistent Effect on Income and Employment? *International Review of Law and Economics* 14: 103–19.

—————. 1994b. The Effect of Criminal Conviction on Income and the Trust "Reposed in the Workmen." *Journal of Human Resources* 29: 162–81.

—————. 1995. Are Fines and Prison Terms Used Efficiently? Evidence on Federal Fraud Offenders. *Journal of Law and Economics* 38: 107–39.

Williamson, Oliver E. 1964. *The Economics of Discretionary Behavior: Managerial Objectives in a Theory of the Firm.* Englewood Cliffs, N.J.: Prentice Hall.

Wilson, James Q. 1983. *Thinking about Crime.* New York: Basic.

—————. 1993. *The Moral Sense.* New York: Free Press.

————. 1994. Culture, Incentives, and the Underclass. In *Values and Public Policy*, edited by Henry J. Aaron, Thomas E. Mann, and Timothy Taylor, 54–80. Washington, D.C.: Brookings Institution.

Wilson, James Q., and Richard J. Herrnstein. 1985. *Crime and Human Nature*. New York: Simon and Schuster.

Witte, Ann D. 1980. Estimating the Economic Model of Crime with Individual Data. *Quarterly Journal of Economics* 94: 57–84.

————. 1993. Some Thoughts on the Future of Research in Crime and Delinquency. *Journal of Research in Crime and Delinquency* 30: 513–25.

————. 1996. Urban Crime: Issues and Policies. *Housing Policy Debate* 7: 731–48.

————. 1997. Crime. In *The Social Benefits of Education,* edited by Jere Behrman and Nevzer Stacey, 219–46. Ann Arbor: University of Michigan Press.

Witte, Ann D., and Pamela A. Reid. 1980. An Exploration of the Determinants of Labor Market Performance for Prison Releasees. *Journal of Urban Economics* 8: 313–29.

Witte, Ann D., and Peter Schmidt. 1977. An Analysis of Recidivism, Using the Truncated Lognormal Distribution. *Journal of the Royal Statistical Society (Applied Statistics)* 26: 302–11.

————. 1979. An Analysis of the Type of Criminal Activity Using the Logit Model. *Journal of Research in Crime and Delinquency* 16: 164–79.

Wynne, John M. 1978. Unions and Bargaining among Employees of State Prisons. *Monthly Labor Review* 101: 10–16.

Zimmer, Lynn, and James B. Jacobs. 1981. Challenging the Taylor Law: Prison Guards on Strike. *Industrial and Labor Relations Review* 34: 531–44.

3

Correctional Privatization in America: An Assessment of Its Historical Origins, Present Status, and Future Prospects

Charles W. Thomas[1]

Correctional agencies in the United States soon will have had two full decades of experience with contracting for the private management of jails and prisons. Although the role played by the private sector was trivial during the 1980s, today privatization is a mainstream alternative throughout the United States and in a growing number of other nations.

Evidence of the magnitude and the rapidity of the change that has taken place is found easily, but a single illustration is sufficient for these introductory comments. Specifically, the Corrections Corporation of America (CCA) did not exist until 1983 and did not receive its first facility management contract until 1984. Today CCA manages sixty correctional facilities in the United States that have a design capacity of more than 60,000 prisoners, an actual prisoner population of approximately 55,000, and operating revenues derived exclusively from facility management contracts with government agencies that are expected to grow greater than $1 billion during 2002. Thus, in less than twenty years, CCA moved from being no more than a concept to a correctional system responsible for a prisoner population that is exceeded in size only by those of the Federal

Bureau of Prisons (FBOP) and the state correctional systems of California, Florida, New York, and Texas. The CCA story is unique, however, only with regard to its magnitude. Analogous stories of growth are to be found in the corporate histories of such management firms as Avalon Correctional Services, Inc., Cornell Companies, Inc., Correctional Services Corporation, Management and Training Corporation, and the Wackenhut Corrections Corporation.

The appeal of privatization obviously has grown rapidly, but the transition from a service delivery area within which government agencies long enjoyed a monopoly to one within which competition between alternative providers is common did not yield applause from everyone.[2] To the contrary, contracting out for the full-scale management of correctional facilities became the most hotly contested innovation that touched the nation's correctional system during the twentieth century.

I remain somewhat perplexed by how strident the privatization debate continues to be. There is nothing novel about private-sector involvement in U.S. corrections. Private firms have played a major role in the management of facilities housing juvenile offenders for many years. Indeed, the origins of the separate juvenile justice system that Americans now take for granted has its roots in private-sector initiatives that began to unfold during the first quarter of the nineteenth century (e.g., Thomas and Bilchik 1985). Although the degree of reliance on the private sector varies broadly from state to state, it is quite common to find individual states where between one-third and two-thirds of the total confined population of juveniles is housed in private rather than public facilities. Further, reliance on the private sector in some areas of adult corrections has been both commonplace and largely noncontroversial for many years. For example, it has long been the practice of the FBOP to contract for the management of 100 percent of its community-based correctional services for adult offenders with private firms. This is not a trivial role for the private sector. As this chapter is being finalized in August 2002, the FBOP is reporting contracts with private firms for the housing of the more than 6,100 offenders in its custody who have been assigned to community corrections facilities.

Finally, for decades, government has been contracting with the private sector for the delivery of a broad array of specialized services (e.g., educational, food, and medical services) within our jails and prisons. Seldom has this reliance on the private sector spawned significant controversy (e.g., Camp and Camp 1984).

What is novel and often highly controversial is the full-scale privatization of the jails and prisons.[3] Beginning with a handful of small contract awards by federal agencies during the early 1980s, privatization proponents advanced a simple hypothesis that had inherent appeal to elected officials who were struggling with rapidly growing prison populations and correctional expenditures.[4] The pursuit of profit by alternative providers of correctional services, contended the proponents, would bring competition into the correctional marketplace, which, in turn, would result in equivalent or superior correctional services being delivered at a lower cost.

I should hasten to add that the viability of this hypothesis did not then and does not today mean that enhanced correctional cost effectiveness can be achieved only if those services are privatized. The logic of the hypothesis expressly recognizes that competition with the private sector should foster increased efficiency and effectiveness within public correctional agencies. Indeed, many have argued that the greatest contribution of privatization will flow from more efficient and effective performance by public agencies. If, for example, privatization initiatives accounted for 10 percent of the nation's correctional system—which would be roughly twice the level of privatization that we see today—and those initiatives yielded equivalent or superior services at a cost 10 percent below the cost of a business-as-usual approach, it would follow that the economies achieved on a national level would be modest. If, however, the competition represented by so modest a role by the private sector energized public agencies to the degree that they began providing equivalent services at even a 5 percent cost savings, the cost savings would be much larger.

At least if approached on an abstract level, there is an apple pie flavor to privatization proponents' two-pronged hypothesis. It is often asserted that placing a high premium on the value of competition is an inherent part of what is said to be "the American way."

Most people would accept the pursuit of equivalent or superior goods and services at the lowest possible cost as a reflection of little more than common sense. In what purports to be the real world, however, the economic and political realities sometimes result in spitting out the apple pie and rejecting common sense. Those who saw potential value in the fostering of fair competition between alternative providers of correctional services learned this lesson in intergroup conflict theory quite early in the game.

Opposition to full-scale privatization materialized almost immediately with the first privatization initiatives. Some academic critics loudly bemoaned the arrival of corporate America in the nation's correctional system—and yes, it is ironic that many of those critics were the same people who previously and equally loudly bemoaned the shortcomings of public correctional agencies. Correctional agencies, understandably disinclined to welcome competitors into an area within which competition was an unfamiliar concept, generally took the position that the private sector would never gain the expertise necessary to establish its credibility. At the very most, argued senior agency executives, the private sector might be able to make a contribution in highly focused settings involving low-security prisoners (e.g., prerelease prisoners and parole violators). Professional organizations such as the American Bar Association adopted what amounted to official antiprivatization policies.[5] Vested interest groups—including the National Sheriffs' Association; the American Jail Association; and the American Federation of State, County, and Municipal Employees—challenged both the legality and the propriety of privatization.[6]

The historical record makes it clear that the opposition did not erase the appeal privatization was developing in the minds of elected officials who were saddled with the responsibility of setting public policy and allocating finite resources. Growing numbers of officials reasoned that if there were a realistic chance that contracting for the full-scale management of jails and prisons might yield equivalent or better correctional services at a lower cost, then public-policy choices should be shaped by that pragmatic fact.

The effect of this reasoning was dramatic. Until the mid-1980s, the number of privatized jails and prisons could be counted on the fingers of one hand. Today there are more than 180 fully privatized jails and prisons in operation or under construction, and multiple jurisdictions now rely on private management firms to operate facilities that house 20 percent or more of their total prisoner population. This rapid change notwithstanding, in many parts of the nation the debate is even more intense today than it was a decade ago. The parameters of the debate, however, have changed in a consequential way. For at least two reasons, the debate can no longer be won or lost based on nothing more than the persuasiveness of emotional or political rhetoric.

First, today the debate must take systematic evidence into account. There is now a wealth of published research as well as an ever-increasing number of privatized facilities. Indeed, a growing number of fully privatized jails and prisons housing local, state, and federal prisoners have now been in continuous operation for more than a decade. Thus, the possibility of meaningful longitudinal analyses is within our grasp.[7]

Second, only the most ideologically committed on both sides of the debate can hope to prevail by treating anecdotal evidence of the success or the failure of privatization initiatives as the equivalent of systematic evidence. When the correctional privatization movement began, the only evidence that was available was necessarily anecdotal. It is not the case, of course, that anecdotal evidence either had or has no value. It can tell us something of value about an event or a series of events that took place at a given public or private facility at a single point or period of time. During 1998, for example, serious problems—including multiple aggravated assaults, homicides, and escapes—were encountered at a new prison in Youngstown, Ohio, within which the CCA housed prisoners under a contract with the District of Columbia. Few if any would be so foolish as to argue that CCA was handling its contractual obligations in even a minimally adequate way. The events at Youngstown made that facility the poster child for opponents of correctional privatization—and you may safely assume that those opponents never updated the caustically critical case they presented when corrective action by CCA and the District of Columbia had the effect of significantly decreasing the incidence of assaults, eliminating escapes altogether, and achieving accreditation by both the American Correctional Association (ACA) and the National Commission on Correctional Health Care.[8]

Do those events offer anecdotal evidence of a failure? Of course they do. But do they offer systematic evidence of CCA's inability to manage the Youngstown facility in a suitably professional manner over time, of CCA's general inability to meet its contractual commitments, or of some general shortcoming of the private sector when it moves into the area of jail and prison management?

Of course not. Meaningful systematic evidence would require comparisons with the performance of public correctional agencies working under at least substantially the same circumstances as those confronted by CCA in Youngstown. There also would be a need for evidence that examined performance at this facility for a longer period of time, evidence that compared CCA's performance at Youngstown with its performance at other similar CCA facilities, evidence that looked at its performance at dissimilar CCA facilities, and, of course, evidence that examined the performance of private firms other than CCA at both similar and dissimilar facilities.

Put more concisely, anecdotal evidence cannot be brushed aside lightly, but it also offers general proof of nothing. Systematic evidence is far more powerful. Identifying the lessons that systematic evidence offers to policymakers will be a core purpose of this analysis.

The Focus and Organization of the Analysis

The body of relevant evidence is far too large to permit a study-by-study examination of it within the confines of a single chapter. What I can and will do, however, is to provide a reasonably detailed overview of that evidence as well as a fairly comprehensive set of references to specific studies.

I first make an honest effort to deal with the troublesome but also unavoidable problem of potential bias that might unintentionally color my assessment of the evidence under consideration. It is the case that I have opinions about the potential value of privatization, and I have not hesitated to express them in numerous articles, speeches, and presentations before elected officials at the local, state, and federal levels.

Thus, it is necessary that those opinions be reviewed in a summary manner as early as is possible in this discussion.

I then provide an overview of the origins and early history of correctional privatization, emphasizing the U.S. elements of that history for the simple reason that I have a better grasp of the relevant issues in the United States than I do of what has taken place elsewhere (but see, e.g., Harding 1997). The purpose of this portion of the analysis is twofold. First, it is important to understand that correctional privatization emerged not as a new innovation but as a logical extension of privatization experience gained by government contracting for the delivery of a host of essential public services in other contexts. Second, it is also important to understand that privatization did not arrive on the correctional scene in the form of a great explosion of insight by policymakers who swiftly went about the business of privatizing everything in sight. If privatization is to be construed fairly as an innovation in corrections, then it is also the case that the diffusion of the innovation was and continues to be slow and cautious.

Next I attempt to provide reasonable answers for a simple question: In an area of governmental responsibility that historically has been strikingly slow to embrace change, why is it that correctional privatization moved from being adopted by no jurisdiction in the nation to being relied on by more than half of all U.S. jurisdictions in less than twenty years?[9] In fact, of course, forging an answer for this general question requires addressing each of its two sides. One side deals with why so many jurisdictions made their initial decisions to contract with the private sector to manage (or more often to design, construct, and manage) correctional facilities. The other, which is in many ways both the more interesting and more important facet of the general question, deals with why 95 percent or more of the facilities with contracts awarded by various jurisdictions remained privatized long after the original contract terms expired.

The final portion of the analysis is necessarily speculative, but there is always a need to reach reasonable conclusions about the prospects of any innovation. Opponents of privatization firmly believe that it is the correctional equivalent to the "dot com" craze of 1999–2001. Proponents of privatization reach the contrary conclusion that the private sector will become an even stronger engine for change in the field of corrections in the years that lie ahead.

As soon will become clear, I endorse neither of these positions. Indeed, my judgment is that we have not yet really begun to explore the potential that true privatization in corrections might have. Without getting too far ahead of myself, my opinion is that the vast majority of all privatization initiatives in place today come closer to demonstrating how government can "governmentalize" the private sector than to demonstrating how the private sector can bring fresh ideas into a service delivery area previously thought of as necessarily being a governmental monopoly. Privatization, after all, presupposes that government will identify goals with some specificity but will defer to the creativity of the private sector to devise the means and the methods to achieve those goals. The vast majority of facility management contracts, however, devote virtually all of their attention to processes and methods and almost none to the setting of short- or long-term performance goals. The effect of this choice is to encourage and often even to require private firms to approach the tasks put before them in much the same fashion as do their counterparts in public agencies, which, to say the least, minimizes incentives for creativity and innovation.

The problems posed by contracting agencies' peculiar obsession with mandating adherence to traditional processes while being strikingly inattentive to outcomes is aggravated by the fact that private management firms have predominantly hired former government employees, who too often bring public-sector ways of thinking with them as they migrate into the private sector. Somtimes these weaknesses have been magnified by top management teams that have no correctional experience.

The bottom line is that both public policymakers and the top management teams of the private corrections firms will need to become more sophisticated than they often have been if correctional privatization is to mature into something capable of having long-term significance. Policymakers will have to encourage rather than inhibit innovation. Private management firms will have to bring creativity to the table that goes well beyond the meaningful contributions they already have made with regard to construction methods, facility designs, and acceptance of technological innovations in such areas as security. Otherwise, government agencies, whether intentionally or otherwise, will have succeeded only in governmentalizing the private sector. I find it difficult to imagine such a cloning exercise being a worthwhile enterprise.

Finding the Foundation for a Rational Public Policy

It is unfortunate that any examination of so controversial a topic as correctional privatization almost inevitably results in its author being characterized as an ideologue. Thus, at this point, I briefly alert the reader to what I believe should provide a foundation for a rational public policy in corrections and to a little of the professional background that I bring to the writing of this chapter.

First, it is often and, I think, accurately said that a society may be judged by the manner in which it responds to those for whom it has the least regard and who have at best meager access to economic and political power. Prisoners are certainly one such group. Thus, if our society is to be judged favorably, the evidence would have to offer proof that we have met our basic obligations to those we have chosen to confine. Those obligations seem fairly obvious. Prisoners are entitled to humane treatment, which at least in part means treatment that meets or exceeds all relevant constitutional, legal, and professional standards. Further, prisoners are entitled to treatment aimed at allowing them to depart from their confinement experience better able to cope with life in a law-abiding manner than they were when their term of confinement began.[10] Sadly, much evidence offers proof of the frequency with which we have failed to meet these obligations and more than a little evidence of our willingness to tolerate deplorable conditions in our jails and prisons. All of the failure notwithstanding, it remains true that the failure is in our conduct and not in the quality of the standards by which that conduct is judged.

Second, the fact that resources are finite strikes me as being self-evident yet nontrivial. It is unsurprising that public employees, public agencies, and private firms routinely lobby for a larger slice of the public resource pie. Nor is it surprising that the lobbyists defend the self-centeredness of their lobbying with claims that they serve the greater good. I am even willing to stipulate that such self-serving claims often are valid. Validity, however, seldom causes the resource pie to grow larger. Thus, the goal of sound public policy must include creating a pie that is adequately large and assuring that the array of public services on which we depend is of sufficient breadth, depth, and quality. Improved efficiency in any service delivery area is to be sought after diligently. Any cost saving that can be achieved without a counterbalancing reduction in the quality of services delivered has the desirable benefit of freeing up resources that then can be allocated to improve services in other important areas, to commence the delivery of new but necessary services, or to return to taxpayers some portion of the funds government took from them but did not need.

Despite the high hurdles that excessive bureaucratization and burdensome tradition place in our path, what I have observed already leads me to conclude that our collective obligation is to guarantee the delivery of correctional services that meet or exceed all applicable constitutional, legal, and professional standards and to do so in such a way as to impose the smallest commitment of the limited resources to which policymakers have access. This does not mean that I wish to avoid providing correctional services whose breadth and depth exceeds the minimum standards, even though the cost of providing such enhanced services would be higher. Especially if enhanced services were to be correlated meaningfully with reduced recidivism rates, which also implies a reduction in the risk of criminal victimization of the rest of us, I absolutely would favor funding the enhancements. This does mean I believe that there is a floor below which we cannot allow the quality of correctional services to fall and that we must allocate whatever resources might be necessary to meet the fundamental standards forming that floor.

The goals that I have outlined imply that the public or private identity of alternative providers of correctional services is a fundamentally irrelevant consideration. What is relevant is the delivery of the best possible correctional services at the lowest possible cost. Often, however, my public support for what I take to be an

intentionally neutral philosophical position on correctional privatization has been the incentive not only for opponents of privatization
to label me as a pawn of corporate America, but also proponents to
imagine that I would be willing to ignore whatever evidence there
might be of their failures. Sometimes I have been amused by both
the opponents' attacks and the proponents' false confidence. But
always I have been certain that both are wrong. Still, the existence
of bias can be impossible to detect for those who are biased. Thus,
at this point, it may be useful for me to offer a bit of information
about my personal history so that readers can make their own assessment of my objectivity.

First of all, my initial experience in a public prison came with
the beginning of my doctoral dissertation research at the Virginia
State Penitentiary in Richmond, Virginia, in 1969. It was a dismal
and often dangerous maximum security facility that had been in use
by then for more than one hundred years. My first experience with
a private facility came in the very early 1980s. It was a remote "last
chance" residential facility for serious and violent juvenile offenders. The term *privatization* was not then a part of my vocabulary.
At this point in time, a privatized jail or prison did not exist anywhere in the United States.

The novelty of privatization being what it was in those days, I
was a bit puzzled when, in 1985, the Florida legislature enacted
enabling legislation that expressly authorized Florida counties and
the Florida Department of Corrections to contract out for the full-
scale management of correctional facilities. With passage of this
legislation, the Bay County Board of County Commissioners
swiftly ended the role its sheriff had in the management of its jail
and vested managerial responsibilities in CCA—which, by the way,
continues to manage the Bay County jail system today. The liberal
though not always thoughtful politics of the academic world being
what they are, my first reaction was that any such intrusion by corporate America into the field of corrections simply had to be
wrong. At first blush, it seemed to me that the private sector would
be "more interested in doing *well* than in doing *good*" (Robbins
1988, 4). As noted earlier, however, my approach to "private versus public" issues is essentially pragmatic. It seemed necessary,

therefore, to actually think through what the proponents of privatization were saying.

I did think through the arguments and found some merit in the positions being advanced on both sides of the debate, but my basic conclusion was that the failures of public correctional agencies were so numerous that meaningful change seemed to be beyond their grasp. With jail and prison populations already growing at an unprecedented rate, it was obvious that change was imperative. I thought the private sector might perform no better than had so many public agencies, but it also seemed improbable that they would perform worse. My conclusion then was that privatization deserved the effort required to implement and to evaluate objectively some number of pilot projects. If such pilot projects yielded the desired outcomes, then obviously the public interest would have been served and a broader reliance on the private sector would be justified. If such pilot projects merely proved the claims of privatization opponents to be valid, then a return to a business-as-usual approach would never be further from our grasp than a few contract terminations.

Nearly two decades have passed since I reached that conclusion. Those years have found me becoming far more intimately involved in the world of privatization than I ever expected to be. Among other things, in the mid-1980s I never imagined a future that would find me serving as a member of the board of directors of three publicly traded corporations.[11] The main change, however, is that privatization is no longer a novelty. It has been tried many dozens of times and has been evaluated objectively. What before was a hypothesis based on soft theory can be stated now with the confidence that comes from a small mountain of empirical evidence. It is clear to anyone who is familiar with that evidence that reasonably structured privatization initiatives yield comparable or superior services at lower or equivalent costs.

Historical Considerations

The history of the U.S. criminal justice system is replete with examples of essential government services being provided by both the nonprofit and for-profit elements of the private sector. At the federal level, for example, the historical roots of the Secret Service have been traced back to a contract award to the Pinkerton detective agency (e.g., Kettl 1993). Similarly, the origins of our separate juvenile justice system are to be found in private rather than in public initiatives (e.g., Thomas and Bilchik 1985; Schlossman 1995). Further, the involvement of the private sector in corrections—albeit often in less than a palatable way—was established even before the United States became a nation (Eriksson 1976; McKelvey 1977; Morris and Rothman 1995; Smith and Morn 2001). Finally, prior to the emergence of correctional privatization as a means of providing for the full-scale management of jails and prisons, it had become common for government to contract with the private sector for a broad array of specific services (e.g., Camp and Camp 1984; Mullen, Chabotar, and Carrow 1985).

Despite the historical linkages between the public and private sectors in the delivery of criminal justice services in general and of correctional services in particular, the privatization of jails and prisons remains controversial. Thus, it is productive and perhaps necessary to provide an abbreviated overview of the history of correctional privatization before attention shifts to the other concerns of this chapter.

The Broader Context from Which Correctional Privatization Emerged

More than a few influential organizations, some having but others lacking an obvious vested interest in whether privatization initiatives move forward, forcefully have opposed contracting decisions. Their rhetoric sometimes gives rise to the incorrect impression that full-scale correctional privatization was a novel concept that leaped from the shadows and ambushed the correctional establishment without warning.

One need not have predispositions either in favor of or opposed to correctional privatization in order to understand that the "ambush theory" is invalid. To the contrary, it is clear that much of the economic and public-policy history of the second half of the twentieth century involved a fundamental change in the general public's and policymakers' judgment regarding both the brightness of the line that distinguishes the public and private sectors and their roles in the delivery of essential public services.

Early on, of course, there was a continuum along which public and private providers of goods and services could be placed with only a modest risk of any point on the continuum simultaneously being occupied by both public and private providers. At one end were traditional public agencies that provided for the delivery of most essential public services (e.g., K–12 education, hospitals, mail delivery services, institutionally based mental health care services, solid waste collection, wastewater treatment, and, of course, correctional services). Toward the middle of the continuum were highly regulated but private providers of other essential services (e.g., electric utilities, railroads, trucking companies, and telecommunications services). Toward the other end of the continuum were private and quite commonly nonprofit firms that provided essential services that were largely supplemental to what traditional government agencies provided (e.g., nonprofit acute care and mental health care facilities) or that in some way competed with public-agency providers of similar services (e.g., private and parochial schools and private providers of welfare services). At the end of the continuum was the whole array of traditional for-profit corporations that generally confined themselves to the production of goods or the delivery of services other than those made available by public agencies.

The world was a very different place for all of us when the oversimplification represented by this continuum bore some relationship with reality. Those were the days before Federal Express, United Parcel Service, and many other companies—obviously including countless Internet providers of e-mail delivery services—delivered mail and important documents. And before large corporations such as WorldCom Group, Inc., Sprint PCS, Nextel Communications, and dozens of others—not to mention the "Baby Bells"—provided a telecommunications alternative to AT&T. And before HCA, Inc., Hospital Management Associates, Tenet Health Care, and others provided hospital management services. And before a myriad of other private firms existed that now collect and handle the disposal of solid wastes, operate air-traffic control systems, guard government buildings, manage public airports, maintain public buildings, operate school bus fleets, provide firefighting services, provide wastewater treatment services, repair government-owned vehicles, and teach K–12 students. And before any of the private corrections-management firms that have received jail and prison management contracts began to transform correctional privatization from a fuzzy concept into a tangible reality.

The line between the public and private sectors has blurred in recent decades for at least three interconnected reasons. First, Americans have a long history of distrusting power in general and governmental power in particular. Much of the language in the Constitution, including but not limited to what one finds in the Bill of Rights, illustrates this distrust. Although the same distrust clearly extends to the exercise of power by private corporations, it is not difficult to identify a set of widely accepted beliefs that, whether correctly or incorrectly, depict the private sector as being more efficient and effective than government. This view is captured succinctly by Donald F. Kettl (1993):

> Americans have long had a reverence for private markets to match their dislike of public power. Markets seek efficiency; government may not. Markets promise choice in quality and price; government does not. Markets offer competition; government has a monopoly...The most profound attacks on government, in fact, have come from comparisons with the market. . . . While competition focuses private marketers clearly on the bottom line, the argument goes, government bureaucrats tend to be rewarded, not for efficiency, but for increasing their size and the size of their budgets; not for responsiveness, but for expanding their power. (1)

This image of both the public and private sectors is sometimes incorrect, but the image exists and creates a predisposition to accept the hypothesis that it is reasonable to turn to the private sector when the need arises to get "a bigger bang for the buck."

Second, the general public remains inclined, on the one hand, to demand both more and better services from government, while, on the other hand, resisting virtually any effort to increase taxes. The pressure this places on elected officials is considerable, and it encourages policy choices that aim to increase both the efficiency and effectiveness of service delivery. Contracting out for service delivery has become one of the means by which policymakers respond to this pressure.

Third, we find ourselves in a time when the notion of "reinventing government" by encouraging government to become more "entrepreneurial" attracts support from both conservatives and liberals (e.g., Osborne and Gaebler 1992). Such concepts encourage policymakers to structure government agencies in a manner that encourages and rewards competitiveness. In addition, however, an obvious byproduct of reinvention is the fostering of a heightened willingness on the part of policymakers and government agencies to contract out for the delivery of a broad array of essential public services when doing so yields equivalent or improved services at the same or a reduced cost.

In short, recent decades have witnessed fundamental changes in how government has gone about the business of delivering essential public services. The day has passed when the dominant view was that the proper role of government involved *both* the making of public policy *and* the delivery of policy-mandated services. The day has arrived when it is altogether common to see government agencies actively involved in shaping public policy regarding the content of essential public services but contracting with the private sector for service delivery. The pivotal reason why privatization by whatever name—*contracting out, forming public-private partnerships, outsourcing,* and so on—has become progressively more commonplace is that it generally yields the desired results of increased competition, a more efficient utilization of available resources, and enhancements in the caliber of the essential public services that are delivered (e.g., Utt 2001). Thus, when the pressures and problems of the prisoner population explosion in the United States began to grow in the mid-1970s, it probably was only a matter of time before the arrival of the private sector on the correctional scene.

The Modern History of Correctional Privatization

The involvement of the private sector in corrections predates the colonial period of U.S. history (Eriksson 1976; McConville 1987; McKelvey 1977; Morris and Rothman 1995; Smith and Morn 2001). To say that more than a few of those forms of involvement represented strikingly callous and exploitative forms of collusion between uncaring and often greedy public officials and their equally reprehensible counterparts in the private sector would be to accord both groups kinder treatment than either deserves. Perhaps especially for those of us whose roots are in the South, even to read about the brutality and the blatant racism that characterized the convict lease system that many Southern jurisdictions adopted following the Civil War is to be embarrassed by the inhumanity of our ancestors (e.g., Oshinsky 1997). To realize that so wretched a system persisted until well into the twentieth century is to recognize a national disgrace that rather conveniently escapes more than cursory inspection even in college-level U.S. history courses.

Disgust with the abuses, economic exploitation, and racism of the convict lease system, of course, played far less a role in its abolition than did a withering away of its economic benefits both to government and to private corporations. Still, an awareness of the abuses associated with it certainly did not encourage a swift return to any significant private-sector involvement in corrections.

Further, during most of the twentieth century, the nation's correctional system did not encounter problems of so great a magnitude that they would create significant pressures in favor of innovation of any kind. Indeed, prisoner populations were relatively stable throughout most of the twentieth century. Between 1940 and 1970, for example, the size of the state and federal prisoner population rose from 173,706 to 196,429, a multidecade increase of only 13.08 percent (Maguire and Pastore 2001, 507). During the same time period, the incarceration rate (i.e., the number of state and federal prisoners per 100,000 persons in the general population) actually fell from 131 to 96, a decline of 26.72 percent. Consequently, there were few incentives to alter traditional ways of delivering correctional services.

Given the benefits of hindsight, there are a host of reasons why the criminal justice system in general and the correctional component of that system in particular should have known that the viability of traditional means of addressing service delivery needs was going to be woefully inadequate as the nation moved into the last quarter of the twentieth century. On a demographic level, for example, it should have been clear that an unprecedented fraction of the general population would move into the high-risk age cohort—roughly eighteen to twenty-five years old—as a consequence of the post–World War II "baby boom." The effect of this circumstance and various other variables was dramatic. In 1960, for instance, 3,384,200 serious felonies were reported to the police. By 1975, the number of serious felonies reported rose to 11,292,400 (Maguire and Pastore 2001, 278).

Further, the judicial activism of the 1960s found the U.S. Supreme Court making it clear that what amounted to the "no rights doctrine" set forth in such early cases as *Ruffin v. Commonwealth* (62 Va. 790 [1871]) and the later "hands-off doctrine," deference to which resulted in the courts being disinclined to interfere with the operation of jails and prisons, was no longer acceptable on constitutional grounds (e.g., Branham and Krantz 1997, 278–92). In the wake of such landmark cases as *Monroe v. Pape* (365 U.S. 167 [1961]), it became clear that prisoners could litigate claims of unconstitutional jail and prison conditions under 42 U.S.C. §1983, do so in a federal rather than a state court, and, by the mid-1970s and pursuant to 42 U.S.C. §1988, be eligible for the award of attorney fees from the defendant party in the civil rights action. These and other major changes either in law or in interpretations of law opened the door for widespread judicial intervention into the operation and management of the nation's jails and prisons. It did not take long for members of the judiciary to walk through the door.

The Initial Contract Awards

The leading edge of the correctional privatization movement began to take form during the early 1980s with small contract awards by the Immigration and Naturalization Service (INS) and the U.S. Marshals Service to such California-based pioneering firms as Behavioral Systems Southwest and Eclectic Communications, Inc.[12] Practically speaking, however, the privatization alternative did not attract serious attention until several key developments materialized a few years later. Specifically, the first county-level award of a management contract came in 1984, when Hamilton County (Chattanooga), Tennessee, awarded a contract to CCA. The first state-level contract award came in 1985, when Kentucky contracted with the U.S. Corrections Corporation. The first significant federal award came in 1984, when the INS contracted with CCA for management of the Houston Processing Center.[13]

The importance of these contract awards to the subsequent development of correctional privatization would be difficult to overestimate. In addition, the fact that all of these contracts remain in force today is not inconsequential for those who would be willing to accept this fact as at least an oblique performance indicator. Each contract provided a real-world opportunity to test the hypothesis that contracting would yield meaningful benefits to government. Each also provided a valuable model that subsequent units of government could examine and improve on in such critical areas as procurement strategies, the formulation of sound contracts, and the creation of effective means of contract monitoring (for a review of these legal issues, see Quinlan, Thomas, and Gautreaux 2001).

Notwithstanding the value of the multidimensional testing ground established by the early contract awards, corrections is a conservative area where the diffusion of innovations is seldom swift. Further, as recently as the early 1980s, no jurisdiction in the United States enjoyed express statutory authority to contract for the operation of either jails or prisons. At least during those years, members of legislative bodies were not inclined to venture into such novel and potentially risky areas of law and policy. Few if any public agencies were enthusiastic about awarding facility management contracts, and more than a few opposed the concept quite vigorously. Public-employee unions were angered by the possibility that one of the rapidly decreasing areas within which their members enjoyed a monopoly would disappear. Other interest groups such as the American Civil Liberties Union voiced harsh opposition to full-scale privatization. The time lag between the adoption of suitable enabling legislation and the initiation of procurement processes, contract awards, and facility openings often was considerable.

Suffice it to say that these and related obstacles precluded any possibility that the initial progress of privatization would be dramatic. Indeed, the early developments were relatively few and far between (e.g., Logan 1990; Mullen, Chabotar, and Carrow 1985; Quinlan, Thomas, and Gautreaux 2001; Thomas 1998; Thomas and Logan 1993). At the same time, however, the early reports of cost benefits of privatization were favorable (e.g., Logan and McGriff 1989), and the pressures confronting the nation's correctional system continued to mount. The stage for further developments was set.

The Transition from Pilot Projects to an Accepted Alternative

Although informed commentators might differ in their judgments regarding when the tide began to turn in favor of privatization, the key influence was quite probably the 1987 Texas Department of Criminal Justice decision to award two 500-bed facility management contracts to CCA and two 500-bed contracts to Wackenhut. All four contracts were made pursuant to a Texas statute that mandated at least a 10 percent cost savings. All four contracts imposed performance standards on the two management firms that were more demanding than the standards that had to be satisfied by the public agency.[14]

To be sure, a different Texas correctional agency and multiple correctional agencies in other jurisdictions had awarded facility management contracts prior to these awards to CCA and Wackenhut (e.g., local-level awards in Florida, Pennsylvania, New Mexico, and Tennessee; state-level awards in California, Kentucky, and Texas; and federal-level awards in California, Colorado, and Texas). Still, the sheer magnitude of this single announcement produced shock waves both throughout and far beyond the boundaries of the United States.

The Present Status of Correctional Privatization

Even as late as 1989, after the Texas contract awards, the prisoner housing capacity of all private, secure, adult correctional facilities in operation or under construction was only 10,973. Although the comparable capacity figure had risen substantially to 63,595 by the close of 1995, the future of the correctional privatization movement was by no means guaranteed. Since then, however, the growth as measured by the number of beds under contract or under construction has continued. As this chapter is being written, for example, the best available evidence documents 184 private facilities (153 in the United States and 31 located elsewhere in the world) that provide a total prisoner housing capacity of 143,021 (of which 119,523 are in the United States and 23,498 are elsewhere). The geographical distribution of private facilities in operation or under construction reveals one or more facilities in twenty-nine states, the District of Columbia, and six other nations (Australia, Canada, England, New Zealand, Scotland, and South Africa).

Here I hasten to note that the average annual growth rates in the number of and the aggregate prisoner housing capacity of private facilities has been essentially flat since the end of 1999. The estimated capacity of all private facilities at year-end 1999 was 145,160. The comparable figure at the end of 2001 was 143,021. This rate does not compare favorably with the growth rates we witnessed as recently as the mid- to late 1990s, when, for instance, the capacity of privatized facilities rose from 63,595 at year-end 1995 to 145,160 by year-end 1999. Also important is the fact that a few jurisdictions within which facility management contracts had been in place either have implemented or have announced publicly plans to end their contractual relationships with the private sector (e.g., Arkansas, North Carolina, and Mississippi).

Because I discuss the future of correctional privatization at more length in the last segment of this chapter, little more needs to be said about the recent paucity of growth in contract awards and privatized correctional capacity. The fact deserving emphasis is that the diffusion of the innovation represented by correctional privatization during the 1990s was dramatic. Put in more quantitative terms, between year-end 1990 and year-end 1999 the design capacity of privatized facilities rose from 15,300 to 145,160—an increase of an astounding 848.76 percent. By comparison, during the same time period the U.S. prisoner population, inclusive of those confined in local jails, rose from 1,148,702 to 1,890,837—an increase of 64.61 percent.

The antiprivatization forces clearly underestimated the breadth and depth of the appeal privatization would enjoy following the initial contract awards of the early 1980s. Because the change has been so much more rapid and so much more pervasive than critics imagined would be possible, a productive purpose is served here by a comparison of privatization critics' key predictions with the lessons of actual experience.

• *Critics predicted that the constitutional and legal barriers to privatization would be so impenetrable that privatization decisions, were any to be made, would be challenged successfully in the courts.* Even if one ignores both what has taken place regarding the privatization of municipal and county jails and contract awards by federal agencies, the most recent data collected indicate that twenty-four states have enacted legislation specifically authorizing the privatization of state prisons and that another nine states perceive existing statutes to be sufficient to allow contract awards (Quinlan, Thomas, and Gautreaux 2001; Thomas and Gautreaux 2000). To date, there is no evidence of any facility management contract awarded by a local, state, or federal agency ever having been invalidated on legal or constitutional grounds.

• *Critics predicted that the ambiguous but heightened exposure to legal liability for any government agencies that chose to contract would yield such prohibitively costly consequences because of the tidal wave of anticipated prisoner lawsuits that this form of outsourcing would be recognized as a failure.* Prisoners are an especially litigious group but two points appear to have escaped critics' attention. First, a general principle of law is that the wrongful acts or omissions of an independent contractor do not provide an adequate foundation for a cause of action against a contracting agency. Second, all or substantially all facility management contracts impose a legal obligation of the private firm to indemnify and to hold harmless the contracting government agency against any and all sources of legal liability associated with the activities of the private firm (e.g., Quinlan, Thomas, and Gautreaux 2001). The result of such factors is that no single contracting agency, as far as I am aware, has expended as much as a dollar either to defend a private firm against a lawsuit or to shoulder the financial burden of any damage award to a prisoner plaintiff who was judged by a court to have suffered some unlawful loss or injury.

• *Critics predicted that the number of prisoners, if any, to be housed in private correctional facilities would be trivial.* By the close of 2001, there were 184 private jails and prisons in operation or under construction that yield an aggregate prisoner housing capacity of 143,021. The lion's share of these facilities and this capacity are to be found in the United States (153 facilities that provide a rated prisoner housing capacity of 119,523) (Thomas 2001).

• *Critics predicted that privatization experiments, if there were any, would be limited to small facilities designed to house special offender populations (e.g., detainees in the custody of the INS).* Privately managed facilities now house a diverse prisoner population. Typical privatized facilities have design capacities of 1,500 to 2,500 prisoners. The largest, as illustrated by a facility in South Africa operated by Wackenhut, are capable of housing more than 3,000 high-security prisoners. To be sure, the private sector is now responsible for various special offender populations (e.g., detainees in the custody of the INS, pretrial detainees in the custody of the U.S. Marshals Service, and special subsets of offenders deemed to require special programs targeted at such issues as substance abuse and addiction). However, the expectation that the private sector would never be permitted to house and provide programs for a broad cross section of the prisoner population proved to be false.

• *Critics predicted that few if any jurisdictions would elect to house their prisoners in privately managed facilities.* In addition to Australia, Canada, England, Scotland, and South Africa, for example, the following states in the United States—in addition to the District of Columbia—presently are housing prisoners in privately managed facilities: Alaska, Arizona, California, Colorado, Florida,

Georgia, Hawaii, Indiana, Kansas, Kentucky, Louisiana, Michigan, Mississippi, Montana, Nevada, New Mexico, North Dakota, Ohio, Oklahoma, Tennessee, Texas, Virginia, and Wisconsin. Further, all three federal U.S. agencies with prisoner custody responsibilities house prisoners in private facilities (i.e., the FBOP, the INS, and the U.S. Marshals Service).

• *Critics predicted that privatization experiments, if there were any, would be limited to facilities housing prisoners with low-security classifications.* CCA opened the first privately managed maximum-security facility in Leavenworth, Kansas, in June 1992. Numerous other privately managed facilities house significant numbers of maximum-security classified prisoners (e.g., both CCA and Wackenhut manage 1,474-bed state prisons in Louisiana that have maximum-security housing units, and in 1997 Wackenhut opened a 1,318-bed prison in Florida that houses both medium- and close-custody prisoners). Similar multi-security-level experience is in evidence in Australia, Canada, South Africa, and Great Britain. Indeed, the only two sectors of the correctional system in which the private sector is not represented today is in the management of facilities that have a death row population and in the management of what have come to be referred to as "supermaximum" facilities.

• *Critics predicted that privatization experiments, if there were any, would fail if for no other reason than that prisoners housed in them would refuse to respect the authority of their private keepers.* Although maintaining control in detention centers, jails, and prisons is a perpetual problem for both public and private managers, the evidence regarding control problems (e.g., inmate-on-inmate assaults, inmate-on-staff assaults, minor disturbances, riots, and escapes) in private facilities does not support the hypothesis that private correctional employees fail to maintain effective control in their facilities.

• *Critics predicted that private management firms, motivated by a desire to maximize profit, would "cut corners" and provide substandard programs and services.* To be sure, one can find illustrations of both public agencies and private firms that either have caused or have allowed substandard correctional services to be provided in one or more of the correctional facilities for which they had operational responsibility. More than one private firm that once had contracts, today has none—although problem-plagued correctional agencies in states such as California seem entirely immune to corrective forces. What the critics failed to anticipate was, among other things, the contracting agencies' ability to draft sophisticated contracts and to guarantee adherence to those contracts by effective on-site contract monitors. They also appear to have ignored the fact that private firms cannot grow and thus achieve heightened profitability if they fail to gain and then to maintain a reputation for being trustworthy, cost-effective providers.

By focusing on the false predictions of privatization critics, I certainly do not wish to convey the impression that privatization proponents were flawlessly precise in the expectations they advanced. In fact, I have to look no further than the nearest mirror to find someone who made more than one incorrect prediction. My own errors include the following.

• I expected that professional correctional management firms had such substantial advantages, including but certainly not limited to very large economy-of-scale advantages, over the vast majority of local-level agencies that the growth prospects for firms capable of managing municipal and county jails was enormous. I was wrong. Although some local units of government have been contracting for the management of their jails for nearly twenty years, I seriously underestimated the political power of sheriffs, who almost always oppose privatization, and overestimated the appeal to other elected local officials of both improving the quality of jail operations and achieving cost savings through contract awards.

• I expected that evidence of the success of contracting out would yield considerable competition between the public and private sectors for the opportunity to manage existing correctional facilities. I was wrong. Only infrequently have existing facilities converted from public to private management, and there is no evidence at all in the United States of fair competition between public agencies and private management firms.

• I expected that the private sector would bring much by way of creativity and innovation to corrections that would then cause the diffusion of innovative approaches to public correctional agencies. I was more wrong than right in this regard. I have seen a great deal of creativity and innovation on the front of facility design and construction as well as in the greater willingness of the private sector to accept technological innovation in, for example, the area of security. Thus far, however, I am unimpressed by the creativity that the private sector has brought to the table in such areas as staffing patterns, performance incentive programs for employees, fringe benefit and retirement programs for employees, and innovative programs for prisoners that include adequately sophisticated measures of in-program and postrelease outcomes.[15]

The point, however, is not that so many proponents made errors in the predictions they advanced about correctional privatization, but that both the critics' negative predictions and the proponents' positive predictions were advanced in an experiential vacuum. In the mid-1980s, neither group could do more than speculate about what the future would bring. However, the seeds of change carried by privatization proponents during the early 1980s clearly found far more fertile ground in which to grow than even the most optimistic among them had imagined at the time.

Explaining Growth in the Appeal of Privatization

It has been established that substantially all of the doom and gloom predictions advanced by critics of correctional privatization in the mid-1980s proved to be wrong. This, however, cannot be taken as evidence that public-policy decisions favoring privatization achieved the objectives that prompted those decisions to be made. To be sure, much systematic evidence reveals that privatization initiatives in other public-service delivery areas had allowed the desired outcomes to be achieved (e.g., Utt 2001), but evidence of success in other areas is not a sufficient basis for making public policy in corrections. Only growth in the body of directly relevant evidence supports the hypothesis that contracting for correctional services reflects sound public-policy decisions. Professor Marvin E. Wolfgang (1998), an internationally recognized criminologist, made this pragmatic point succinctly when he wrote, "The privatization of criminal justice from crime reporting to enforcement, mediation, prosecution, and prison management should be seriously considered, empirically evaluated, and if found to be positive, implemented" (xvii).

Fortunately, we now have access to nearly twenty years of contracting experience and to what has become a voluminous research literature (for a comprehensive bibliography, see Quinlan, Thomas, and Gautreaux 2001). It is the case that published studies have reached both favorable and unfavorable conclusions, but one should be surprised (and perhaps also distrustful) only if all the evidence were to point only in a positive or a negative direction. The key, I think, is to look for patterns in the best available evidence. Prudent public policy must look to what is typical rather than atypical. If what is typical also is positive regarding an innovation such as correctional privatization, then another key is to find whatever appears to have increased the likelihood of success in the typical contexts and to have decreased the likelihood of success in the atypical contexts. Sound policymaking, after all, builds on the lessons learned from prior successes and failures.

Competition

The least-often discussed or researched, but perhaps also the most powerful potential advantage of correctional privatization is its ability to generate competition between alternative providers of correctional services and thereby to motivate public agencies both to improve the quality of the services they provide and to control or reduce their costs (Harding 1997). Arguably one of the most fundamental problems of a government monopoly is the absence of incentives that encourage them and their employees to become more efficient and effective (Kettl 1993; Logan 1990). When policymakers encourage or require public agencies to compete for the opportunity to be the providers of essential public services, the public interest is served without regard to whether a public or private entity prevails in the competition—as long, of course, as the rules of the competition favor neither public nor private entities.

It is the case, of course, that government agencies and public employees often are the most outspoken opponents of privatization.

Their desire to preserve a comfortable status quo is not difficult to understand. Although everyday life experience provides evidence that we perform better in competitive settings, noncompetitive settings are understandably appealing to most if not all of us. The appeal of what amounts to easier challenges, however, obviously does not mean that monopolies give rise to creativity or to greater degrees of cost effectiveness. To the contrary, a growing body of evidence strongly suggests that privatization can be a powerful stimulus for change in how public agencies perform.

It is worth emphasizing that policymakers have been slow in recognizing and exploiting this potential benefit of privatization. Regarding jurisdictions within which one or more facilities have been privatized, this shortcoming has at least two dimensions. First, policymakers either intentionally or unintentionally have looked the other way while their correctional agencies effectively disallowed true privatization by mandating strict adherence to the very same traditional agency policies, procedures, and practices that in many ways created the initial appeal of privatization. Second, both policymakers and correctional agencies have done a truly wretched job when it comes to recognizing the need to evaluate fairly the performance of private firms and to compare the results of such evaluations with comparably objective assessments of the performance of public agencies.

Beyond these serious shortcomings, however, is a larger weakness. Specifically, the lion's share of any improvements in efficiency and effectiveness within public agencies clearly appears to have come from those agencies' desire to avoid privatization to the maximum extent possible and, when it could no longer be avoided, to confine the scope of privatization initiatives as much as they could.

The dubious distinction of winning first place in this foot-dragging contest must go to the FBOP. I recall the top executives of the FBOP proudly proclaiming twenty years ago that they housed no prisoners in privately managed prisons. On an amusingly hypertechnical level, they were telling the truth. In Eden, Texas, for example, the FBOP then (and also today) had entered into a noncompetitively procured contract with the City of Eden (i.e., what is referred to in government circles as an *intergovernmental agency agreement* or IGA). They did so with the full knowledge that the City of Eden had no intention of managing the Eden Detention Center and, instead, would contract with a private management firm for each and every service mandated by the agreement with the FBOP. Thus, although today there are more than 1,200 FBOP prisoners housed in the Eden Detention Center, and although all necessary services are being provided by CCA (which, by the way, also owns the Eden Detention Center), the FBOP continues to claim that its contract is with the City of Eden and thus that it does not contract with the private sector for the management of the facility.

In addition, the FBOP has claimed repetitively that the nation has had so little experience with privatization that the federal government must deem the private sector to be capable of handling nothing more difficult than prisoners with low- and minimum-security classifications. Ignoring the real and relevant fact that assigning security classifications to prisoners is an activity that often results in virtually any prisoner being pushed into any pigeon-hole in the classificatory system that contains an empty bed, the FBOP position can be described most gently as being ridiculous and as serving nothing beyond the parochial limits of that agency's political agenda. Prisoners with medium-security, close-custody, and maximum-security classifications have been housed for years in privately managed facilities both in the United States and elsewhere in the world. Indeed, the same is true of federal prisoners in the custody of the U.S. Marshals Service. Thus far, however, Congress has chosen to ignore the fact that the FBOP's assertions are devoid of a factual basis.

My point, however, is not merely to poke fun at the FBOP and at the silliness of the positions it advances to protect its own bureaucratic interests. Instead, my point is that policymakers have lacked the insight and the will to devise means by which *all* reasonably qualified providers of correctional services are encouraged or required to compete with one another for the opportunity to manage the nation's jails and prisons. Instead, somewhat like crumbs being brushed from an overflowing table, a small percentage of the nation's correctional facilities have been contracted out following competition between various numbers of private management firms.

I am aware of no statute in the United States that authorizes or requires public agencies to compete for the opportunity to manage a jail or a prison. I am aware of no example in the United States that reveals fair competition between public and private providers of correctional services. Until both of those policy failures are corrected, achieving many of the potential benefits of privatization will be impossible.

Construction Time and Cost Savings

No informed person on either side of the privatization debate will deny that one benefit of privatization is the ability of the private sector to move far more swiftly with the construction of new correctional facilities and to do so at a substantially lower cost. The construction times of new privatized facilities are generally 50 percent or more below those of government projects. Construction-cost savings of 15–25 percent are quite typical.

One fairly recent example of this dual benefit is provided by a case study of a fairly large facility in Delaware County, Pennsylvania (Kengor and Scheffler 1999). Prior to the decision to privatize, construction costs had been estimated at $93 million. Wackenhut received a contract to design, construct, and manage the needed facility and did so at a cost of $55.84 million. Further, observe Kengor and Scheffler, when "Wackenhut broke ground for the new facility, a similar state prison in Chester County was over a year-and-a-half underway, yet Delaware County completed its prison before the government finished its facility" (9).

Research reports with comparable conclusions regarding construction-cost savings have become routine. For instance, the Florida OPPAGA, the research arm of the Florida legislature, published a detailed statistical analysis on the construction-cost savings achieved by Wackenhut (OPPAGA 2000). Here it was possible to make a direct comparison between the costs of constructing the 1,318-bed private prison and a nearby traditional public prison of equivalent size and mission. The total construction and financing costs of the private prison was $69.9 million; the comparable cost of the traditional public prison was $85.7 million.

Access to Construction Capital

The construction of new correctional facilities places a substantial financial burden on government. Construction costs expressed on a per bed basis are quite commonly in the range of $50,000 to $80,000. Either government must divert the needed funds from its present-year budget or arrange for the sale of bonds, which allows the construction-cost burden to be spread over a period of twenty or more years. However, government sometimes finds itself in the awkward position of confronting pressing needs for new jails or prisons at the very same time that its tax revenue stream is constrained or that its existing level of debt undermines its ability to borrow more capital through the sale of tax-exempt bonds.

Suffice it to say that many jurisdictions favoring privatization have shifted the burden of obtaining construction capital onto private management firms (e.g., Arizona, Colorado, Georgia, Kentucky, Oklahoma, and the FBOP). Although the private firms certainly hope to recapture their investment of capital, I am not aware of any contract that includes a guarantee that this hope will be realized. Nonetheless, it is the case that many government agencies define the private sector's ability and willingness to commit large amounts of private capital to the construction of new facilities as a significant advantage of privatization.

The benefits of this advantage can be multifaceted. In 1998, for example, CCA assessed the need for prisoner housing space for either state or federal prisoners in California to be so great that it committed more than $100 million of private capital to construct a 2,304-bed medium-security prison located in California City, California. The company made the commitment without any contract that guaranteed the utilization of the facility. More important, not a penny of public capital was put at risk by CCA's decision to move forward with the project prior to a contract award. Soon after the construction was completed, however, the largest prisoner housing contract ever awarded by the FBOP was announced. The net effect of this decision was that the FBOP was able to gain access to a new state-of-the-art facility immediately following the contract award, to do so at a construction cost far below the norm set by recent FBOP construction projects, and to achieve significant daily operating-cost savings for federal taxpayers.

Other illustrations of the access to capital advantage provided by the private sector are identified easily. In 1999, for instance, Cornell Companies, Inc., committed more than $30 million of private capital to the construction of the New Morgan Academy in New Morgan, Pennsylvania. This modern 214-bed facility was constructed in only eighteen months and today provides intensive programs and services for some of the most difficult juveniles in the nation. Although the corporate decision to move forward with the project was based on its internal assessment of government needs rather than a preconstruction contract award, the fact that the facility is already operating at close to its design capacity offers evidence of how prudent risk taking by the private sector can yield a tangible benefit to government.

Here it once again seems necessary to inject something of a qualification about the benefits government can gain when it shifts the burden of obtaining construction capital onto the private sector. Government agencies too often have exposed themselves to unnecessary risks by failing to protect their own legitimate interests when the ownership of important infrastructure assets is private rather than public. This is most particularly the case when the private management firm that operates the facility is the same as the private entity that owns the facility. Such an arrangement easily can place the public interest at risk if the caliber of services being provided fails to meet expectations. If such a circumstance were encountered, then a contract termination would be impossible unless the government agency involved has sufficient excess capacity and thus can absorb the increased prisoner population. Obviously, however, this risk can be mitigated by contract terms that permit the government agency either to purchase the facility at an agreed upon price in the event of the termination of the management contract or to assign to another private firm the right to purchase the facility at the same agreed-upon price.

Operating-Cost Savings

Everyday operating-cost savings achieved by privatized facilities routinely are found to be between 10 and 15 percent (for a review of recent literature, see, e.g., Brakel and Gaylord this volume, Segal and Moore 2002). For example, a few years ago I received a contract from the Arizona Department of Corrections for the purpose of evaluating whether its first privatization initiative in 1994, which involved a management contract award to Management and Training Corporation (MTC), had yielded cost and performance benefits (Thomas 1997). The overall conclusion, endorsed by the Arizona Department of Corrections, was that cost savings of no less than 13.8 percent had been achieved and that the quality of the services provided by MTC had been either equivalent to or superior to the services provided in public prisons housing inmates with comparable security classifications.

Altogether expectedly, various opponents of privatization, including the FBOP Office of Research and Evaluation, were quick to criticize my research (Gaes, Camp, and Saylor 1998). The criticism notwithstanding, my results regarding cost savings and performance were cross-validated recently by a two-year study conducted by the Arizona Department of Corrections itself (2000). This study broadened the focus of the comparisons to include both the MTC facility and two newer facilities operated by Correctional Services Corporation. The three private facilities were compared with fifteen public facilities that house prisoners with comparable security classifications. The report concluded that "the private prisons performed at or above the aggregate performance of Level 2 public prisons 62.3 percent of the time" (2000, 2) and did so at a cost per prisoner per day of "less than $41.00 versus a comparable public-prison cost of $46.72 in 1998 and $45.85 in 1999." This figure translates into an average operating-cost savings of 13.62 percent in fiscal year 1998 and 10.84 percent in fiscal year 1999 (Arizona Department of Corrections 2000, 46–47).

Because the provisions of many state laws flatly require evidence of consequential cost savings as a precondition for any contract award, findings of the type reported in my Arizona research and reinforced by the more recent analysis should not come as a shock to anyone. Still, this often-demonstrated advantage of privatization has been the subject of far more controversy than the construction-cost savings. To be sure, the vast majority of the published cost comparisons in the United States, as well as those coming from Australia and Great Britain, document attractive cost savings (Brown 1994; Coopers and Lybrand 1996; Crants 1991; Davenport 2001; Dunmore 1997; Gold 1996; Kengor and Scheffler 1999; Logan and McGriff 1989; Loux 1996; McDonald 1990; OPPAGA 2000; Segal and Moore 2002; Texas Sunset Advisory Commission 1991; Thomas 1997; Wilson 1998; Woodbridge 1997). Indeed, the most recently published literature review indicates that twenty-two of twenty-eight separate studies found significant cost savings (Segal and Moore 2002). The conclusion of another influential study is quite straightforward: "The most rigorous studies clearly find positive cost savings" (Volokh 2002, 1875). Still, privatization critics continue to contend either that the documented savings are unpersuasive or that they will diminish over time (e.g., Gaes, Camp, and Saylor 1998; U.S. General Accounting Office 1996).[16] Despite this criticism, the same body of evidence as well as other studies that focus only on the quality of services provided in privatized facilities make it equally clear that cost savings do not come at the expense of the caliber of the correctional services provided (Brakel 1988; Logan 1992, 1996; Quinlan, Thomas, and Gautreaux 2001; Thomas 1997; Wilson 1998).

Quality of Service Enhancements

To achieve cost savings through privatization is a meaningful public-policy objective, but to pursue those savings blindly in the absence of clear evidence that the precontract quality of services is being preserved or enhanced would achieve no productive purpose. In recent years, for example, I watched closely while Arkansas and North Carolina ineptly privatized two state prisons in each of those jurisdictions. Both either knew or reasonably should have known that the services required by their contracts could not possibly be delivered at the prices they agreed to pay. All four initiatives failed, which many suspect was the true goal in both states. Now, however, the operating budgets for all four facilities will be pushed significantly and unapologetically higher as they return to the publicly managed side of the ledger.[17]

Fortunately, those responsible for more thoughtful privatization initiatives have recognized the distinction most of us make between "good value" and "cheap" in our everyday economic lives (e.g., Alaska, Arizona, Florida, Hawaii, Oklahoma, Tennessee, Wisconsin, and the FBOP). Policymakers in those jurisdictions had the sophistication to pursue reasonable cost savings and to do so at the same time that they demanded meaningful programs and services.[18]

The research evidence quite clearly shows that government agencies that qualify as being what Kettl (1993) refers to as "smart buyers" can and do obtain enhanced correctional services by privatizing. In the previous discussion of cost savings, I identified many of the individual studies that support this conclusion, and there is other evidence that improved services made possible by privatization may yield meaningful long-term benefits. Indeed, the results can be dramatic. Recent research in Florida, for instance, compared recidivism among prisoners released from a medium-security prison operated by the CCA and from a similar facility operated by Wackenhut with recidivism among a similar group of releasees from prisons operated by the Florida Department of Corrections (Lanza-Kaduce, Parker, and Thomas 1999). Recidivism was measured in terms of differentials in rearrest, technical violations of the conditions of release, and resentencing for post-release crime. The research results revealed significantly lower recidivism among the releasees from the private prisons. For example, releasees from the private prisons were more than 28 percent less likely than releasees from the public prisons to be returned to prison following their release (Lanza-Kaduce, Parker, and Thomas 1999, 36). More important, a follow-up study that examined differentials in recidivism among the same prisoner population for a significantly longer time period documented lower levels of recidivism among the releasees from private prisons (Lanza-Kaduce and Maggard 2001).[19]

Heightened Accountability

It simply is not possible to argue against the hypothesis that heightened accountability is an important benefit of privatization (Harding 1997; Quinlan, Thomas, and Gautreaux 2001; Volokh 2002). The reason is simple. The legal link between government policymakers and private management firms is a management contract. The performance requirements in such contracts are commonly quite specific with respect to numbers of employees the private firm is obliged to hire, the training standards those employees must meet, the array of programs and services the private firm agrees to provide, the fraction of the prisoner population that must be involved in programs, and so on. Private firms risk significant financial performance penalties if the terms and the conditions of their contracts are violated, and either serious or chronic contract violations justify contract terminations. Further, most contracting agencies are sophisticated enough to appreciate the value of full-time monitors whose presence in private facilities serves as an additional guarantee of contract compliance. Nothing similar to such contracts and fully independent contract monitors exists in facilities managed by public agencies.

Heightened accountability, of course, is a means to an end and should not be viewed as an end in and of itself. Still, much experience gained since the first management contracts were awarded in the mid-1980s offers persuasive proof that the prospects for the success of privatization initiatives is enhanced greatly by the dual accountability mechanisms of properly drafted contracts and fair but firm monitoring of contract compliance.

Operational Flexibility

Change and flexibility are two concepts that are difficult to translate into meaningful action in government agencies. Absent a meaningful ability to implement change swiftly and to respond flexibly to changing circumstances, virtually any private corporation will fail to survive. This general weakness in government and this general strength in the private sector make it unsurprising that flexibility is an advantage of correctional privatization.[20]

Private management firms, for example, regularly add, significantly modify, or replace various educational, vocational, and treatment programs. It is difficult and often impossible for government agencies to be as open to change or to be as flexible in their operations. Although part of this flows from their bureaucratic habits and traditions, a large part is tied to civil service job-security guarantees. To be sure, it is at least theoretically possible to eliminate a government program, but the general effect of this elimination is merely to transfer all of the involved employees to some other government program. Far too often the consequence, therefore, is change without either cost savings or program improvements.

Reduced Exposure to Legal Liability

A voluminous body of case law, the vast majority of which involves cases that have been decided by state and especially by federal courts since the early 1960s, makes three things painfully apparent: (1) violations of the constitutional and statutory rights of prisoners are so common as to blemish many public agencies' reputation; (2) prisoners are such a litigious group that their claims, most but not all of which are frivolous, provide employment opportunities for a small army of lawyers; and (3) the annual costs of litigation, settlements of cases, and damage awards consume tens of millions of dollars. As though to make matters even worse, the flow of prisoner lawsuits is erratic, and the magnitude of the outcomes is so highly variable that it is difficult to create reasonable forecasts of budgetary needs.

Contracting with the private sector does not get rid of the exposure to legal liability associated with cases brought by prisoner plaintiffs. There is certainly no credible evidence that suggests that prisoners are averse to bringing suit against a private rather than a public actor. What does change dramatically is that the burden of exposure to legal liability is shifted almost entirely from the shoulders of government agencies to those of private firms. A general principle of civil law is that a government agency cast in the role of prime contractor cannot be held liable for the wrongful conduct of an independent contractor on which it relies for the delivery of an essential service. Thus, an independent contractor will incorporate into its management proposal the legal costs that it foresees. I have never seen a facility management contract that required a contracting public agency to shoulder any legal costs above an agreed upon dollar amount, unlike other risks sometimes shared with the public agencies (e.g., medical costs rising above a certain amount). Further, the general rule is that the cost proposal must provide a cost saving to government in the range of 5 to 10 percent. One seldom if ever sees legal costs included when government estimates its own facility operating costs for the purpose of comparison.

My judgment is that the net effect of all of this evidence is not subject to debate. The practical consequence of correctional privatization is to limit the government's legal-liability costs to whatever amount is included in the cost proposals that private management firms submit to it, which shifts the real risk of litigation from the public to the private sector. In a sense, of course, this practice is not fair. It places a heavier burden on private management firms than it does on government agencies. On the other hand, however, the unfairness of such arrangements also gives rise to a powerful set of financial incentives and disincentives for the private sector, which, in turn, encourages private firms to be more attentive to the legal rights of prisoners than publicly managed facilities typically are. If private management firms drop the ball, they pay for each bounce it takes in the courtroom. If public agencies drop the ball, each bounce yields a new charge only to the taxpayers.

The Future of Correctional Privatization

When it is recognized that only twenty years ago there were no fully privatized correctional or detention facilities housing adult prisoners anywhere in the United States, it becomes clear that proponents of the privatization movement have much to which they can point with a sense of satisfaction. A small mountain of empirical data accumulated since the mid-1980s provides persuasive evidence that well-conceptualized privatization initiatives can bring new prisoner capacity on line far faster than can traditional government construction methods; that construction-cost savings of at least 15–25 percent are commonplace; and that everyday operating cost savings of 10–15 percent are common. Much additional evidence offers proof that the considerable cost benefits of privatization are not achieved at the expense of the quality of services. For example, it is undeniable that privatized facilities have been far more likely than publicly managed facilities to earn the distinction of ACA accreditation. Still other evidence coming from jurisdictions such as Florida reveals that levels of participation in, and completion of, programs aimed at offender rehabilitation are substantially higher in privatized facilities than they are in publicly managed facilities. Not surprisingly, therefore, related research findings document lower levels of recidivism among prisoners released from privatized facilities. Finally, few would be so foolish as to challenge the contention that the existence of a private alternative to a business-as-usual approach in corrections has caused public agencies to pursue various means of controlling their costs and of improving the quality of the services they provide.

The accumulated privatization has yielded much useful information regarding the design of procurement processes, fairly evaluating proposals submitted by alternative providers, methods of structuring contracts that maximize the probability of success, and means of monitoring the performance of independent contractors that quite substantially increase the likelihood of contract compliance (e.g., Quinlan, Thomas, and Gautreaux 2001).[21] This experience allows policymakers to have far greater confidence in public agencies' ability to implement privatization initiatives in a suitably sophisticated manner. The diverse types of privatized facilities that have proved to be successful have broadened significantly the settings within which privatization might be appropriate. Thus, candidates for privatization are no longer limited to small facilities housing inmates with low-security classifications and now routinely include facilities with capacities ranging from 1,500 to 3,000 prisoners with all possible security classifications.

Despite these accomplishments, more than a few critics are of the opinion that the future will yield no more than anemic growth in the fledgling private corrections industry. For nearly twenty years, vested interest groups, such as the public-employee unions, have been predicting the demise of the correctional privatization movement. Such groups were stating their hopes rather than making predictions. But not all of the skepticism one confronts today can be characterized as self-serving ideological rhetoric. The appeal of investing in the stock of publicly traded management firms, for example, has diminished dramatically. The pace of growth in new contract awards has slowed to a crawl during 2000–2002. Indeed, backward rather than forward movement has been more common since the beginning of 2001. For example, privatized facilities have been returned or soon will return to management by public agencies in such states as Arkansas, Mississippi, North Carolina, and Utah, as well as in Puerto Rico. Growth in the nation's prisoner population and thus the demand for new capacity in prisoner housing continued on the moderating path it began to follow in 1995. The average annual growth in the state and federal prisoner population between 1990 and 2000, for example, was 6.0 percent. Between the end of 2000 and the end of 2001, however, the prisoner population rose by only 1.1 percent (Harrison and Beck 2002).

Such factors provide a rational basis for concern if not also skepticism about the future prospects of the correctional privatization movement. To be sure, private-sector involvement in areas such as juvenile and community corrections is accepted widely. There are examples of privately managed facilities being returned to public agencies in a handful of jurisdictions, but such examples attract attention primarily because they are exceptions to the rule. The rule is that virtually all contracts that have come up for renewal or extension have yielded decisions favoring continued private management. Further, those who imagine that there will be no new contract awards are demonstrably wrong. As this chapter is being finalized in August 2002, for example, the FBOP has announced its award of a contract to CCA to manage a McRae, Georgia, 1,500-bed facility that CCA designed, constructed, and owns. Similarly, it is generally believed that the INS is poised to award a management contract to the Correctional Services Corporation for at least a 500-bed facility to be located in Tacoma, Washington. Further, as illustrated by the opening of a 1,200-bed facility last November by Management and Training Corporation in Ontario, Canada—the first Canadian prison ever to be privatized—contracting activity persists outside of the United States. More such international activity is expected this year in Australia, Great Britain, Costa Rica, and perhaps also in Chile and Peru. Indeed, Wackenhut issued a press release in which it announced its financial results for the second quarter of 2002 and indicated that during the coming year it expected to compete for the award of contracts for facilities having an aggregate capacity of approximately 25,000 beds.

On balance, I see a combination of both challenges to and opportunities for growth. The mixture of the two makes me optimistic about the contributions the private corrections industry is likely to make in the years ahead, but the magnitude of the external and internal obstacles the industry must overcome if it is to realize its potential is considerable. A decade ago, I might well have described my optimism as unqualified enthusiasm. Today, I would describe my position as one of cautious optimism. Thus, it seems appropriate to close this discussion of the future of correctional privatization with what I take to be the most influential threats to the prospects of the industry.

The Politics of Privatization

A decade ago I overestimated the sophistication or perhaps simply the common sense that policymakers at the local, state, and federal level bring to the table when decisions about the delivery of essential public services are being made. I wrongly imagined that facts would be more influential than rhetoric. Thus, I also wrongly imagined that there would be a high and positive correlation between evidence regarding the cost effectiveness of correctional privatization and its appeal to policymakers. Perhaps growing more cynical about the political process as I grow older—but also perhaps growing more aware of reality as I became more experienced—I have seen both meaningful opportunities for privatization pushed to the sidelines by antiprivatization groups' effective lobbying and decisions to award contracts made in the absence of any persuasive reason that doing so would serve the public interest. It turns out that the political power of special interests usually trumps the facts.

It is true, of course, that both proponents and opponents of privatization make efforts to influence the political process. The antiprivatization forces, however, are better organized, far more sophisticated in the tactics they employ, and seemingly more capable of committing very consequential financial resources to the ongoing battle. The strikingly powerful position enjoyed by the California Correctional Peace Officers Association, a public-employee union in California, is an excellent illustration of this commitment. Despite the acute state budget shortfall of more than $24 billion, California Governor Davis recently (2002) approved a multiyear contract for correctional employees that will give them a 37 percent salary increase as well as various other fringe benefits. In an article that appeared in the *San Francisco Chronicle* on July 31, 2002, Greg Lucas reviewed the relevant background on the approval of this new contract. According to Lucas, "between 1998 and January 2002, the union gave Davis some $200,000 and hosted golf fund-raisers for the Democratic governor that brought in an additional $356,000. He received another $251,000 in March, one month after the contract was signed. . . . Over the past decade, the prison guard union has become one of the most powerful special interests in Sacramento. In 2000 alone, prison guards contributed nearly $1.9 million to dozens of state senators and Assembly members of both parties."

To the degree that the prime directive for many elected policymakers is the preservation of their positions, large public-employee unions' ability to channel substantial campaign contributions to these policymakers and to energize consequential numbers of voters continues to be the major threat to the growth prospects of the private corrections industry.

The Threat Posed by Public Corrections Agencies

I cannot recall a time when a decision to privatize a jail or a prison was made as a consequence of the senior executives of a local, state, or federal correctional agency reaching the conclusion that the public interest would be served more efficiently and effectively by a private management firm. For the vast majority of these executives, such a decision would be an admission of both personal failure and the failure of the agencies for which they are responsible. Far more commonly, elected officials—usually those elected officials who endorsed conservative political ideologies and whose political futures were thus not dependent on how enthusiastically they responded to the agenda of organized labor—forced the executives to make such decisions.

Public agencies are strange creatures. Theoretically politically passive component parts of the executive branch of government whose powers and budgets are shaped by those in the legislative branch, they in fact lobby aggressively for the roles and resources that they determine to be most appropriate. When either the head of the executive branch (e.g., a governor) or the legislative branch (e.g., a state legislature) force certain courses of action on such agencies, they can be particularly adept at undermining the efficacy of initiatives with which they disagree. For example, agency executives regularly take the position that elected officials will come and go, but that the management class is the permanent and semiautonomous group that really formulates public policy. Thus, it is not uncommon to see agencies avoid initiatives with which they disagree merely by delaying their implementation until the political climate is more supportive of their position. Alternatively, bureaus sometimes choose to implement a decision in such a way as to maximize the probability of its failure.

These kinds of tactics by public agencies have plagued correctional privatization efforts from the beginning and continue to be serious threats today. In Florida, for example, the state legislature enacted the necessary authorizing legislation in 1985 and soon thereafter began to pressure the Florida Department of Corrections to award facility management contracts. Multiple times the Department of Corrections initiated procurement processes with no apparent intent to actually award contracts. In mid-1993, a thoroughly frustrated legislature finally gave up on the prospect of its state correctional agency getting the job done. Instead, notwithstanding the strident opposition of the Florida Department of Corrections and a threatened veto of the legislation by Florida's governor, it created a new state agency, the Florida Correctional

Privatization Commission, and charged it, rather than the Department of Corrections, with contracting responsibilities. Contracts for the design, construction, and private management of two 750-bed medium-security prisons were awarded within months of the creation of the commission. Today the commission is responsible for the everyday management and operation of five privately designed, constructed, and managed facilities that have a design capacity of more than 4,000 beds. The commission's success notwithstanding, its very existence is challenged annually by those who are committed to a business-as-usual approach in Florida. Indeed, the ongoing political struggle in Florida may well have reached a point at which it no longer serves any useful public-policy purpose.

Governmentalization

A very significant threat to the future of privatization comes from agencies that do not understand that real privatization means more than contracting with the private sector. Contracting agencies are obliged to set the major goals that independent contractors are expected to achieve, to maximize the flexibility those independent contractors have in devising innovative methods for achieving those goals, and to monitor contract performance with at least two objectives in mind. One objective, of course, is to guarantee compliance with the terms and conditions of contracts and to impose reasonable sanctions on contractors if and when they fail to deliver what they promised to provide. Another objective is to identify innovative methods that can be adopted in publicly managed facilities.

Far, far too often, contracting agencies have conceptualized independent contractors as nothing more than an extension of their agencies and have required substantially all methods of service delivery to mirror the methods previously devised by the public agency.[22] This approach includes but is surely not limited to requirements that independent contractors comply with all rules and regulations applicable to the public agency (such standards, of course, having been promulgated by the public agency); adhere to staffing patterns substantially identical to those the contracting agency adopts; offer salaries equivalent to the salaries of agency employees and do so without regard to the economics of local labor markets; provide programs that are the same as those provided in public facilities; allow public agencies to approve or disapprove of the employment of key personnel of independent contractors; and even require that mundane dimensions of facility operation, such as food service, be precisely the same as those of the public agency.

A recent example of the point I am trying to make is provided in a report on privatization in Arizona prepared by the auditor general of Arizona. An especially relevant portion of it reads as follows:

> The Department requires that private prisons mirror state-operated facilities, and performs extensive oversight activities to ensure that its contractors meet its requirements. In order to maintain uniform standards for state and private prisons, the Department requires contractors to follow Department Orders, Director's Instructions, Technical Manuals, Institution Orders, and Post Orders. These requirements extend to specific details, such as following the same daily menus as state-operated facilities. (Davenport 2001, 9)

Such an approach, of course, misses the point of privatization.[23] The core appeal of correctional privatization is linked closely to the excessive bureaucratization of government agencies, to those agencies' aversion to innovation, to endless regulatory and reporting requirements that focus far more on processes than on outcomes, and, perhaps most important, to public agencies' frequent operational failures. To the degree that government agencies design privatization initiatives in such a way as to make private firms clones of public agencies, real privatization has not happened. It makes little difference whether efforts to governmentalize privately managed facilities are caused by public agencies' intellectual mediocrity or by their malice. What matters is that this practice undermines private management firms' ability to devise and then implement creative solutions for our correctional problems.

Pressures favoring governmentalization rather than privatization notwithstanding, perhaps the greatest blessing the private corrections industry enjoys is that it competes primarily with public agencies that are setting the height of efficiency and effectiveness hurdles at so low a level that they can be cleared by a heavy turtle that has really "no rise" (to use the language I often hear from my younger son). Looked at from a public-policy point of view, however, this blessing is a curse. Competition is a dynamic process that feeds on its own successes. A vitally important aspect of the dynamism is that performance standards be driven higher over time. Governmentalization fails to achieve that desired objective. In practice, it typically either leaves performance standards unchanged or causes performance standards applied to private firms to be more demanding than the standards applied to public agencies. It is likely that the private corrections industry will maintain its edge over the public agencies, but so long as the overseeing public agencies set standards in so unsophisticated a way as continues to be common, we are unlikely to see the innovation, experimentation, and rapid advances that competition brings to other areas of the economy.

Are There Best Practices that Mitigate the Risks of Governmentalization?

The threat that governmentalization poses to realizing the potential of true privatization deserves whatever words of condemnation I may be able to offer. In fairness, however, one can sift through two decades of contracting experience and find evidence of greater sophistication in what government agencies have done, or at least a basis for reasonable inferences about what could have been done better. Thus, before concluding this discussion, I feel it is worth taking a moment to identify what might be construed to be best practices whose value has been proven, and the means by which more progress may be achieved.

Understanding the Need to Identify the Costs of Government Agencies

A core failure of virtually all service delivery efforts by all levels of government is the general absence of credible data regarding the true costs at which those services are delivered. This is not a unique failure of correctional agencies. It is a generic failure, and it is bewildering to anyone who becomes aware of it. No private corporation of any kind could possibly remain viable were its understanding of its cost of doing business so incomplete and superficial as is common at public agencies. With regard to correctional privatization, this fundamental shortcoming of government is pushed into sharp relief by policies and often by statutory requirements that management contracts not be awarded or renewed absent hard evidence of cost savings of a specific magnitude (most commonly either 5 or 10 percent). The reality, of course, is that it is altogether impossible to confirm cost savings achieved by private firms without first calculating public costs using standard accounting principles.

At least some jurisdictions have recognized and made efforts to respond to this problem (e.g., Arizona, Florida, Ohio, and Tennessee in the United States, as well as Australia and Great Britain on the international scene). Such jurisdictions' good faith efforts have proved to be valuable with regard to what they have provided and to what they have identified as being shortcomings in the cost-accounting process. Florida provides an example of both. The statutory language its legislature enacted in 1993 requires that the Office of the Auditor General establish a benchmark price against which cost proposals are to be compared to verify compliance with Florida's mandated 7 percent cost savings.

Unfortunately, what Florida did following its efforts to establish estimates of its public agencies' service delivery costs was to contract for the construction of private facilities that were substantially unlike any publicly managed facilities in size, programs, and missions. The effect, of course, was largely to negate whatever value might otherwise have been created by the efforts to identify public-agency construction and operating costs.

It certainly is good public policy that public agencies of all types be able to identify continuously the unit costs of the services they deliver. But whatever value may flow from requirements for cost savings can be achieved only if the type of privatized operation has reasonable points of comparison in the public sector. This does not mean that jurisdictions should not contract with the private sector for novel types of facilities or programs or both. To the contrary, many jurisdictions successfully have taken advantage of this opportunity (e.g., Arizona, California, Michigan, New Mexico, Ohio, and Texas). When this strategy is followed, however, it makes little sense to apply precise cost-savings requirements because there are no viable points of cost comparison in the public sector. Instead, agencies must solicit multiple bids and rely on the competitiveness of the bidding process to establish reasonable levels of costs. In other areas (e.g., highway maintenance), public agencies have been allowed to compete on an equal basis with private firms in tendering bids; if the public correctional agencies can be put on an equal footing with private firms with regard to cost accounting, this approach might be followed in correctional services also.

Progress in Avoiding the Pitfalls of "Low-Ball" Cost Proposals

Cost-saving requirements and ignorance of true public costs have sometimes led agencies to fixate on low-cost proposals that give short shift to service quality and to firms' qualifications. Various kinds of goods and services are procured so commonly and standardized so thoroughly that it is reasonable to view the lowest-cost bid as being the best bid (e.g., many types of commodities, office supplies, and equipment). In these cases, encouraging or requiring contract awards to be given to low bidders makes good sense. It is not reasonable, however, in selecting an independent contractor for the design, construction, and everyday management of something so variable and complex as a correctional facility.

Today most jurisdictions have become sufficiently astute as to realize that costs are *a* variable and not *the* variable. Indeed, in the world of best practices, most experienced people would agree that no more than a modest weight in any evaluation scheme should be assigned to cost proposals per se. Any weighting of more than approximately 30–35 percent of the total number of points the evaluative scheme makes available is widely believed to be an invitation to "low-ball bids." The reason is that higher weightings severely undermine well-qualified and experienced firms' ability to compete with firms whose commitment to quality is more dubious.

Here I should note that in one manner or another I have been involved in dozens of procurement processes in the United States and in a few elsewhere in the world. I have witnessed many disputes within government agencies regarding the degree to which cost savings alone deserved the top priority when proposals from alternative service providers were being evaluated and also when the final details of contracts were being drafted. During more than a few of those disputes, I have seen that overemphasizing cost per se had a simple motive. The people in charge of procurement believed they would gain status in the eyes of their superiors if they focused on cost savings. Large but myopic egos, however, are not the most perplexing problem. More perplexing—at least to me—is the common predisposition government bureaucrats in the corrections field have to be very concerned about the "excess" profitability of private management firms. They thus often respond with major efforts to push contract costs down even if the consequence is lower-quality services.

What is most perplexing about this practice is that it appears confined to corrections. I have been involved in government procurement processes of one kind or another during my years in the military, my three decades in the academic world, and my many years of experience with correctional privatization. Almost never have I seen government officials focus much, if any, attention on the potential profitability of their contracting decisions for those to whom they often were transferring many millions of dollars. This was the case whatever the nature of the goods or services that were the object of the procurement effort. The focus instead was on getting as much of what could be gotten at the highest value that was possible given the limits of budgetary constraints.

Perhaps the implied irrelevancy of provider profitability was a consequence of procurement initiatives that focused on goods or services that the government needed but could not provide itself. In these cases, nobody knew about or even cared about the profit margins of the automobile manufacturer, the building contractor, the computer manufacturer, the lawyer, the telecommunication provider, the travel agency, and so on. In corrections, however, there often is a kind of green-eyed jealousy and resentment about the transfer of funds from the public to the private sector. The jealousy acts as a maximizer of the bureau's interest rather than of the public's interest. What is relevant to the public interest is obtaining high-quality services at a lower price than available from the government sector. To the degree that profitability is an issue, it is so only to the extent that the fostering of fair competition between alternative providers almost always exposes profit margins to market forces. If private providers are capable of providing better services than government, doing so at a lower cost, and also preserving profit margins that reasonable people perceive to be too high, the reasonable conclusion is that the "excess" profits reflect the extreme nature of government inefficiency.[24]

The Growing Sophistication of Procurement and Contract Documents

Many if not most government agencies have used their growing experience with correctional privatization to improve the sophistication of their requests for proposals (RFPs) and of the contracts they award. An important dimension of the increased sophistication is the greater specificity one now finds in RFPs and contracts regarding the scope of services that independent contractors are obliged to deliver. There was a time when vague terms such as *suitable programs, adequate medical services,* and *properly qualified staff* evidently made sense to someone. Clearly, however, such imprecision makes accountability impossible. Thus, those who draft documents for public agencies today quite properly are making efforts to set service delivery in far more precise and measurable ways. When this is done reasonably, the effect is a set of performance requirements that is clear to the contracting agency, clear to the independent contractor, and clear to anyone who has the responsibility of evaluating contract compliance.

Not surprisingly, the movement toward sophisticated procurement documents and contracts remains far from complete, even though most parties involved are aware at least both of what should be done and what should be avoided. Public agencies remain most comfortable with laying out processes and procedures in ponderously detailed ways—and yes, it is the case that federal agencies, especially the FBOP, are masters of this dubious skill.

Documents within which one finds numerous "incorporate by reference" entries make countless pages of obscure regulations a legal though not a physical part of many privatization contracts. Many of the process and procedure details reflect efforts to governmentalize rather than to privatize. Putting aside these very real flaws, we are left with the even more remarkable and common error of silence about outcomes. It is not uncommon, for example, that the eligibility standards, certification requirements, and program participation standards are laid out in ponderous detail for whatever educational, vocational training, and therapeutic programs may be required. At least in the abstract, this detail is entirely appropriate, but all of it focuses on the process rather than on the product. Rather than controlling inputs, contracts should measure and reward output. If, for example, some prisoners are required to participate in an English as a second language training program, English-language skills should be measured before and after entering the program. That is common sense, but if there are contracts that include product-oriented requirements that go beyond mere evidence of participation, then they are contracts I have never read.

Reliance on Third-Party Standards as a Best Practice

In everyday life, we rely on the existence of multiple third-party standards. The habit many people have of shaping their consumer behavior after consulting publications such as *Consumer Reports* is but a single illustration of the reality. Tens of thousands of electrical products carry the UL seal of quality from Underwriters Laboratory. Food is certified kosher by Star-K Kosher Certification or by other certifying organizations. Indeed, third-party standards set at least the minimum standards for virtually every good or service (Klein 1998). It is true, of course, that considerable care must be taken to understand the nature of such standards and the degree to which adherence to them warrants our trust. Their existence, however, provides us with an increased level of assurance that the product or service under consideration has met or exceeded the quality standards set by a third party that has no financial interest in the choices we make.

Various third-party standards pertain to the design, construction, and operation of correctional facilities. The most familiar of these standards are the ones developed by the ACA, which is the largest and the most prestigious of the professional organizations that represent the interests of those working in the field of corrections. ACA standards are subdivided as mandatory or nonmandatory. For a public or private correctional facility to achieve ACA accreditation, it must past muster during an on-site audit by a multimember ACA audit team, which, at a minimum, means compliance with 100 percent of all mandatory standards and compliance with no less than 90 percent of all nonmandatory standards. The accreditation is in effect for three years. To maintain the accreditation, the facility must move satisfactorily through a new ACA facility audit.

It has become common for policymakers, whether by statute or by contract requirement, to require that private firms to whom management contracts are awarded achieve ACA accreditation within a specific period of time following the opening of privatized facilities (typically within eighteen to twenty-four months), and that accreditation be maintained thereafter. To be sure, ACA accreditation is not a 100 percent guarantee of quality performance. I doubt that one can identify a well-managed facility that has sought but failed to achieve accreditation, but there are certainly weak facilities that have received accreditation. On balance, however, the trend toward mandating accreditation deserves to be viewed as a best practice. If the practice has any obvious flaw, then the flaw is related to privatized facilities being required to achieve accreditation when policymakers neither recommend nor require the accreditation of public facilities in the same jurisdiction (e.g., Florida and Texas).

Performance Incentives and Disincentives as Best Practices

The early privatization contracts were unsophisticated, and the consequences of deficient or superior performance by independent contractors were limited to contract termination or little more than a "thank you," respectively. More recently, however, many public agencies have drafted contracts that create a wide range of sanctions when poor performance is detected, and sometimes even include the option of allocating financial rewards for superior performance. The drafting of fair and meaningful contract language that, on the one hand, authorizes financial-type performance penalties for deficient vendor conduct and, on the other hand, financial-type performance incentives for superior conduct is challenging. However, there is no question that penalty-and-reward contract provisions encourage independent contractors to focus on what allows them to avoid the former and to earn the latter.

Three problems continue to tarnish the appeal of performance-incentive and performance-disincentive provisions. One is that the amounts involved commonly have little or no correlation with the true magnitude of what independent contractors accomplished or failed to accomplish. Another is that the dollar value of the reward or sanction is often too trivial to encourage superior performance or to deter defective performance. Finally, what is virtually never recognized is that there is a fundamental unfairness to the inclusion of financial-type performance incentives and disincentives. If it is believed that there is a motivating power to such incentives and disincentives—and I believe there absolutely is such a power—then there is no good public-policy reason why this approach should not be applied to both private management firms and public agencies. I am not aware of this dual application ever having happened. Still, does it make any public-policy sense for us either to tolerate substandard performance by public employees or to deprive them of rewards for superior performance? I think not.

Enhancing Success Prospects via On-Site Contract Compliance Monitors

Perhaps the most easily identified best practice that characterizes all jurisdictions that can legitimately claim to understand the fundamentals of correctional privatization is the existence of a policy or a statute that requires government officials as full-time and on-site contract compliance monitors. Given my academic background, I often think of the outcomes I am confident I would find were I in a position to contrast the performance of students taking a difficult final examination while I am physically present in the room with that of students who performed the same task in my absence. Whether fortunately or otherwise, the difference often would be dramatic. Part of the difference, of course, would be that the probability of students' succumbing to the temptation to seek and to receive a bit of improper assistance would be substantially lower in my presence than it would be in my absence. Beyond that, however, one easily can imagine benefits to my presence that would go well beyond my ability to deter students from cheating. For example, better student performance can be achieved simply because a professor's presence contributes to a quiet setting, which gives rise to a minimum of distractions, and because the professor can clarify the meaning or purpose of questions.

Much the same applies with regard to on-site contract-compliance monitors. There is a real sense in which their presence encourages the likelihood of desired behavior and discourages the likelihood of undesired behavior, but their presence provides an array of additional benefits as well. Such monitors can offer authoritative interpretations of various contract requirements. They can identify many problems at a point when resolution can be achieved before more serious problems arise. Their presence encourages prisoners to understand that the keepers' behavior is not invisible to the contracting agency. They can see and appreciate the need to modify the terms and conditions of contracts. Thus, when used wisely, on-site contract-compliance monitors are a valuable resource.

As with any useful tool, it is of course the case that on-site contract compliance monitors also can undermine as well as enhance performance. There certainly have been settings where the monitors' qualifications were dubious. There have been more settings where monitors conceptualized their roles as being analogous to that of police officers charged with creating a speed trap zone and with evaluating each person's performance largely in terms of the number of tickets issued. Generally speaking, however, both common sense and growing experience points to the assignment of on-site contract compliance monitors as deserving a best-practice designation.

Conclusions

Current circumstances have in some ways reduced the optimism I had in the mid-1990s. At that time, the tide seemed to be turning in a major way. The correctional privatization movement had more momentum than anyone would have imagined possible when the first contracts were awarded in the 1980s. Who, for example, would have imagined it to be possible for facility management contracts to be awarded in such heavily pro-union places as Australia, Canada, Great Britain, Ohio, Michigan, and Pennsylvania?

Today the modest growth in the nation's prisoner population places far less pressure on elected officials and public agencies to pursue innovative approaches. Privatization proponents are learning that the sleeping giant of organized labor has decided that nap time is over. It is a challenging time for the private corrections industry. The internal threats to its prospects are many, but the potential for the private sector to make meaningful contributions strikes me as being at least as great today as it seemed to be twenty or more years ago. Ironically, we now have far more evidence that privatization works than we had when the movement began. Realizing the very real potential that privatization can offer will take elected officials who have a commitment to the public interest that is at least equivalent to their desire to maximize their reelection prospects by pandering to vested interest groups; public agencies whose top executives come to understand that the effective management of their resources often requires them to take advantage of the talent that now exists in the private sector; and private firms whose top executives are committed to the long-term future of the industry rather than simply to the quarter-on-quarter measures of financial performance that they report to Wall Street.

It will seem improbable to many readers that these prerequisites will be met. Such readers should remember, however, that the alternative to correctional privatization is public-agency monopoly. Those public agencies, to use my son's language yet again, "just ain't got no rise." Twenty years of experience have provided at least a modest and generally successful challenge to the existence of such a monopoly, but far more can and should be done to raise the performance hurdles both public agencies and private firms must clear if they are to deserve the right to be providers of correctional services. No answer is yet possible to the question whether elected policymakers will be blessed with the fortitude required to push efficiency and effectiveness to higher levels through fair competition between alternative providers of correctional services. One can only hope that their past behavior will not serve as a predictor of how they will shape public policy in the future.

Notes

1. The author is indebted to Alexander Tabarrok of the Independent Institute and Rhonda M. Zingraff of Meredith College for their reviews of drafts of this chapter and their thoughtful recommendations regarding both content and style.

2. I say more about this later, but even at this point I think it necessary to make two important qualifications. First, many state correctional systems continue to ignore the considerable body of positive evidence regarding full-scale privatization. Second, the goal of fair competition between alternative providers of correctional services has not been realized in the United States. To be sure, many dozens of private providers of facility management services compete with one another for contract awards. The full potential of the correctional privatization movement cannot be realized, however, until policymakers devise means by which the private sector competes with the public agencies for the opportunity to manage both new and existing correctional facilities.

3. It has become common to distinguish between partial and full-scale privatization when discussing privatization initiatives. Readers should take care not to interpret this distinction too broadly. To be sure, the comparatively narrow focus of contracting decisions that fall within the scope of what is meant by partial privatization is obvious. *Full-scale* privatization, however, is not as expansive as the term may imply. Even when a private firm becomes the independent contractor responsible for most jail and prison management functions, it remains true that government cannot and, as a matter of prudent public policy, should not delegate all correctional functions to its independent contractor. The core policymaking function

remains governmental. Further, the power to make critical decisions regarding the liberty interests of prisoners remains in government rather than in corporate hands (e.g., decisions to confine, to determine the length of sentences, to determine the facilities to which prisoners will be assigned, to allocate or to take away "good time" credits, to release on parole prior to sentence expiration dates, and so on). See, for example, Florida statute §957.06, *Powers and duties not delegable to contractor.*

4. The prisoner population explosion that began in the mid-1970s can be illustrated by considering what took place during the decade before and the decade after the correctional privatization movement began to take form in 1984. Between year-end 1974 and year-end 1984, this population rose from 204,211 to 429,050, an increase of 110.10 percent (Langan, Fundis, and Greenfield 1988). Between year-end 1984 and year-end 1994, this population rose from 429,050 to 1,012,463, an increase of 135.98 percent (Beck and Gilliard 1995). The nation's correctional system was totally unprepared to cope with either such a large or such a rapidly growing prisoner population.

5. It should be noted that the antiprivatization position of the American Bar Association, initially adopted in 1986, was modified significantly in 1989 following such key decisions as the holding announced by the United States Supreme Court in *West v. Atkins,* 487 U.S. 42 (1988).

6. It is worth noting that the largest and most prestigious of the organizations that represent the interests of those in corrections—the American Correctional Association—never joined the antiprivatization lobbying groups. Its official policy position remains more practical than ideological: "Government has the ultimate authority and responsibility for corrections. For its most effective operation, corrections should use all appropriate resources, both public and private. When government considers the use of profit and nonprofit private-sector correctional services, such programs must meet professional standards, provide necessary public safety, provide services equal to or better than government, and be cost-effective compared to well-managed governmental operations." See the ACA's policy statement at http://www.bmi.net/wca/priv_sector.

7. Illustrations of this continued presence are numerous, but it is worth providing a few examples. The 411-bed Immigration and Naturalization Service (INS) facility in Houston, Texas, managed by CCA, first received prisoners in May 1984. The 414-bed county facility in

Hamilton County (Chattanooga), Tennessee, also managed by CCA, first received prisoners in September 1984. The 250-bed Eden Detention Center in Eden, Texas—originally managed by the Eden Detention Center, Inc. and now, its capacity having been increased over the years to 1,215 beds, managed by CCA—first received prisoners in October 1984. The 258-bed INS facility in Laredo, Texas, managed by CCA, first received prisoners in March 1985. The 276-bed county jail in Bay County (Panama City), Florida, which is one of the two county jail facilities that are managed by CCA and that have a combined prisoner housing capacity of 670 beds, first received prisoners in October 1985. The 500-bed state prison in St. Mary, Kentucky, originally managed by the U.S. Corrections Corporation and now managed by CCA, first received prisoners in January 1986. The 201-bed local facility in Santa Fe, New Mexico, originally managed by CCA and now managed by Cornell Companies, Inc., first received prisoners in August 1986. The 300-bed INS facility in Aurora, Colorado, managed by Wackenhut, first received prisoners in May 1987.

8. I find no flaw whatsoever in privatization critics' condemning CCA's performance during its initial years of operating the Youngstown facility. Bad performance deserves to be condemned. Bad performance by a private management firm deserves to be met by meaningful financial penalties and, if appropriate, by the termination of management contracts. There is no question whatsoever about CCA having been punished severely by what took place at its Youngstown facility. Indeed, today the facility stands empty, and CCA is obliged to shoulder the substantial financial penalty of meeting debt-service obligations on a facility that required roughly $75 million in construction funds, in return for which CCA now receives no revenue whatsoever. The public-policy irony, however, is that recent decades have yielded mountains of evidence of equivalent or worse performance by public agencies. Now and then such flaws in public agencies' performance have required that the head of a director of corrections be offered up as a symbolic sacrifice, but generally the risk of persistent substandard performance by a public agency is inconsequential. A rational public-policy approach would not and should not long tolerate independent contractors' dropping the ball in public-service delivery. Neither, however, would a rational public-policy approach tolerate the various forms of quite incredible misconduct that seem common in some publicly managed systems (e.g., the California Department of Corrections).

9. It may seem internally inconsistent to say, on the one hand, that the diffusion of the innovation represented by correctional privatization has been slow and to note, on the other hand, that policymakers in so large a proportion of U.S. jurisdictions took advantage of the innovation during so brief a period of time. Thus, it should be noted that today one would find only approximately 5 percent of U.S. prisoners being housed in privately managed facilities. This modest percentage certainly does not indicate that we have witnessed a tidal wave of contract awards. At the same time, however, it is noteworthy that so many jurisdictions have awarded at least one facility management contract and that so many jurisdictions have enacted provisions of law that expressly authorize contract awards at the local, state, and federal levels of government.

10. Here I need to qualify my meaning fairly carefully. In particular, I do not mean that I believe offenders should be confined for rehabilitative purposes, any more than I believe offenders should be confined for (rather than as) punishment. The tyranny of rehabilitative zealots is neither better nor worse than the tyranny of those who lack the intellectual ability to differentiate between just and harsh treatment of prisoners. It follows that the amount of time offenders serve should have no relationship to their program participation or, for that matter, to their refusal to participate in programs. However, I also believe that it is in both the public's and the offenders' interest that those who are confined be presented with opportunities to improve their future life chances. It matters not at all to me whether those opportunities are described as habilitative, rehabilitative, or treatment programs. It does matter to me that we have the common sense to allocate scarce resources in such a way as to maximize the probability that the match between program type and prisoner type will yield the desired outcome.

11. From early 1997 through late 2000, I was a member of the board of directors of Prison Realty Trust, a publicly traded real estate investment trust that owned many of the jails and prisons managed by CCA. Following the merger of CCA and Prison Realty Trust in the fall of 2000, I served on the CCA board of directors. When I left the CCA board, I became and continue to be a member of the board of directors of Avalon Correctional Services, Inc., which is one of the larger private firms that specialize in the management of community corrections facilities. Thus, the good news is that I have had years of board-level

experience in multiple privatization-related firms, as well as two decades of academic research experience on the topic. The bad news is that the depth and quality of my experience may undermine my ability to control whatever potential bias this experience has passed my way.

12. Behavioral Systems Southwest no longer operates secure adult correctional facilities. Eclectic Communications, Inc., now operates as a wholly owned subsidiary of Cornell Companies, Inc.

13. The first contract awards outside the United States are of even more recent vintage, the first coming in 1989 from the State of Queensland, Australia, to the Corrections Corporation of Australia (the Australian extension of CCA until it was acquired by Sodexho), and the first non-Australian award coming in 1991 from the United Kingdom to Group 4 Prison Services, Ltd.

14. It merits note that the terms and conditions one finds in facility management contracts quite often unabashedly impose requirements on contract vendors that are more demanding than those imposed on public agencies. At the very same time, cost savings in the range of 5 to 10 percent are required as a standard of success and contract renewal. Private firms share a portion of the responsibility for such requirements because they often have uttered the "better, cheaper" promise as a part of their marketing mantra, and it was not long before more than one cynical public agency decided to put that theory to the test. The result, however, is that the level playing field required for real privatization takes on a tilt that looks rather like the slope of Mt. Everest. The problem is worsened when the net effect is a contractual arrangement that obliges the independent contractor to do everything precisely the way the contracting agency does it, but to do it both with more demanding performance requirements and at a significantly lower cost. Privatization of the public sector becomes replaced with governmentalization of the private sector, a problem I discuss at greater length in the text.

15. Some of this weakness, but by no means all, flows from the terms and conditions of contracts that government agencies have drafted. Contract requirements often inhibit private firms' implementation of creative approaches. In fairness, however, private management firms' actions do not always reflect their flexibility to behave more innovatively.

16. Space limitations in this chapter preclude a thorough critique of the body of work on privatization that opponents have produced. Suffice

it to say that very little of it has an independent quantitative base and that much of it advances claims that cannot, even in principle, be refuted by empirical evidence. Often, for example, I have debated privatization critics who advanced the claim that the cost and quality benefits of privatization will diminish over time. When I have pointed out that there is evidence of cost savings still being achieved by contracts now in place for nearly twenty years, the response has been that the time will come when those savings will cease to exist. It should be obvious that it is absurd for either opponents or proponents to base a significant portion of their case on the evidence they imagine will exist at an undefined point in the future. One certainly can hope, however, that the competition privatization creates will drive public agencies toward more efficient and effective methods for delivering any essential public service, thus causing the often quite wide gap between the performance of public agencies and private firms to shrink.

17. It would be reasonable, of course, to raise questions about the quality of the judgment of the private firms that entered into contractual relationships with correctional agencies when they knew, or reasonably should have known, that they could not provide the services they agreed to provide at the agreed upon price. Indeed, the private firms involved in the Arkansas contracts (Wackenhut) and in the North Carolina contracts (CCA) are the two largest firms in the private corrections industry. My belief is that both firms were so focused on increasing their market share and so confident that necessary adjustments in their contracts could be negotiated after the initial contracts were executed that they accepted a known risk—a risk they were not able to mitigate after the contracts were in force. Clearly, however, when a private firm takes so large a risk and the risk becomes a reality, then the firm must accept the financial and reputation damage that goes with having failed. On the other hand, when a public agency drops the ball, then almost always it is the public at large rather than the failed public agency that must pay the bill. It also should be noted that there have been instances when it would be reasonable to conclude that private management firms submitted "low-ball bids" to maximize the likelihood of receiving a contract award with the intention of playing a "bait and switch game" thereafter. Often government agencies imprudently include contract clauses that significantly reduce the risk of the low-ball bid approach. For example, one routinely finds so-called termination-for-convenience clauses that permit independent contractors

to escape from the performance obligations that contracts impose merely by giving the involved government agencies a brief notice of their decisions to bring the contractual relationships to an end. It is not easy to understand how the public interest is served by the inclusion of this kind of penalty-free escape clause in a contract.

18. One can only wonder if the time ever will arrive when policymakers apply the same performance and accountability standards to publicly managed facilities that the best of them already apply to privately managed facilities.

19. See also Knight and Hiller 1997.

20. One reviewer of this chapter, Professor Rhonda M. Zingraff at Meredith College, raised a possible criticism of this assertion. Her question pertained to whether the hypothesized weakness of government and strength of the private sector might be more an artifact of organizational size than of the public-private distinction. Here I note merely that the size variable is relevant almost by definition, but I also believe that virtually any comparison of public and private entities of roughly equivalent size would yield evidence of greater flexibility among the private entities. Still, placed in the context of this chapter, Professor Zingraff's point is quite relevant. Based on my experience with most of the private corrections-management firms, it seems clear to me that the larger firms have reached a size at which the complexity of their organizational structures and of the corporate cultures that have evolved within those structures over time makes it more difficult for them to respond as swiftly and as flexibly as was possible previously.

21. It should go without saying that private firms are not perfect, and they must be monitored and disciplined to prevent weak performance. On countless occasions, I have argued for the inclusion of meaningful financial penalties in management contracts, for fair but firm on-site contract compliance monitoring, and for the termination of contracts awarded to private firms that subsequently do not meet the commitments they have made with respect to cost savings, programs, and services. Note, however, that I have never urged the adoption of a double standard that imposes a heavier burden on the private sector than it does on public agencies. Accountability is not a trivial concept. If prudent public policy requires that correctional services meet or exceed all applicable constitutional, legal, and professional standards at the same time that those services are pro-

vided at the lowest possible cost to taxpayers, then it follows that the mandate should apply equally to both public and private providers of those services. It is disappointing, though certainly not surprising, that so much effort has been expended toward achieving the goal of holding private management firms accountable while at the same time withholding accountability from public agencies in their service delivery obligations. Sadly, there is a public and certainly a political perception that government and its employees cannot be held to the same standards of accountability that apply to the private sector. In fact, however, the toleration of poor performance does little more than to encourage its persistence.

22. Indeed, purely as a matter of law it can be argued that many firms described as independent contractors are in point of fact agents of the involved public agencies. The liability implications to government of such a transformation are considerable and not generally recognized.

23. The Arizona approach can result in modest cost savings. My own published research offers evidence of the contracting experience in Arizona yielding value. But the relationship between Arizona practice and true privatization is very weak. We can and we should do better.

24. Competitive bidding would, of course, lower truly excessive profit margins.

References

Arizona Department of Corrections. 2000. *Public-Private Prison Comparison*. Phoenix: Arizona Department of Corrections.

Beck, Allen J., and Darrell K. Gilliard. 1995. *Prisoners in 1994*. Washington, D.C.: U.S. Bureau of Justice Statistics.

Brakel, Samuel J. 1988. Prison Management, Private Enterprise Style: The Inmates' Evaluation. *New England Journal on Criminal and Civil Confinement* 14: 175–244

Branham, Lynn S., and Sheldon Krantz. 1997. *The Law of Sentencing, Corrections, and Prisoners' Rights: Cases and Materials*. St. Paul, Minn.: West.

Brown, Allan. 1994. Economic and Qualitative Aspects of Prison Privatisation in Queensland. In *Private Prisons and Police: Recent Australian Trends,* edited by Paul Moyle, 194–218. Leichhardt, New South Wales: Pluto Press Australia.

Camp, Camille, and George M. Camp. 1984. *Private Sector Involvement in Prison Services and Operations.* Washington, D.C.: National Institute of Corrections.

Coopers and Lybrand, Inc. 1996. *Review of Comparative Costs and Performance of Privately and Publicly Operated Prisons for HM Prison Service.* Report no. 1. London: H.M. Prison Service.

Crants, R., III. 1991. Private Prison Management: A Study in Economic Efficiency. *Journal of Contemporary Criminal Justice* 7: 49–59.

Davenport, Debra K. 2001. *Arizona Department of Corrections Private Prisons: Performance Audit.* Report no. 01-13. Phoenix: Arizona Office of the Auditor General.

Dunmore, James. 1997. *Review of Comparative Costs and Performance of Privately and Publicly Operated Prisons, 1995–96.* Prison Service Research Report no. 2. London: H.M. Prison Service.

Eriksson, Thorsten. 1976. *The Reformers: An Historical Survey of Pioneer Experiments in the Treatment of Criminals.* New York: Elsevier Scientific.

Gaes, Gerry G., Scott A. Camp, and William G. Saylor. 1998. Appendix 2: Comparing the Quality of Publicly and Privately Operated Prisons, a Review. In *Private Prisons in the United States: An Assessment of Current Practice,* edited by D. McDonald, E. Fournier, M. Russel-Einhorn, and S. Crawford. Boston: Abt Associates.

Gold, Martin E. 1996. The Privatization of Prisons. *The Urban Lawyer* 28: 359–99.

Harding, Richard W. 1997. *Private Prisons and Public Accountability.* New Brunswick, N.J.: Transaction.

Harrison, Page M., and Allen J. Beck. 2002. *Prisoners In 2001.* Washington, D.C.: U.S. Bureau of Justice Statistics.

Kengor, Paul, and Mark Scheffler. 1999. *Prison Privatization in Pennsylvania: The Case of Delaware County.* Report no. 99-09. Pittsburgh, Penn.: Allegheny Institute for Public Policy.

Kettl, Donald F. 1993. *Sharing Power: Public Governance and Private Markets.* Washington, D.C.: Brookings Institution.

Klein, Daniel. 1998. Quality and Safety Assurance: How Voluntary Social Processes Remedy Their Own Shortcomings. *The Independent Review* (4, spring): 537–55.

Knight, Kevin, and Matthew L. Hiller. 1997. Community-based Substance Abuse Treatment for Probationers: 1-year Outcome Evaluation of the

Dallas County Judicial Treatment Center. *Federal Probation* 61: 61–68.

Langan, Patrick A., John V. Fundis, and Lawrence A. Greenfeld. 1988. *Historical Statistics on Prisoners in State and Federal Institutions, Year End 1925–1986.* Washington, D.C.: U.S. Bureau of Justice Statistics.

Lanza-Kaduce, Lonn, and Scott Maggard. 2001. The Long-Term Recidivism of Public and Private Prisoners. Unpublished paper presented at the annual conference of the Justice Research Statistics Association.

Lanza-Kaduce, Lonn, Karen F. Parker, and Charles W. Thomas. 1999. A Comparative Recidivism Analysis of Releasees from Private and Public Prisons. *Crime and Delinquency* 45: 28–47.

Logan, Charles H. 1990. *Private Prisons: Cons and Pros.* New York: Oxford University Press.

———. 1992. Well Kept: Comparing Quality of Confinement in Private and Public Prisons. *Journal of Criminal Law and Criminology* 83: 577–613.

———. 1996. Public vs. Private Prison Management: A Case Comparison. *Criminal Justice Review* 21: 62–95.

Logan, Charles H., and Bill McGriff. 1989. *Comparing Costs of Public and Private Prisons: A Case Study.* Research in Brief Report no. 216 (September/October). Washington, D.C.: National Institute of Justice.

Loux, Steven. 1996. *Prison Privatization in Pennsylvania.* Harrisburg, Penn.: Commonwealth Foundation for Public Policy Alternatives.

Lucas, Greg. 2002. State will pay dearly for Davis' prison deal. Auditor: guards' raises will cost $518 million. *San Francisco Chronicle,* July 31.

Maguire, Kathleen, and Ann L. Pastore. 2001. *Sourcebook of Criminal Justice Statistics 2000.* Washington, D.C.: U.S. Bureau of Justice Statistics.

McConville, Sean. 1987. Aid from Industry: Private Prisons and Prison Crowding. In *America's Correctional Crisis: Prison Populations and Public Policy,* edited by Stephen D. Gottfredson and Sean McConville, 221–242. New York: Greenwood.

McDonald, Douglas C. 1990. The Cost of Operating Public and Private Correctional Facilities. In *Private Prisons and the Public Interest,* edited by Douglas C. McDonald, 86–106. New Brunswick, N.J.: Rutgers University Press.

McKelvey, Blake. 1977. *American Prisons: A History of Good Intentions.* New Jersey: Patterson Smith.

Morris, Norval, and David J. Rothman. 1995. *The Oxford History of the Prison: The Practice of Punishment in Western Society.* New York: Oxford University Press.

Mullen, Joan, Kent J. Chabotar, and Deborah M. Carrow. 1985. *The Privatization of Corrections.* Washington, D.C.: National Institute of Justice.

Office of Program Policy Analysis and Government Accountability (OPPAGA). 2000. *Private Prison Review: South Bay Correctional Facility Provides Savings and Success; Room for Improvement.* Report no. 99-39. Tallahassee: Florida Office of Program Policy Analysis and Government Accountability. Available online at http://www.oppaga. state.fl.us/reports/crime/r99-39s.html.

Osborne, David, and Ted Gaebler. 1992. *Reinventing Government.* Reading, Mass.: Addison-Wesley.

Oshinsky, David M. 1997. *Worse Than Slavery: Parchman Farm and the Ordeal of Jim Crow Justice.* New York: Free Press.

Quinlan, J. Michael, Charles W. Thomas, and Sherril A. Gautreaux. 2001. The Privatization of Correctional Facilities. In *Privatizing Governmental Functions,* edited by Deborah Ballati, 10.1–10.75. New York: Law Journal Press.

Robbins, Ira P. 1988. *The Legal Dimensions of Private Incarceration.* Washington, D.C.: American Bar Association.

Schlossman, Steven. 1995. Delinquent Children: The Juvenile Reform School. In *The Oxford History of the Prison,* edited by Norval Morris and David J. Rothman, 363–89. New York: Oxford University Press.

Segal, Geoffrey F., and Adrian T. Moore. 2002. *Evaluating the Costs and Benefits of Outsourcing Correctional Services: Reviewing the Literature on Cost and Quality Comparisons.* Los Angeles: Reason Public Policy Institute.

Smith, Beverly A., and Frank T. Morn. 2001. The History of Privatization in Criminal Justice. In *Privatization in Criminal Justice,* edited by Michael J. Gilbert and David Schichor, 3–23. Cincinnati, Ohio: Anderson.

Volokh, Alexander. 2002. A Tale of Two Systems: Cost, Quality, and Accountability in Private Prisons. *Harvard Law Review* 115: 1868–90.

Texas Sunset Advisory Commission. 1991. Information Report on Contracts for Correctional Facilities and Services. In *Recommendations to the Governor of Texas and Members of the Seventy-second Legislature,* Chapter 4, Austin, Texas: Texas Sunset Advisory Commission.

Thomas, Charles W. 1997. *Comparing the Cost and Performance of Public and Private Prisons in Arizona.* Phoenix: Arizona Department of Corrections.

————. 1998. Issues and Evidence from the United States. In *Privatizing Correctional Services,* edited by Stephen T. Easton, 15–62. Vancouver, British Columbia: Fraser Institute.

————. 2001. Private Adult Correctional Facility Census. Available online at http://www.crim.ufl.edu/pcp/.

Thomas, Charles W., and S. Bilchik. 1985. Prosecuting Juveniles in Criminal Courts: A Legal and Empirical Analysis. *Journal of Criminal Law and Criminology* 76: 439–79.

Thomas, Charles W. and Sherril Gautreaux. 2000. The Present Status of State and Federal Privatization Law. Electronically published on the web site of *The Center for Studies in Criminology and Law at the University of Florida,* www.crim.ufl.edu/pcp/html/statelaw.html.

Thomas, Charles W., and Charles H. Logan. 1993. The Development, Present Status, and Future Potential of Correctional Privatization in America. In *Privatizing Correctional Institutions,* edited by Gary W. Bowman, Simon Hakim, and Paul Seidenstat, 193–240. New Brunswick, N.J.: Transaction.

U.S. General Accounting Office. 1996. *Private and Public Prisons: Studies Comparing Operational Costs and/or Quality of Services.* Washington, D.C.: U.S. Government Printing Office.

Utt, Ronald D. 2001. *Improving Government Performance Through Competitive Contracting.* Report no. 1452. Washington, D.C.: Heritage Foundation.

Wilson, Tim. 1998. Contractual Management of Custodial Services in the United Kingdom. In *Privatizing Correctional Services,* edited by Stephen T. Easton, 63–92. Vancouver, British Columbia: Fraser Institute.

Wolfgang, Marvin E. 1998. Foreword to *To Serve and Protect: Privatization and Community in Criminal Justice,* by Bruce L. Benson, xiii-xvii. New York: New York University Press for The Independent Institute.

Woodbridge, Jo. 1997. *Review of Comparative Costs and Performance of*

Privately and Publicly Operated Prisons, 1996–97. Report no. 3. London: H.M. Prison Service.

4

Prison Privatization and Public Policy

SAMUEL JAN BRAKEL AND

KIMBERLY INGERSOLL GAYLORD

The U.S. correctional system, which, along with the police and the courts, constitutes the official machinery for dealing with crime, is beset by population and cost pressures that have intensified since the 1980s. Reformers have suggested various ways of relieving these pressures. Some of their proposals target matters better left to those who manage correctional facilities and services. Other reformers recommend changing sentence severity and certainty, devising alternatives to incarceration, and delimiting the classes of offenders within the scope of such policy reforms.

This chapter examines an approach to corrections that is applicable regardless of the specific policies in place. In short, we defend a modest proposal: "privatize" parts of the correctional machinery. Privatization, we believe, would make the corrections system more responsive to the system's various demands in less time and at lower cost—that is, more efficient. Privatization also would carry the potential for improving overall quality.

Since its introduction in the early 1980s, the idea of delegating correctional functions to private companies has become a commonplace, if not established fact of correctional life. Overall, privatization of and contracting out for corrections has worked well. Privatization of corrections can save substantial costs in the management of prison facilities, in the construction (or renovation) of prison facilities, and in the financing of prison facility construction projects. Private companies also can finance and carry out construction projects relatively quickly—a special bonus at a time when many states are struggling to build facilities as fast as the inmate population rises. And all this significantly has come at no reduction in quality. Private prison construction and management often is of higher quality than that provided by the public sector.

Despite the evidence for these claims, there remains strong opposition to the concept of privatizing corrections. Some of this opposition stems from a philosophic position that holds it to be "just plain wrong." Sometimes the opposition is articulated in terms of legal concerns, other times in symbolic imagery ("Do we want to put inmates at the mercy of the ACME Correctional Company?"). Some opposition reflects pure self-interest. For example, public-employee unions are among the most vocal critics because they fear union members will lose their jobs.

Much of this opposition is ill founded. Although unions in some states (e.g., Illinois and New York) have effected the passage of statutes prohibiting contracting out with private corrections companies, there are no principled legal arguments to support this selective curtailment of the delegation of authority. Arguments based on governmental philosophy merely substitute preconceived opinion for analysis, and the symbolic objections misperceive both the central social and economic experience of our country and public attitudes toward government.

Public employees' fears can be allayed by pointing out that privatization need not and will not result in immediate and drastic overhauls of employment within the enterprise: no wholesale firings without cause, no real loss in fringe benefits, and no sudden changes in procedures that are demonstrably functional. Moreover, the state and the private provider can agree contractually to these guarantees. Good contracts and good contracting procedures can guarantee many other features of sound correctional management.

Some analysts believe that only a decreased reliance on incarceration will solve our prison population and cost problems. (They disagree on whether crime policy should deemphasize incarceration for all offenders, for certain classes of offenders, or for all but a few presumably identifiable hard-core offenders.) Many of these analysts further contend that certain types of conduct presently prohibited and prosecuted under the law (namely, "victimless crimes") ought to be "decriminalized" altogether. The level of empirical, moral, or political support that exists for these positions is at best uncertain, as is the question whether voters can be persuaded of their merit. However, even if the nation ultimately was to head in the direction of deincarceration and decriminalization, the efficient and effective management of its prison facilities remains an imperative. In addition, the privatization approach has substantial relevance to the alternatives-to-incarceration movement. There are already many private companies in the nonprison correctional enterprise, ranging from drug treatment to electronic monitoring programs, and the privatization option deserves to be considered for prison correctional functions as well.

The National Problem

The "generic" problems facing corrections systems nationwide are *overpopulation* and *rising costs*. Many of the nation's systems are in crisis, although a few states have escaped these deleterious trends.

The 1990s saw a continuation of the steep rise nationwide, which began in the 1970s, in the total number and percentage of adults on probation, in jail or prison, or on parole. In 1990, 4,348,000 adults were under some form of correctional supervision. By mid-2000, that number had risen to 6,467,200—a 48.7 percent increase.[1]

The adult prison population (i.e., convicted offenders)—traditionally the target of the bulk of the correctional system's efforts and resources—increased, along with the more comprehensively defined correctional population (all those under correctional control, including probationers, parolees, and jail detainees). Figures 1 and 2 indicate the explosion in the prison population that has occurred since the mid-1970s both in terms of absolute numbers and as a percentage of the population.

Figure 1

Sentenced prisoners under jurisdiction of State and Federal correctional authorities on 31 December

United States, 1925–2000

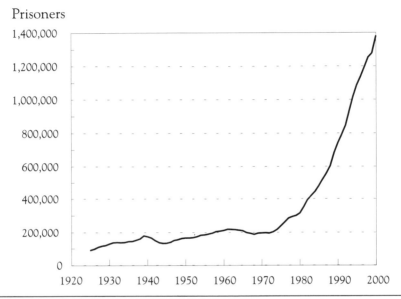

Source: Sourcebook of Criminal Justice Statistics 2000, U.S. Department of Justice, Bureau of Justice Statistics, Table 6.1 at 505.

One Solution

Large, systemic problems require large, systematic solutions. The solution we propose, which represents only one of several possible (not mutually exclusive) modes of attack, is privatization. We recommend not a precipitous, wholesale divestment of the state's responsibility for correctional facilities and services, but a more gradual, quasi-experimental approach. Each state should consider, as an initial step, privatized management of at least three facilities, according to size and security, that roughly represent the range of adult correctional experiences in that state. When possible, the states

Figure 2

Rate (per 100,000 resident population) of sentenced prisoners under jurisdiction of State and Federal correctional authorities on 31 December

United States, 1925–2000

Number of sentenced prisoners
per 100,000 residents

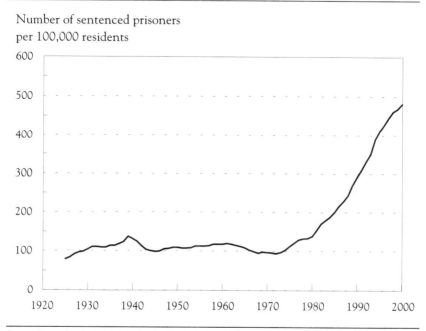

Source: Sourcebook of Criminal Justice Statistics 2000, U.S. Department of Justice, Bureau of Justice Statistics, Table 6.4, at 506.

would distribute the initial privatization contracts in such a way as to permit performance comparisons between similar institutions. For example, a state with two high-population prisons might privatize one and compare its performance with the publicly managed prison. Similarly, if a state needs new prisons, it might contract out the construction of one prison to a private contractor, who also would be responsible for arranging its financing.

The objective is to implement privatization in a way that will allow the states to learn from the experience. The idea is to introduce competitive forces into the current correctional state-monopoly environment to test the effectiveness both of the states' traditional "public" efforts and of the private prison-service providers. The ultimate goal is to build a competitive partnership between the state and private enterprise rather than simply to hand over corrections to the forces of the market.

What Does Privatization Entail?

Privatization is the transfer of ownership, operation, and responsibility from the public sector (i.e., the government) to the private sector. Privatization can be implemented either through the wholesale divestiture of major government-run enterprises or the contracting out of discrete services to private vendors. The "denationalization" of British Gas, British Airways, British National Oil, British Aerospace, and many other basic enterprises during the 1980s under the Thatcher regime constituted privatization on a grand scale. The role of government in the service and manufacturing industries in the United States has never been comparable to that in Great Britain because the United States was never as "nationalized" as Great Britain; consequently, there has been less to denationalize (Brakel 1988a, 1988b). One would have to envision the U.S. government selling NASA, AMTRAK, the U.S. Postal Service, and the like for something to begin to compare the U.S. experience to the British experience.

Privatization was a global phenomenon in the 1980s, as governments of developed and developing nations transferred public tasks and properties to private hands. In the 1990s, privatization became central to the economic reforms in eastern and central Europe in the wake of the political collapse of the communist governments.

The motivation for embarking on a course of privatization often contains two elements: (1) a philosophical component that holds that the government should not manage enterprises that it is not particularly good at managing, and (2) a pragmatic recognition that the private sector tends to be more efficient than the public sector and that governments can save money by selling assets or contracting out to private vendors.

Privatization of public goods and services in the United States, although comparatively small, is by no means untried. During the 1980s and 1990s, many cities began to contract out basic services such as garbage collection, parking meter upkeep, rent and fine collection, fire prevention and control services, park maintenance, and a host of similar "public" functions (Kent 1986; Savas 1982). County governments, like the federal government, got into the privatization act in certain small select areas, but the states showed greater reluctance. Nevertheless, by the early 1980s, the stage was set for privatization as a serious policy option for an increasing range of public goods and services.

Privatization of Justice Services

Correctional services, the police, and the courts constitute the three interlinked components of law enforcement (or "justice") services. Yet, among this triad, corrections consumes on average as much as what the states spend on the other two.[2]

Privatization of justice services has roots that go back to the *lex mercatoria* (merchant law) that first developed to govern trade in medieval Europe (Benson 1998). Private security firms that included detective, patrol, prosecution, and insurance services have been around for longer than public police departments and were common in nineteenth-century England (Davies 2002). More recently, private security services have grown tremendously in the United States. Today, the U.S. private security industry employs more workers and (in monetary terms) provides more justice services than does government (Chaiken and Chaiken 1988). Private courts and related arbitration services are also a large and fast-growing industry (Benson 1998).

Privatized Corrections

Corrections in the form of prisons began in this country as a private (albeit nonprofit) enterprise run by Quaker societies at the end of the colonial period and briefly in postcolonial times

(Rothman 1980). This private cottage-industry approach to corrections, steeped in benevolent intentions, did not last long as the society grew in size and complexity. Along with the increase in public regulation in general, corrections, too, became a largely exclusive governmental responsibility. Even so, there was always some private involvement.

Just as for other public works, the private sector has long been involved in the building of prisons. Private-sector participation in the internal operation of prisons also occurred previously. Particularly in the southern states, a long-surviving practice was to hire out prisoners to private ventures and adventurers who, at best, exploited cheap prison labor. At worst, chain gangs and their connotations of slavery marked this type of prisoner-for-hire experience. However, private firms also have hired prisoners to work in-house on clerical work such as answering phones. One hopes that this practice has instilled usable skills, alleviated boredom, and paid a wage of some worth to the inmates, to the jurisdictions bearing the cost of their incarceration, or to both. (It should be noted that most prison labor has been and is performed at the direction of the state and federal government and is not done for private firms. The issue of prison labor is therefore distinct from that of privatized prisons.) The private management of "treatment-oriented" facilities such as juvenile homes and halfway houses is also quite significant (Rothman 1980). In addition, private vendors have long provided prison services with respect to education, food, and health care on a contract basis.

The privatization model proposed in this chapter, however, is part and parcel of a distinct and far more recent phenomenon. It involves the management, sometimes construction, and occasionally the financing of entire prison facilities by private correctional companies under contract to federal, state, and local governments. This movement began in the early 1980s with a few contracts to manage a youth camp, a small county jail, and a minimum-security prison. Today it comprises the gamut of available residential correctional experiences, including (1) relatively small detention facilities for undocumented immigrants or citizens charged with federal crimes; (2) state and county facilities of widely varying style and type, including women's units and special prerelease centers for offenders nearing the end of their sentences; and (3) several sizable medium- to heavy-security institutions. (See Charles Thomas's chapter in this volume for more information.)

Potential and Proven Benefits of Privatized Corrections

Few would argue that incarcerating and trying to rehabilitate offenders convicted by the state is not the business of government; there is no compelling philosophic argument for government to divest itself of this responsibility and its burdens. The issue is instead pragmatic: What is the optimum way to discharge this responsibility?

Private firms must keep costs low and quality high or else their profits will fall, their customers will leave, and if the problems are not fixed in time, they will go bankrupt. The theory that competition and the profit incentive enhance efficiency has been tested in countless and varied settings wherein public and private operations have been compared (Kent 1986; Savas 1982).[3] It would be surprising if corrections were different, but empirical investigation is warranted still, and we must also ask whether noneconomic costs render privatization prohibitive irrespective of efficiency gains.

Costs must be considered regarding three aspects of corrections operations: (1) the construction (or renovation) of facilities; (2) the management of facilities and programs; and (3) the costs of financing construction projects.

By contracting out to private vendors, at least in the short term, states can guarantee themselves cost savings in all three areas, because, in the tradition of governments' contracting with private parties for correctional services, contracts can be approved only if they save the government money. In an era when companies are still trying to get a foothold in the market, they are willing to take initial losses. Therefore, governments are able to obtain contractually favorable cost terms, irrespective of the long-term viability of these terms to the vendor.

However, it would be shortsighted for governments to embark upon a privatization course if there were no prospects for long-range viability. If the terms are not lastingly viable, the vendor will withdraw prior to or upon contract expiration. The state may be able to get another vendor willing to play the loss-leader game, but the process is sustainable only for a limited period. Thus, long-term viability on costs is ultimately in both parties' interest.

After almost three decades of experience with privatized corrections, there is strong evidence that the cost savings are both substantial and sustainable.

The Evidence on Construction Costs

The evidence shows that the private sector can construct correctional facilities more quickly and at lower cost than the state sector. For example, the Florida Office of Program Policy Analysis and Government Accountability (OPPAGA), a research arm of the Florida legislature, published an analysis of the construction costs associated with two Florida prisons. The two prisons were designed to have the same housing capacity (1,318 prisoners) and were constructed in the same general area of the state. Total construction and financing costs for the private prison were $69.9 million, whereas total construction and financing costs for the public prison were $85.7 million, 23 percent higher (OPPAGA 2000). Construction-cost savings on the order of 15–25 percent are in fact typical (Thomas 1997).

Another notable example is the Corrections Corporation of America's (CCA) construction of a 350-bed, minimum-security facility in Houston for the Immigration and Naturalization Service (INS) for the detention of undocumented immigrants. It was completed in the early years of CCA's operations at a cost of $14,000 per bed, a figure that compared very favorably to the estimated $26,000 per bed that it cost the public sector to build a minimum-security facility at that time (Grant and Bast 1987). A more recent example is CCA's construction in 1991–92 of its Metro-Davidson medium-security facility in Nashville, Tennessee. The total cost of building this 870-bed unit was $18 million, or $20,700 per cell (Ramirez 1994).[4] Equally important is the CCA Silverdale facility contract, alluded to earlier, under which the company spent $1.6 million dollars in construction additions and improvements, not a penny of it coming from the county. The pattern of private companies' amortizing their prison construction costs in the fees they charge the government for management is a common one. With private management fees typically lower than public ones, the economic advantage gained by "privatizing" becomes so certain that its consideration becomes a virtual imperative for state and county governments.

Construction efficiency not only means lower costs but also greater speed, independent of whether and how the speed of construction may affect costs. In a context where legislation regarding prison overcrowding may mandate the release of prisoners regardless of crime or time served, time itself can be an important concern. Again, privatization offers major advantages.

The relevant facts include the following: CCA built the Houston INS facility referred to earlier in six months, as compared to the INS's own average of two and one-half years (Grant and Bast 1987). Another useful illustration of private-sector efficiency concerns the conversion of nonprison facilities into correctional facilities. In one of the earliest correctional privatization experiences, the state of Pennsylvania in 1975 turned to a private contractor to deal with a newly imposed legal mandate that juvenile offenders could no longer be incarcerated with adult offenders. In ten days, the private company was able to put into operation an "intensive treatment unit" for juveniles by converting a building complex already owned by the state (Brakel 1989).

Lower costs at the expense of lower quality is, of course, no cost saving at all. The evidence, however, is that the design and building techniques used by private vendors in the construction of prison facilities have not compromised quality. To the contrary, there is today a store of knowledge on how to build prisons that are safer by virtue of their physical layout, their use of automated locking systems, and their applications of the latest technology for surveying the inmate population. All these improvements have the added benefit of requiring less labor to operate the facility. In addition, in order to meet quality standards, construction materials do not need to be uniform. They can be selected in accordance with the particular security needs of the particular facility being constructed. Private companies have reduced construction costs by taking advantage of these innovations in design, selection of materials, and other technologies (DeWitt 1986).

It is certainly true that a private vendor *might* forego the efficiencies of, say, prefabrication or modular construction, and that public providers *might* make every effort to exploit cost-reducing opportunities (undoubtedly both of these things have happened). But private firms have much stronger incentives to minimize costs than do public bureaucracies. On average, therefore, it is not surprising that private firms produce at lower cost.

It is often difficult to find public and private prisons that are exactly the same. As a result, comparisons between them are subject to contention. Yet the search for identical facilities misses the point. Private prisons cost less (per bed) in part because they are designed and sited differently than public-sector prisons. As a result, cost savings typically are larger the more authority the private firm has to choose where and how to build prison facilities.

The Evidence on Management Costs

Prison construction costs may loom large, particularly during an era such as the present one, when governments have been trying unsuccessfully to build their way out of the overpopulation crisis, but the day-to-day operational costs are in fact far larger. Even during the prison-building boom of the past ten years, these highly visible "capital" costs represent on average no more than 5–10 percent of total correctional expenditures. At one point during the late 1980s, construction projects were estimated to be proceeding at a pace of $60 to $70 million per week (Meese 1988). Indeed, they briefly may consume a larger share of the budget in individual jurisdictions. All the rest, however, is "management." Therefore, any savings in operational costs will have a significant impact on total correctional outlays.

Crude comparisons of publicly available cost figures have been made, and largely substantiate the economic advantage of turning over prison management to private vendors. Savings in the range of 3 to 30 percent have been reported (Grant and Bast 1987; Massachusetts Legislative Research Council 1987), but getting good cost comparisons is difficult because few private and public facilities are similar (as noted earlier, comparing similar facilities may not be the right type of comparison to make to the extent that cost savings occur precisely because private firms make different decisions than do bureaucracies). Despite these difficulties, the literature repeatedly finds modest yet meaningful cost savings for private prisons. Moore (1998), for example, summarizes fourteen studies, twelve of which found private prisons to be lower in cost than government prisons by between 5 and 28 percent.

Among the most important studies, Archambeault and Deis (1996) compared the cost of three prisons that were built from the same plans and had similar populations. Two of the prisons were run privately; the third was a Louisiana State prison. Archambeault and Deis concluded that "the two private prisons significantly outperformed the government operated prison." Cost savings were in the region of 6–14 percent.

Several other studies compare the same prison before and after it was turned over to private control. The first management-cost study was done on CCA's Silverdale Detention Center, a county facility in Hamilton County, outside Chattanooga, Tennessee. This facility "went private" in 1984, and actual costs and projected costs were analyzed for the first full year of operation under CCA (1985–86) and for the two subsequent years (1986–87 and 1987–88.) The investigators were Charles Logan, an associate professor of sociology at the University of Connecticut, and Bill McGriff, a CPA and county auditor for Hamilton County.

Logan and McGriff (1988) concluded that CCA was saving the county 3.8 percent in 1985–86, when its fee was $21 per inmate per day; 3.0 percent in 1986–87, when it raised its fee to $22; and

8.1 percent in 1987–88, when the fee was kept at $22. Logan and McGriff emphasize the "conservative nature of the county cost estimates," adding that actual savings were "certainly more than this." In a footnote, they estimate that a more realistic projection of a prison guard's pay, for example, would put the 1986–87 savings at 7 percent rather than 3 percent. They also note that the county gained $1.6 million in CCA's new construction, which was incorporated into the management fee, and the "capital and labor in repair and preventive maintenance of the physical plant" invested by CCA because the company inherited from the county a facility that was "in a state of deterioration and neglect." Only a fraction of these costs were factored into the county cost projections, in the event it might wish to take back the facility and reimburse CCA for the construction cost.

The second set of comparative management-cost findings are from a study of a women's prison in New Mexico, which CCA took charge of in 1989–90. The study by Logan, DiIulio, and Thomas reported in Logan (1991) focused mainly on management quality; it attempted "no formal cost analysis" but nonetheless provides useful information on this subject. In 1989, it cost the state $80.00 per day per inmate to operate the prison. CCA's fee for 1990 was $69.75, 12.8 percent below the state's expenditures one year earlier. Logan listed a long series of costs incurred by but unaccounted for by both CCA and the state, the results of which conceivably would alter the precise amount either the CCA or the state spent in running the prison, which in turn would alter the comparison of costs. However, it would change neither the gross quantum nor the direction of the savings. Both Logan and "financial analysts in the New Mexico Corrections Department" concluded that "the contract surely was saving the state money."

Many other studies compare a variety of prisons by statistically controlling for any differences in public and private prisons. A comparison study done by Charles W. Thomas (1997) for the Arizona legislature, for example, compared a private prison to fifteen other state prisons and found operating-cost savings of at least 17 percent. Similarly, a recent comparative study by the Florida OPPAGA

(2000) points to a 3.5 percent cost savings in one fiscal year and a 10.6 percent cost saving in the following year.

If all of the studies on cost savings published in the United States, Australia, and Great Britain were taken as a group, one would end up with an estimate of operating-cost savings in the range of 10–15 percent. The private companies are able to achieve such savings because they (1) use staff more efficiently (in part through improved morale and better prison design); (2) may lower the cost of fringe benefits for staff by substituting stock options for traditional pension plans; (3) use more efficient purchasing arrangements for basic prison goods, services (including insurance), and equipment; (4) make more efficient use of the goods and equipment; and (5) reduce legal, property, and other costs of inmate idleness and discontent by providing additional and improved programs for prisoners (Brakel 1988a; see also Ramirez 1994).

States would do well to consider privatization from the perspective of management costs alone. It is also worth noting that these gains are sustainable efficiency gains. The privatization of prison industry services can be profitable for the governments who buy prison services and for the firms that sell such services. The private-prison industry has amassed a wealth of correctional experience and expertise, and the purchase and sale of prison services today can be done with no more than normal business risk on both sides.

The Quality of Private-Prison Management

Even many opponents of private prisons concede that privatization may save the state some money, but they perceive the correctional enterprise as a zero-sum game—if costs are falling, then quality *must* be falling also. Yet this perception is contradicted by the facts.

One of the writers of this chapter (Brakel) conducted one of the earliest studies on the quality of private prisons. The study (Brakel 1988a) focused on the previously mentioned Silverdale facility near Chattanooga, Tennessee. In an examination of sixteen major aspects of prison conditions and procedures, Brakel concluded that the takeover of the prison by the private vendor (CCA) had resulted in substantial gains in the following areas: (1) the physical plant, including its general upkeep and cleanliness; (2) safety and security, in particular improved prisoner classification; (3) staff professionalism and treatment of inmates; (4) medical services; (5) recreation programs and facilities; (6) religious and other counseling services; (7) disciplinary procedures; (8) inmate grievance and request procedures; and (9) legal access. In the remaining areas, CCA's performance was roughly equivalent to the country's performance, but in no area was a diminution in quality found.

Brakel (1988a) pointed out that the improvements achieved by CCA came in a setting where a great deal of improvement was needed. The county's own management record contained many glaring deficiencies, a fact that figured heavily in the county commissioners' decision to go private in the first place. From one perspective, these prior deficiencies might appear to diminish the significance of CCA's accomplishments. On the other hand, they might be interpreted to augment those accomplishments. The company was dealt a difficult hand at Silverdale: a dilapidated facility with long-standing management problems, situated in a resource-poor environment, contracted out at a per diem fee rate that left the private provider only the slimmest possible profit margin. The fact that the company was able, against these odds, to achieve overall institutional respectability within two and one-half years of the takeover can be viewed as strong evidence of the private sector's capacity to contribute to quality prison management.

Logan conducted a more recent study of private-prison management in 1990–91. Already mentioned in reference to the cost issue, this investigation involved a 200-bed, multi-security-level facility in New Mexico for the state's entire population of sentenced women felons. The now familiar CCA managed the prison beginning in 1989 and built the physical plant.

With more detail than the Silverdale analysis, Logan (1991) measured management quality in eight standard "dimensions"— security, safety, order, care, activity, justice, conditions, and management.

Each of these dimensions in turn was broken down into more specific components, yielding a total of 333 quality "indicators." Logan compared the results of the CCA management experience for the first six months (June–November 1989) against the state-operated situation one year earlier (June–November 1988.) In addition, he threw in a third point of comparison by replicating the investigation in a federal women's prison at Alderson, West Virginia.

The analysis presents rich reading and is recommended to anyone who is interested in the subject of prison privatization. For our purpose, however, the main conclusion offered in the study's summary will suffice: "While all three prisons are regarded as having been high in quality, the private prison outperformed its governmental counterparts on nearly every dimension" (Logan 1991).

Many other studies of the quality of private prisons have been performed (see Harding 1997 for a somewhat outdated list). In Great Britain, the director general of Her Majesty's Prison Services concluded after one study that the private prisons "are the most progressive in the country at controlling bullying, health care, and suicide prevention" (quoted in Moore 1998). The director general then took steps to see that the public prisons emulated the techniques of the private prisons. Surveys of prisoners also find that prisoners prefer private prisons because they are cleaner, health care is better, staff use force less often, and, perhaps most important, violence among prisoners is better controlled (Brakel 1988a; Hackett et al. 1989).

Prison escapes are rare events in public or private prisons. Despite the occasional sensationalistic media account, there is no evidence that escapes are more common in private than in public prisons. Given the high costs of bad publicity to a private prison from an escape, one would expect that, if anything, the rate of escape from private prisons would be lower than the rate of escape from public prisons.

The charge has long been leveled that private corrections companies are willing and able to take on management responsibilities only in relatively low-security settings. The implications are (1) they lack "true" corrections experience and therefore will fall short if they undertake the management of a high-security ("real") prison; and (2) they are cream-skimming by taking on the "easy" populations in an effort to look good in comparison to public corrections agencies, which must deal with both nonviolent and hardened offenders funneled to them by the courts.

These charges are false. In the very early years of privatization, some states (for example, Kentucky) limited private prisons to minimum-security prisoners. Today, however, the most common class of prisoner one finds in privatized facilities are medium-security prisoners, and the housing of maximum-security prisoners in private jails and prisons is not uncommon.

Both of the privately run facilities Brakel examined most closely—the 305-bed Silverdale "jail" near Chattanooga, Tennessee, and the 204-bed New Mexico women's prison—are essentially multi-security prisons and house some pretty tough offenders, although, with respect to the New Mexico prison, it is true that women prisoners do not pose the level and type of security problems presented by male inmates. In Chattanooga, CCA was dealing with an overflow of state felons that comprised 33 percent of the facility's total population. These men were serving sentences from one to six years on a "campus" that housed 90 to 100 convicted women offenders, in addition to convicted misdemeanants and pretrial detainees—a situation that made the security situation even trickier (Brakel 1988a).

Besides these two examples, several other private correctional experiences belie the low-security-only charge. Prominent examples include: (1) the state of Louisiana's contract with CCA for the management of its large (1,382-bed) Winn Correctional Center; (2) the state of Tennessee's contract for the management of its 870-bed Metro-Davidson facility in Nashville, a medium-security prison; (3) the Federal Bureau of Prisons (FBOP) contract for the management of the Leavenworth Detention Center in Kansas, a 256-bed multi-security prison with a substantial maximum-security component (CCA 1992); (4) the FBOP contract with CCA for a 2,304-bed correctional facility located in California City, California (this facility was designed, constructed, and owned by Prison Realty Trust; the base term of the contract is for three years and provides for seven one-year renewal options; the value of the ten-year contract is approximately $530 million, and the contract is believed to be the largest awarded to a private corrections firm in the history of the private corrections industry);[5] and (5) South Africa's recently opened (February 2002) Kutama Sinthumule Maximum Security Prison, at 3,024 beds perhaps the largest prison of its type in the world, which was built and operated by Wackenhut and its local partners.[6]

The cream-skimming charge is not only false but also irrelevant. No serious researcher of prisons has ever compared government maximum-security prisons to private minimum-security prisons. The responsible studies that have been done are before-and-after privatization comparisons of the same facility or comparisons between similar facilities, often aided by the use of statistical techniques to control for the differences that do exist.

Financing the Costs

Financing problems come into play primarily with facilities construction and their high one-time-only costs. Governments traditionally have financed capital improvements in their prison facilities with current operating revenues or, in the case of state and local governments, from the sale of general obligation or revenue bonds. The private sector may play a tangential role by serving as the underwriter and marketer of government bonds. Recent developments, however, signal the prospect of a substantially expanded private-sector role in financing.

Financial intermediaries—including investment-banking firms that specialize in corrections financing, prison construction, and prison management companies—increasingly are becoming the primary financiers of prison construction projects. They have done so via lease-financing techniques that allow government to hurdle imposing barriers to current revenue, "pay-as-you-go" financing, and the economic and political costs of bond issuance. Lease financing includes straight lease, lease-purchase, and even leaseback arrangements. In a leaseback arrangement, the government entity rents the prison facility from the private owner-builder, with or without an option to buy, thus spreading construction costs over the long term, conceivably the life of the facility, and avoiding the extraordinary strain on current revenues or the need to obtain political approval for sudden large increases in operating budgets. Leasing arrangements are often preferable to bond-issue financing because they avoid the time delays and costs incurred in the process of floating bonds (Mullen, Chabotar, and Carrow 1985).

Questions have been raised regarding the political and legal propriety of lease-type financing arrangements because they preclude public participation in the approval of government expenditures. With lease financing, legislative appropriation and taxpayer approval is bypassed (Mullen, Chabotar, and Carrow 1985). In view of the small annual impact of costs spread out over the long term, these concerns may not be of paramount importance. Concern may be allayed further by pointing out that public oversight is preserved in other ways, most notably via a contract that may be more "visible" than typical public accounting mechanisms. Finally, the concern over the propriety of privatized financing all but disappears where, as seems to be the pattern, the private builder-manager wholly absorbs construction costs. These costs are reflected only in the management fee, paid out quarterly or annually, which is, in fact, lower than the government's own operating-cost experience and projections.

If policymakers try to privatize the management and construction of some of a state's correctional apparatus, they should consider privatizing the financing aspects as well.

Matters That Cannot Be Proved: The Propriety of Private Corrections

Evidence shows that private corrections companies can manage and build prison facilities more efficiently than the public sector without compromising quality and, in fact, can improve quality in many respects. This evidence should go a long way toward making privatization a viable option, in an attempt to deal with the large problems of prison overpopulation and its attendant cost burdens.

Some critics, however, reject the empirical evidence as irrelevant. They view the propriety of prison privatization as essentially a moral, legal, or even symbolic issue, unaffected by whether privatization leads to good or bad consequences.

Legality

Not surprisingly, lawyers often have articulated the propriety issue as a legal one. In 1986, the American Bar Association (ABA) passed a resolution that essentially called for a moratorium on any further prison privatization until all the legal and constitutional questions could be explored fully. It then commissioned a study of these questions, selecting as investigator an American University law professor with a record of unequivocal opposition to the privatization of corrections. This study, Robbins (1988), published two years later, produced a model contract and a model statute for jurisdictions wishing to follow the privatization route. Although useful in some details, the models overall were marred by positing minimum standards and conditions so (needlessly) onerous that they threatened to make privatization unprofitable for vendors, rendering the concept unworkable. In the many attendant pages of commentary on the models, the study found no specific legal impediments to privatizing corrections, but left some constitutional issues "unresolved." In short, the ABA effort hardly gave prison privatization a "green light."

This is unfortunate because, from a legal standpoint, the resistance is patently unnecessary. The only real question about the legality of privatizing corrections is whether the government has the authority to delegate correctional responsibilities to non-government entities. The answer to this question is unequivocally affirmative. The delegation of central state authority to subagencies, both public and private, is one of the most common and unavoidable features of modern government. As the writer of the ABA report himself pointed out, no such delegation had been invalidated by the United States Supreme Court in more than fifty years (Robbins 1988). There is no identified constitutional

Table 1

Prison Privatization Lawtable

State	Statutory Authority	Active Contracts?
Alabama	None identified.	No
Alaska	ALASKA STAT. § 33.30.031(a) (1998).	Yes*
Arizona	ARIZ. REV. STAT. § 41-1609 et seq. (1998).	Yes
Arkansas	AR. ST. § 12-50-101 et seq. (1987).	Yes
California	CAL. PENAL CODE § 6256 (1997).	Yes
Colorado	COLO. REV. STAT. § 17-1-201 et seq. (1995).	Yes
Connecticut	CONN. GEN. STAT. § 18-86b(a) (1995).	No
Delaware	None identified.	No
Florida	FLA. STAT. ch.957.01 et seq. (1997); ch. 944.105(1) (1990).	Yes
Georgia	Permissive statutory interpretation.	Yes
Hawaii	Permissive statutory interpretation.	Yes*
Idaho	IDAHO CODE §§ 20-209(2), 20-241 et seq. (1997).	Yes
Illinois	Statutory prohibition, ILL. REV. STAT. Ch.730, 140/1 (1991).	No
Indiana	IND. ST. CODE 11-8-3-1 (1979).	Yes
Iowa	Permissive statutory interpretation.	No
Kansas	Permissive statutory interpretation.	Yes
Kentucky	KY. REV. STAT. ANN. § 197.500 et seq. (Baldwin 1994).	Yes
Louisiana	LA. REV. STAT. ANN. § 39:1800.1 et seq. (West 1992).	Yes
Maine	None identified.	No
Maryland	Permissive statutory interpretation.	No
Massachusetts	None identified.	No
Michigan	MICH. COMP. LAWS ANN. § 791.220g (West 1998).	Yes
Minnesota	Permissive statutory interpretation.	Yes
Mississippi	MISS. CODE ANN. § 47-4-1 et seq. (1997).	Yes
Missouri	Permissive statutory interpretation.	No
Montana	MONT. CODE ANN. § 53-30-602 (1999).	Yes
Nebraska	NEB. REV. STAT. § 83-176(2) (1997).	No
Nevada	NEV. REV. STAT. § 209.141 (1997).	Yes
New Hampshire	N.H. REV. STAT. ANN. § 21-H:8(VI) (1997).	No
New Jersey	None identified.	No
New Mexico	N.M. STAT. ANN. § 31-20-2(G) (1993); § 33-1-17(A) (1995).	Yes
New York	Statutory prohibition, N.Y. Correction Law § 72 (McKinney 1997).	No
North Carolina	N.C. GEN. STAT. § 148-37(g) (1999).	Yes
North Dakota	Permissive statutory interpretation.	Yes*

State	Statutory Authority	Active Contracts?
Ohio	OHIO REV. CODE ANN. § 9.06(A) Yes (Baldwin 1998).	
Oklahoma	OKLA. STAT. ANN. tit. 57, § 561 (1997).	Yes
Oregon	Permissive statutory interpretation.	Yes*
Pennsylvania	None identified.	No
Rhode Island	None identified.	No
South Carolina	Permissive statutory interpretation.	No
South Dakota	None identified.	No
Tennessee	TENN. CODE ANN. § 41-24-101 et seq. (1991).	Yes
Texas	TEX. GOV'T CODE ANN. § 495.001 et seq. (West 1991).	Yes
Utah	UTAH CODE ANN. § 64-13-26(1) (1989).	Yes
Vermont	None identified.	No
Virginia	VA CODE ANN. § 53.1-261 et seq. (1996).	Yes
Washington	None identified.	Yes*
West Virginia	W. VA. CODE § 25-5-1 et seq. (1990).	No
Wisconsin	WIS. STAT. § 301.08(1)(b)(1) (1997).	Yes*
Wyoming	WYO. STAT. § 7-22-101 et seq. (1997).	Yes*

Federal	Statutory Authority	Active Contracts?
Federal Bureau of Prisons	18 U.S.C.A. § 3621 (1998).	Yes
Immigration and Naturalization Service	8 U.S.C.A. § 1103 (1996).	Yes
U.S. Marshals Service	18 U.S.C.A. § 4013(a)(3) (1994).	Yes

Other	Statutory Authority	Active Contracts?
District of Columbia	D.C. CODE ANN. § 24-495.1 et seq. (1998).	Yes
Puerto Rico	P.R. LAWS ANN. tit. 4 § 1112(o) (1994).	Yes

*Indicates that the correctional authority of the jurisdiction has one or more contracts for the housing of sentenced prisoners in force at this time but only for those prisoners to be housed in private facilities outside of the jurisdiction. For more details see source.

Source: Charles Thomas and Sherril Gautreaux. The Present Status of State and Federal Privatization Law (last updated 3/19/00). Online document available at http://www.crim.ufl.edu/pcp/, last accessed October 2002.

principle threatening the legality of delegating correctional authority in particular, and, as Logan (1987) has argued with considerable persuasiveness, no recognized precept of governmental philosophy (from which a constitutional challenge might be fashioned) prohibits a delegation of such authority. Indeed, virtually all the established law on the issue supports the legality of privatization and, in some cases, specifically encourages it.

Federal law is strongly favorable to privatization of correctional functions. The key federal statute remands all federal offenders to the custody of the attorney general for confinement in "any available, suitable, and appropriate institution or facility, whether maintained by the Federal Government or otherwise."[7] Based on an analysis of the legislative history of this law and its amendments, the general counsel to the FBOP has concluded that "there is authority to contract with private facilities, both half-way houses and traditional . . . facilities" (President's Commission on Privatization 1988). More generally, since 1955, the federal government has been under a mandate to compare in-house costs of all commercial services with those obtainable from private suppliers and to opt for the least-expensive supplier of the appropriate quality of service (Butler 1986).

On the state level in a few jurisdictions, there were, until a decade or so ago, legal barriers to the privatization of so-called public functions, including corrections. However, the trend is now in the opposite direction, with many states having enacted laws that go toward "clarifying and granting statutory authority . . . to permit contracting" (Hackett et al. 1987). In the 1980s, a dozen or so states passed laws specifically authorizing the private provision of prison space and services (Hackett et al. 1987). Twenty-eight states presently have enacted statutes that expressly authorize contracts for private prisons, and another ten states are of the opinion that broader language in their general corrections statutes provides all the legal authority they require to authorize contracts for private prisons. Only two states have statutes that prohibit contracting (Illinois and New York).[8]

Privatized correctional facilities have long been a part of corrections in the United States. All three federal agencies that have prisoner custody responsibilities—the FBOP, the INS, and the U.S. Marshals Service—have housed sentenced federal prisoners in private facilities continuously for nearly twenty years: they are an operative fact in many states today—a minority, perhaps, if one counts only traditional prison facilities, but an overwhelming majority if one includes youth homes, halfway houses, and the like.[9]

There are only a few court cases on point. They support—indeed, strongly affirm—the authority of government to delegate its correctional responsibilities.[10] A holding of "obvious state action" was the result in a federal case involving the INS's liability for an incident of fatal negligence on the part of a guard employed by the private security firm that had the contract for managing the INS facility.[11] Thus, there was dual liability for the harm. The federal government and the private provider shared responsibility, and the decision, often cited by opponents of correctional privatization because of its damaging facts, in effect strengthens the privatization concept. It affirms both the government's final responsibility for the functions it delegates and the claimant's right to proceed against either or both the government and the private provider.

The holding of this case also eliminates one of the advantages governments may seek in delegating correctional authority: the avoidance of liability. However, that objective can be recaptured largely by contractual terms requiring the vendor to indemnify the government for damages incurred.

The Morality Issue

Even with the legal issue out of the way, in some circles there remains opposition to prison privatization on the ground that the incarceration of offenders convicted by the state is a uniquely governmental function whose delegation to nongovernment entities is "just not right." This view is often stated more pejoratively, particularly in relation to vendors who are in the business to make a profit. "Making a buck off the backs of prisoners" is the phrase used to describe the presumably unseemly character of this business.

Although this position has some intuitive appeal, if judging only from how frequently it is parroted by privatization opponents, it does not stand up well to more-reasoned analysis. The mistrust of the profit motive seems distinctly out of place in a society whose social and economic engines are driven largely by this motive—indeed, whose creative (and moral) strength is believed to be a very function of this motive, collectively and individually. In addition, the notion that the quest for profit is somehow "worse" than competing motivations, such as power or convenience (to name two that have considerable currency in the public and in other nonprofit settings), remains to be explained. Last, it might be asked what the critical difference is between rewards paid out in salaries as opposed to dividends ("profits"), not to mention that all those who work for profit-making companies—in prisons, everyone from the warden on down to the line guards—are virtually salaried employees.

There is yet the matter of symbolism that causes resistance to prison privatization. Robbins (1988), the ABA reporter, has written derisively of prison guards with the logo "ACME Prisons" on their uniforms. Donahue and DiIulio have invoked the White House/President analogy to illustrate what they see as the moral or symbolic bankruptcy in the idea of privatizing corrections. Donahue (1989) posits the "who should paint the White House versus who should guard the President" dichotomy, finding it self-evident that the former is a job for private business, whereas the latter is a function to be performed by public servants. DiIulio (1988) paints a rent-a-President scene in which an actor "President" plus an entourage of musicians and dignitaries of the "Medals Corporation of America" play out on the White House lawn the role of giving out the National Medal of Honor to deserving citizens. According to DiIulio, it is clear that such a scenario would not satisfy us. The appeal is primarily to our moral intuition, though Donahue brings in the complexity of the guard-the-President task as among the more concrete reasons for having a public Secret Service rather than a private protective force.

However, the message of these illustrations is not nearly so self-evident as their creators think. The question that might be posed in response to Robbins' ACME illustration is whether citizens necessarily find the private-sector identification less appropriate or less confidence inspiring than the public-sector identification, even for traditionally "public" services. Does the Federal Express or United Parcel Service logo suggest to the average consumer a performance quality that is in any way inferior to that of the U.S. Postal Services? To the

DiIulio rent-a-President example the response should be: let the President or other public officials do the symbolic acts, while private providers do the real work. The answer to Donahue's complexity argument is a rhetorical question: Is the public sector or the private sector better at handling complex, responsibility-laden tasks? If one thinks of the air-transport industry, the utility of government oversight might generate some consensus, but surely there is no call in this country today for the government actually to "be" in the airline business. Rationally functioning partnership between government and private vendors is what the prison privatization idea is all about. Opponents of the idea might be less resistant if they thought in more limited terms, instead of in all-or-nothing, moral, and symbolic propositions.

Perhaps the final and most persuasive response to the moral and symbolic concerns about prison privatization is the evidence that the prisoners themselves do not share these concerns. The Silverdale study, one of whose main investigatory components was a survey of inmate views, showed that the prisoners' dominant concern was whether they were treated fairly and lawfully (Brakel 1988a). Precisely where the ultimate authority of their keepers resided or what logo was on the staff's uniforms mattered little to them. They had no beef with privatization at Silverdale because they were treated no worse and, in several respects, were treated better than they were led to expect from their experience in the same facility under public management or from their experience in other public facilities. There exists no plausible theory why "private" managers of prisons or their staff would treat inmates worse than their public counterparts: the motivations are to the contrary (mistreatment fosters discontent, lawsuits, riots, and so on), and the empirical evidence provided by the inmates themselves clearly confirms this conclusion.

The Role of Contracts in Legitimizing Private Corrections

The demonstrable weakness of both the principled and pragmatic arguments against prison privatization suggests that other concerns or interests drive much of the opposition. Prominent among these ulterior motives is self-interest: the fear that privatization will lead to loss of jobs or "turf." It explains why agencies such as public-employee unions are among the staunchest and most vocal critics of privatization. Because the persuasive power of abstract arguments is limited, the better strategy for dealing with entrenched opposition to privatized corrections is often to get down to the specifics. Good contracting procedures and good contracts can substantially allay fears and concerns of all manner of derivation. What follows is a set of contracting characteristics—not abstract ideals, but elements based on prison-contracting experience in the real world. Thus, they are replicable and go far toward assuring the legitimacy of privatized corrections for all sides, parties, or interests (Brakel 1989).

1. *Continuity.* When a private vendor takes over the responsibility for managing a correctional facility or service, no abrupt break with past experience is likely to be necessary or advisable. Gradual change in staffing patterns, practices, and procedures—change that builds on past experience and the continuance of things that were not "broke"—is the key to successful transition. The contract between the government and the vendor should articulate this principle via provisions that guarantee the retention of public employees so long as they perform adequately and substantial continuity in employment benefits. Over time, the company will be able to put its administrative stamp on the facility through the process of selective termination, hiring, and attrition, as well as the gradual substitution of new procedures where experience shows the old methods to be dysfunctional.

2. *Flexibility.* Contracts for the management, construction, and financing of correctional facilities are the mechanism by which continued government oversight of the corrections enterprise is assured and by which continued governmental responsibility and accountability of both parties are made concrete. The fulfillment of these contractual obligations typically is effectuated through compliance-monitoring devices and personnel. Obviously, the more detailed the contractual terms agreed to, the more control the government retains over the enterprise. However, there is a caveat here: the danger of contractual overspecification. A substantial element of flexibility is needed for the vendor to make

efficient staffing, purchasing, and subcontracting decisions that ultimately lower the cost of the enterprise and that allow profits to be made and tax dollars to be saved. A sound privatization contract should be built around a set of basic terms whose details should be left to the vendor's discretionary implementation.

3. *Legality.* Good contracts include terms regarding the liability of both sides for negligent or willfully wrong performance of correctional functions, such as insurance-purchasing mandates that cover the risks of misperformance and that realize the potential claimants' rights and the providers' responsibilities. Governments cannot escape liability by contracting out, but indemnification provisions, whereby the vendor agrees to pay the cost of any judgments against the government as well as the costs of mounting a legal defense or concluding a negotiated settlement, are common. Also recommended are provisions of varying detail that emphasize that the rule of public law continues to apply in privatized corrections. Furthermore, the specification of the parties' legal accountability serves as a symbol for moral accountability as well.

4. *Fee Structures and Incentives.* The typical contract for private prisons includes a fee-structure calculation based on the total inmate population housed in or processed through the facility. Though no practical evidence supports its actualization, the theory is that this fee structure gives the industry as a whole an incentive to keep the prisons full (presumably implemented via legislative lobbying for long or mandatory sentences or both.) Where the financial terms of the contract state that the vendor's fee in fact shall vary directly with the size of the inmate population, the incentive to keep the facility filled is more direct.[12] Although we need to be careful about creating incentives that may influence release decisions (assuming the vendor has control over such decisions), control over intake invariably stays with the government. Therefore, the flat fee, even if initially based on population, is the better arrangement, provided allowance is made for dramatic and unexpected population changes. It has been suggested that financial incentives that would move the vendor to decrease the inmate population should be built into the contract (e.g., via bonuses), but the wisdom of such arrangements depends on the wisdom of early-release policies, about which there

may be doubt. It also has been proposed that vendors be rewarded for rehabilitative success in the facilities they run. Bonuses would be paid, for example, for a proven decrease in recidivism among the population released from the facility. The concept may appear appealing, but there are doubts about whether it is realistic, because adequate definitions of, and proof of, decreased recidivism are difficult to come by. Furthermore, the tracking of former prisoners, apart from being difficult, must be a long-term proposition if it is to have any meaning in terms of the ultimate goal of public safety.

5. *Competition.* It makes no sense from either the efficiency or quality perspective to replace the state's monopoly over corrections with a single private-vendor monopoly, and the contractual process must be structured to prevent this from occurring. Reasonable contractual time limits (three to four years, with an option to renew for a year or two thereafter), preterm termination or buy-out provisions that can be activated under certain circumstances, and an open rebidding process in which the government can be an applicant if it so chooses comprise the features that safeguard a healthy competition and its attendant efficiency and quality benefits.

Privatization and Correctional "Reforms"

Advocates for prison reform often have articulated the position that government efforts to solve correctional problems (or crises) by building more prison space are misguided. They say that the provision of more space merely guarantees, by some law of nature that they pass off as empirically validated, that it will be filled—that is, that it will only enlarge the problems (Robbins 1988).[13] The thrust of our efforts, they advocate, should be precisely in the opposite direction, toward reducing our reliance on incarceration in favor of "nonincarceration alternatives." The prison population, they say, can and should be decreased, thus obviating the need for all this building frenzy, irrespective of whether it is driven by private or public providers.

The merits of this position are at best debatable. Some of its support appears to derive from misinformation. There is also the suggestion that some of its supporters indulge in overly hopeful assumptions.

First, the misinformation is that our prisons presently are populated by large percentages of nondangerous first offenders who do not need to be locked up. Although the "war on drugs" has resulted in the occasional incarceration of nonpredatory first offenders, the reality remains that prisons, in virtually every state, are filled overwhelmingly with the worst offenders who come in contact with the criminal justice machinery. The prison population is dominated by repeat offenders, individuals with tellingly long rap sheets whose penchant for "antisocial" conduct was demonstrated at an alarmingly (and on the average increasingly) early age and whose recidivism, in many cases, virtually can be guaranteed despite their incarceration experience.[14] On the other hand, the comparatively rare first offender who lands in the penitentiary will have committed a very serious first offense, with few exceptions (as noted earlier).

Second, regarding those other prisoners for whom it is at least plausible to argue that they do not need to be locked up—that is, property or other nonviolent offenders, perpetrators of so-called victimless crimes, and the like—the assumption that all or even most of them pose no threat to society is too facile. The assumption is premised on value judgments about what is socially tolerable and what is intolerable, judgments that are by no means universally shared. The assumption also fails to appreciate that the initial commission of relatively nonserious crimes can lead to—and in many cases has been shown to lead to—a career of increasingly serious criminal conduct. And, finally, there is no empirical support for the contention that the criminal justice system can identify and segregate (with or without help from corrections experts, mental health experts, and so on) the presumably few dangerous individuals whose known offenses are nonserious, from the "genuinely harmless" nonviolent offenders. Jeffrey Dahmer was perceived to merit only a slap on the wrist when he was arrested for a sexual solicitation offense prior to the final arrest that led to the revelation of his seventeen sexually driven murders. Whether this mistake was the result of genuine misdiagnosis, poor information gathering, soft-headed optimism, or considerations of prison space allocation hardly matters. The criminal justice and corrections records are filled with too many similarly grievous miscalculations.[15]

This is not to say that there is no merit at all in attempting the difficult and risky business of sorting out from among those imprisoned the individuals or groups who need imprisonment less from those who need it more. The charge that our current antidrug policies—which place heavy emphasis on criminal processing and prison sentencing and less emphasis on drug treatment—are futile and counterproductive has some basis in empirical reality, although the easy conclusion that there will be no individual harms or social consequences from wholesale "decriminalization" stretches plausibility. Nevertheless, these issues are matters of public policy: legislative or political matters in which corrections, as such, let alone private corrections, has no voice. The job of corrections is to contend with the results of these policy decisions.

Finally, whatever the deincarceration movement's ultimate merits prove to be, deincarceration is decidedly against the current prevailing winds of public sentiment. The public today wants to be "tougher" on crime and to imprison more offenders longer, and the politicians, for the most part, have followed the direction indicated by their constituents.

Privatization is not a substantive reform movement. It tends to follow the basic set policy and to respond efficiently and effectively to the needs identified within this policy framework. If efficient and effective performance is seen as "reform," or if it produces institutional conditions that reformers like, that is fine, but it is incidental. For example, private vendors place emphasis on rehabilitative programs in their prisons because such programs are cost effective.[16] Reform, as such, however—in particular "revolutionary" reform— is not the crux of the privatizers' agenda.

In the sense that private vendors, as a group or individually, "profit" from swelling prison populations, their interests, as we noted, indeed run directly counter to the nonincarceration reformers. It was suggested that this might not be very consequential, given the limited influence the industry has or is likely to have on "intake policies," either on the facility level or on the larger sentencing policy level. Furthermore, fees can be structured to counteract any "perverse" incentives that individual vendors of prison services otherwise may have.

What we suggest here is to go one step further. If nonincarceration reforms are indeed good, and if a political consensus develops to push such reforms, then it is both advisable and possible to "co-opt" the vendor industry, so to speak, by aligning its interests with those of the incarceration alternatives movement.

Privatization's Stake in Prison Alternatives

There are a variety of dispositional alternatives to imprisonment. Some are long-standing; others are of more recent origin, for a variety of offender classes. These alternatives include: probation, with or without rehabilitative treatment conditions; early release, conditional and otherwise; direct diversion into treatment-style, nonprison facilities on a full-residence or "outpatient" basis; house arrest or weekend-only incarceration, often with "electronic monitoring" safeguards; and shorter-term "shock incarceration" in "boot camps," usually in rural settings, but now also contemplated in urban and other high-population environments.

Private vendors traditionally have had a sizable stake in the more traditional of these nonprison treatment approaches. They are in the vanguard of taking the more novel approaches, such as electronic monitoring. If prisons are viewed as the wrong answer to our crime problems, and the nonincarceration drive is to be pursued with optimum efficiency and effectiveness, then the idea should be to increase the role of private industry in the latter enterprise. All the measures for harnessing the entrepreneurial drive in the service of the public good of corrections (i.e., good contracts and good competitive contracting procedures) that were identified relative to prison privatization can and should be applied equally to these alternative correctional means and methods.

The Privatization Choice

The nationwide trend of corrections provides an opportunity to try out the privatization concept as a way of enhancing the efficiency and, more incidentally, the effectiveness of a nation's response to the growing problem of crime. Privatization tends to be neutral on policy matters, with its primary purpose being to respond in the context of given policies. As such, the main thrust of the new (renewed) privatization movement in corrections has been to improve the management, construction, and financing of prison facilities.

Even in a course in which greater reliance is placed on alternatives to imprisonment, the privatization option remains both relevant and available, with the addition of private-sector resources and experience as well.

Which policy, policies, or policy emphasis to pursue in tackling crime is up to the citizens of each state and to their political representatives. Implementing policy choices with optimum efficiency is, however, not a matter of choice, but rather an imperative. The objective of this chapter has been to lay out the evidence and arguments regarding privatization choices and to indicate where that imperative might take the decision makers.

Notes

1. *Sourcebook of Criminal Justice Statistics 2000* 2001, table 6.1 at 488.

2. *Sourcebook of Criminal Justice Statistics 1992* 1993, table 1.7 at 7. The precise percentages vary according to whether local (county and municipality) expenditures are counted or only state expenditures.

3. Even medical drugs, that bugaboo of so many groups and individuals who complain about private profiteers gouging the public, cost some three times as much when their development is through government-funded research than when they are developed and marketed in the private sector.

4. The precise bed count of 870 is from CCA's annual report (Ramirez gives the figure as "nearly 900").

5. Information culled from the Web site of Charles W. Thomas, professor of criminology (retired), Center for Studies in Criminology and Law, University of Florida, http://web.crim.ufl.edu/pcp, "Breaking Privatization News," 9 June 2000.

6. See the 29 January 2002 press release from the South African Department of Public Works available at http://www.publicworks.gov.za/pressreleases/2002/29jan2002.htm last accessed 16 Sept. 2002.

7. 18 U.S.C. § 4082(b).

8. Information culled from the Web site of Charles W. Thomas, professor of criminology (retired), Center for Studies in Criminology and Law, University of Florida, http://web.crim.ufl.edu/pcp, "Frequently Asked Questions," last updated on 23 April 2000.

9. Ibid.

10. Ibid.

11. *Medina v. O'Neill*, 589 F. Supp. 1028 (S.D. Tex. 1984).

12. Contracts in which the per-diem price decreases with population are also possible. The per diem price at CCA-operated and Prison Realty Trust-owned correctional facilities located in Coffee County and Wheeler County, Georgia will be $46.83 until the prisoner population exceeds 1,400 and $44.98 thereafter. See the Web site of Charles W. Thomas, professor of criminology (retired), Center for Studies in Criminology and Law, University of Florida, http://web.crim.ufl.edu/pcp, "Breaking Privatization News," 14 September 2000.

13. This point tends to be repeated ad nauseam by organizations such as the American Civil Liberties Union's National Prison Project.

14. See *Sourcebook* 1993, note 3, table 6.70 at 623. Nationwide, 54.6 percent of state prison inmates are incarcerated for violent crimes. Who can contend rationally that property offenses, with burglaries by far the highest percentage (16.5 percent) in that category, are "nonserious" either in terms of actual or potential threat to the victims?

15. The potential of an undeterminable percentage of sex offenders to commit or recommit crimes of appalling character and magnitude has led a number of states to pass special legislation permitting "civil commitment–style" detention of such individuals after their prison sentence, if any, is served and to require some form of notification or registration upon their release into the community. A series of gruesome, sexually motivated child murders in Washington resulted in that state being the first to pass such legislation regarding "sexually violent predators" (Wash. Rev. Code §§ 71.09.010–71.09.120). Other states have had similar experiences, most notably New Jersey with the widely publicized murder of seven-year-old Megan Kanka, resulting in mounting pressure to enact legislation similar to Washington's (but resulting only in a sex offender registration law in 1994). Not until 1998 was a Washington-style commitment law passed in New Jersey.

16. See Ramirez 1994 and Haynie and Associates 1994 for documentation on the point that private prison-service providers emphasize rehabilitative programs (as well as the motivation behind them).

References

Archambeault, William G., and Donald R. Deis. 1996. *Cost Effectiveness Comparisons of Private versus Public Prisons in Louisiana: A Comprehensive Analysis of Allen, Avoyelles, and Winn Correctional Centers*. Baton Rouge: Louisiana State University School of Social Work.

Benson, Bruce L. 1998. *To Serve and Protect: Privatization and Community in Criminal Justice*. New York: New York University Press for the Independent Institute.

Brakel, J. 1988a. Prison Management, Private Enterprise Style: The Inmates' Evaluation. *New England Journal on Criminal and Civilian Confinement* 14: 175–244.

————. 1988b. Privatization in Corrections: Radical Prison Chic or Mainstream Americana? *New England Journal on Criminal and Civilian Confinement* 14: 1–39.

————. 1989. *Privatization and Corrections*. Federal Privatization Project, Issue Paper no. 7 (January). Los Angeles: Reason Foundation.

Butler, E. 1986. *Privatizing Federal Services: A Primer*. Heritage Foundation Backgrounder (February). Washington, D.C.: Heritage Foundation.

Chaiken, M., and J. Chaiken. 1988. *Public Policing—Privately Provided*. Washington, D.C.: National Institute of Justice.

Corrections Corporation of America (CCA). 1992. *CCA Annual Report*. Houston: Corrections Corporation of America.

Davies, S. J. 2002. The Private Provision of Police during the Eighteenth and Nineteenth Centuries. In *The Voluntary City*, edited by D. T. Beito, P. Gordon, and A. Tabarrok, 151–81. Ann Arbor: University of Michigan Press.

DeWitt, N. 1986. *New Construction Methods for Correctional Facilities*. Construction Bulletin (March). Washington, D.C.: National Institute of Justice.

DiIulio, J. 1988. What's Wrong with Private Prisons? *The Public Interest* 92 (summer): 66–83.

Donahue, J. 1989. *The Privatization Decision: Public Ends, Private Means.* New York: Basic.

Grant, D. C., and J. S. Bast. 1987. *Corrections and the Private Sector: A Guide for Public Officials.* Policy Study no. 15 (May). Chicago: Heartland Institute.

Hackett, J. C., H. P. Hatry, R. B. Levinson, J. Allen, K. Chi, and E. D. Feigenbaum. 1987. *Issues in Contracting for the Private Operation of Prisons and Jails.* Report (February). Washington, D.C.: Council of State Governments and the Urban Institute.

————. 1989. *Contracting for the Operation of Prisons and Jails.* Washington, D.C.: U.S. Department of Justice.

Harding, Richard W. 1997. *Private Prisons and Public Accountability.* New Brunswick, N.J.: Transaction.

Haynie and Associates. 1994. *Privatization of Prison Management.* Report furnished by Darrell Massengale, vice president, finance secretary, and treasurer. Houston: Corrections Corporation of America.

Kent, Calvin A. 1986. *Privatization of Public Functions: Promises and Problems.* Policy Study no. 8, February 18. Chicago: Heartland Institute.

Logan, C. 1987. The Propriety of Proprietary Prisons. *Federal Probation* 51 (September): 35–40.

————. 1991. *Well Kept: Comparing Quality of Confinement in a Public and a Private Prison.* Washington, D.C.: National Institute of Justice.

Logan C., and B. W. McGriff. 1988. *Comparing Costs of Public and Private Prisons.* Research in Brief (proposed), October 6. Washington, D.C.: National Institute of Justice.

Massachusetts Legislative Research Council. 1987. *Report Relative to Prisons for Profit.* House no. 6225, July.

Meese, Edwin. 1988. Why We Need More Federal Prisons. *Chicago Tribune*, February.

Moore, Adrian T. 1998. *Private Prisons: Quality Correction at a Lower Cost.* Policy Study no. 240. Los Angeles: Reason Public Policy Institute.

Mullen, J., K. Chabotar, and D. Carrow. 1985. *The Privatization of Corrections.* Washington, D.C.: National Institute of Justice.

Office of Program Policy Analysis and Government Accountability (OPPAGA). 2000. *Private Prison Review: South Bay Correctional*

Facility Provides Savings and Success; Room for Improvement. Report no. 99-39, March. Tallahassee: Florida Office of Program Policy Analysis and Government Accountability. Available online at http://www.oppaga.state.fl.us/reports/crime/r99-39s.html. Accessed 11 May, 2001.

President's Commission on Privatization. 1988. *Privatization: Toward More Effective Government*. March. Washington, D.C.: Government Printing Office.

Ramirez, A. 1994. Privatizing America's Prisons, Slowly. *New York Times,* 14 August C1, C6.

Robbins, I. 1988. *The Legal Dimensions of Private Incarceration*. Washington, D.C.: American Bar Association.

Rothman, David J. 1980. *Conscience and Convenience: The Asylum and Its Alternatives in Progressive America*. Boston: Little, Brown.

Savas, E. 1982. *Privatizing the Public Sector.* Chatham, N.J.: Chatham House.

Sourcebook of Criminal Justice Statistics 1992. 1993. Washington, D.C.: U.S. Department of Justice, Bureau of Justice Statistics.

Sourcebook of Criminal Justice Statistics 2000. 2001. Washington, D.C.: U.S. Department of Justice, Bureau of Justice Statistics

Thomas, Charles W. 1997. *Comparing the Cost and Performance of Public and Private Prisons in America*. Phoenix: Arizona Department of Corrections.

5

Do We Want the Production of Prison Services to Be More "Efficient"?

BRUCE L. BENSON[1]

1. Introduction

Would private, for-profit firms provide prison services more efficiently than the government? Should prison services be contracted to the private sector?

Although these questions are separate from one another, they are closely related in many people's minds. Supporters of contracting out typically stress the reasons to believe that a private, for-profit prison firm in a competitive market would be less expensive than a publicly run system. Opponents of prison contracting counter that the costs saved by contracting would result in lower quality. Their arguments are unconvincing, however, in light of the growing empirical evidence that private firms under contract actually produce higher-quality services at lower costs (Archambeault and Deis 1996; Benson 1998, 26–40; Brakel 1992; Logan 1990). But even if contracting out is *proven* to be more efficient than publicly run prisons, does it necessarily imply that prison services *should* be contracted out? No. Whether or not prison services should be contracted out is a strictly normative question whose answer depends on which norm or standard is invoked.

This study examines several normative arguments about contract prisons. One normative argument against contracting out holds that private firms *should not* be in the business of using force or of producing punishment because this power should be reserved to the state. Another argument to be considered, previously addressed in Benson 1994b and 1998, focuses on "liberty": an individual *should* be free to do as he or she pleases with his/her person and property as long as no other individual is prevented from doing the same.

Because the concept of efficiency plays an important role in the debate about prison contracting, it is helpful to clarify its meaning at the onset. *Efficiency* is the norm presumably applied by advocates of contracting out; it makes the positive arguments for contracting appear to be relevant. Note, however, that the term *efficiency* has more than one meaning. The two most common notions of efficiency are *technological efficiency* and *allocative efficiency*. An increase in technological efficiency refers to (1) an improvement in the quality of a given quantity of goods or services produced at a given cost; (2) a reduction in the cost of producing a given quality of goods or services; or (3) an improvement in quality accompanied by a reduction in cost. An increase in allocative efficiency refers to the redirecting of scarce resources from uses having a lower value to uses having a higher value.

The evidence supports the view that contracting out prison services improves technological efficiency, but does contracting out also improve allocative efficiency? As with so many public-policy questions, the answer depends on *opportunity costs*—i.e., on the value of the alternative uses of publicly controlled resources. For instance, the resources directed to the expansion of prison capacity (whether they are privately or publicly built and managed) have alternative uses, including school construction, housing construction (either public housing or private housing through tax relief), hospital construction, and so on. Is building more prisons the highest and best use of such resources just because the prisons can be built less expensively through contracting out? The answer depends in part on policy objectives. Consider the role of imprisonment in the "war on drugs" (this particular use of prisons is examined in detail below). If the goal of imprisoning drug users is to reduce the level of drug use, for example, then a recent study issued by the Rand Corporation (Rydell and Everingham 1994) concluded that there is a better option: a dollar spent on treatment was estimated to be seven times more effective at reducing cocaine use than a dollar spent on criminal justice resources, including prisons. One opportunity cost of the taxes used to support prison building and management is the forgone drug treatment programs that might be funded (the opportunity cost of using prisons to achieve other objectives of the war on drugs, such as general crime control, are considered later in this essay).

In section II of this study, the implications of contracting out are considered for the various normative perspectives listed above. Some of these perspectives appear to be valid, whereas others do not. For example, it appears that prison services should be contracted out if the normative objective is to increase technological efficiency (although this conclusion is subject to certain conditions considered in section 5). This section also contends that contracting out cannot be rejected on the premise that only the state should produce punishment. The state, after all, never produces *anything* without contracting out with private individuals.

The validity of the allocative efficiency and liberty norms cannot be determined without consideration of the politics of crime and punishment, which are examined in sections 3 through 4. Section 3 considers the politics of crime and punishment in general, and section 4 focuses on the politics of one particular category of crimes: the sale and use of illicit drugs. In light of these issues, section 5 reexamines the technological efficiency norm to see whether or not political influences can affect its likely validity. Section 6 contains my concluding remarks.

2. Normative Arguments Regarding Contracting for Prison Services

Are certain actions, such as incarceration or punishment, by their nature so important or special that only the government should perform them? This question is one of the most frequently cited normative issues in the debate over prison-service contracting.

As Logan (1990, 49) notes, critics often contend that only government should mete out punishment. There is, however, at least one significant logical flaw in this argument.[2]

The fact is "the government" never actually produces anything without contracting with private individuals and organizations (Benson 1998, 15–17). The individuals who work within a bureaucracy such as the Department of Corrections are *private parties working under contract.* They contract to provide their labor services because they expect to be better off than they would be in an alternative job.[3]

In this light, the normative view that "government" must be the only organization with punishment powers, for fear that private entities might abuse such powers, makes little sense. Because an individual civil servant under contract with the government, such as a corrections officer in a public prison, is a private citizen who has been given a substantial amount of power and discretion, he also is in a position to abuse the power that he is given. After all, this private citizen works as a corrections officer under contract with an organization that has virtual monopoly power over the right to coerce, and there is relatively little to constrain his tendencies to abuse his position. His supervisors, after all, are also private citizens under contract. They have similar motivations and incentives, including a desire to avoid tarnishing the image of their bureaucracy by revealing abuses by those whom they supervise (the bureaucrats may have a variety of motives here, such as the belief that tarnishing the bureaucracy's image will reduce their ability to pursue their vision of the public interest or will threaten their job security, support for their families, comfortable lifestyle, discretion, power, or authority). Not surprisingly, many types of abuses (corruption, physical abuse of prisoners, sales of drugs and other goods that are supposedly illegal in prisons) occur in great numbers—and the strong incentives to avoid scandal suggest that we see only the tip of the iceberg (Benson 1988). Therefore, if abuse of power by private entities is the concern that motivates the argument against contract prisons, the argument is not legitimate.

The point is that the idea of government production is a fiction. There is no alternative to contracting out with private providers of punishment. The differences between contracting with a private firm, which in turn contracts with private providers of labor services, and contracting with individual laborers (or with their union) is simply a difference in the organization of contracts: Is the nexus of contracts a private entrepreneur or a private individual who has a contract to manage a bureaucracy? This difference does affect incentives, of course, so it must be considered, but not for the reason suggested by this private versus public production argument.

Technological and Allocative Inefficiencies with Government Production

The strongest normative case for contracting out is that under the right circumstances (see Benson 1994b and 1998, 40–47, as well as the discussion in the following subsection as well as in section 6), the costs of providing the service will be lower, and the quality of the service will be superior when it is produced by a private firm rather than by a public bureau. These gains in technological efficiency through contracting arise largely because the incentives and constraints facing private citizens working as public officials and bureaucrats are very different from those facing private producers providing goods or services in a competitive market.

An understanding of the relative advantage of markets requires an understanding of some basic economic principles. The fact underlying these principles is *scarcity*. There simply are not enough resources (labor, land and other natural resources, capital, knowledge) to produce everything that people want. Choices must be made. Every good or service that is produced requires resources that might be used for something else. Because there are always tradeoffs, scarce resources must be rationed among potential alternative uses. But many different rationing mechanisms might be established, and the rationing process that is established (the rules of the game) determines the nature of the competition that arises.

First consider the rationing of scarce resources through the processes used in government organizations. Governments have the power to tax, and they can use that power of *coercion* to produce "services", whether or not "buyers" (taxpayers) value them relative to the costs. Of course, in a democracy, taxpayers supposedly can "throw the rascals out" if they are forced to buy something they do not want or to pay more for something than they are willing to pay. Unfortunately, the typical voter-taxpayer does not really know what is being purchased with tax revenues, let alone how cost-effective the production of some particular service happens to be.

This lack of knowledge is perfectly rational because citizens have very weak incentives to obtain the information required to evaluate government performance effectively, even in a democracy. After all, voters do not choose individual products like consumers choose among products. They generally vote for a political candidate who is offering to advocate the production of a bundle of goods and services, some of which may be desirable for a particular voter, whereas others are not. To make a "good" decision (i.e., obtain enough information to vote for the candidate who will advocate the policy bundle closest to the voter's preferred bundle), the voter has to determine what each candidate is actually offering (not always an easy task given the obfuscation that politicians often practice in an effort to keep voters from finding out about the costs they are likely to bear if the candidate is elected), weigh the attractive parts of each candidate's offered bundle against the unsatisfactory parts, and then compare these weighted bundles of costs and benefits.

Furthermore, the expected benefits in time and effort of making this investment are small, and the costs to a voter of making a "bad" decision (e.g., voting for a candidate who will not advocate the voter's preferred bundle of policies) are also very low. After all, if the voter makes the considerable investment in time and effort that it takes to make a "good" decision, there is still no guarantee that the preferred candidate will win, or that if he wins, he will be able to achieve the goals he promises to advocate, or that he will even advocate the promised policies. And even if the candidate who wins is inept, false, or totally corrupt, the individual voter who supported the candidate because of an "uninformed" decision will bear only a small part of the costs. These costs are shared by widely dispersed taxpayers, some of whom voted for the same candidate, and many of whom (nonvoters and voters for other candidates) did not.

In light of such relative costs and benefits, most voters have relatively weak incentives to inform themselves. Indeed, most potential
voters do not even bother to vote (not because they are apathetic:
many people are very concerned about what the government is
doing for or to them, but they rationally choose not to invest in
information about candidates), and virtually everyone who does is
far from fully informed.

Most citizens also have weak incentives to gather information
about the general workings of the bureaucracies that actually carry
out government policies, although they may know a great deal
about some policies that have large effects on their well-being. In
general, however, for most people, the cost of gathering information about individual government activities exceeds the likely
benefits of doing so. This imbalance generates an environment con-
ducive to interest-group influence on government decisions, of
course, because members of focused interests invest time or money
to organize and to purchase specialists (lobbyists, spokespersons for
bureaucracies) in order to influence and then monitor performance
in government production related to the issues that have large
impacts on them. The concentrated benefits may be produced at
very high costs, but the costs are widely dispersed (e.g., across all
taxpayers), so per capita costs are small. Those who bear small per
capita costs from such actions have very weak incentives to organize, so they are not represented when decisions are made.

Even the interest groups that gain benefits are likely to have relatively poor information about the actual costs of producing the
service from which they benefit. They probably are not very interested in information about the costs to taxpayers. But whether they
are or are not, they certainly do not want information about those
costs (or about the magnitude of their benefits) to be readily available for fear that those actually paying the costs will find out the full
total of those costs. Bureaucrats (whether they want to capture personal benefits or believe strongly that the public benefits they
produce are very important) also do not want the full costs of their
activities known (Benson 1995), so the interest groups and bureaucrats tend to be allied in this regard. Thus, for instance, Breton and

Wintrobe (1982, 39) emphasize that bureaucrats selectively release both true and false information to the press, the public, the interest groups benefiting from their activities, those who might opposed these groups, and the legislature.

Such "selective distortion" means that the costs of truly effective monitoring will be quite high, and given the low expected benefits for most taxpayers, not much time or effort is expended in *monitoring* the cost-effectiveness of bureaucratic performance. As a consequence, bureaucrats generally have a great deal of discretion, particularly in areas where they are not monitored closely by an interest group, so they can produce in a way that generates personal benefits, often at the expense of technological efficiency. Indeed, there is a good deal of evidence suggesting that bureaucratic budgets exceed the level that would minimize the cost of producing the goods and services they produce (see Benson 1995 for a review), in part because bureaucratic managers value discretionary budgets and in part because it is virtually impossible to replace inefficient or inept civil servants owing to the strong protections they have achieved through the political process. Furthermore, the bureaucratic environment is one in which corruption can flourish (Benson 1988).

If the government does not explicitly establish a rationing institution to allocate a good or service, the fallback ends up being rationing by the principle "first come, first served," but this practice leads to congestion. Those who most want the product rush to line up early and wait to be served, and only those willing to wait can get the product. "First come, first served" is a prevalent method for rationing many publicly provided goods and services, and it clearly applies to law enforcement services (Barnett 1984; Benson 1988, 1990, 97–101, 1994a; Benson and Rasmussen 1991; Benson and Wollan 1989; Neely 1982; Rasmussen and Benson 1994, 18–32). Public-court backlogs are tremendous in some states, for instance. Clearly, such delay is costly for the person who cannot collect damages to pay for ongoing expenses, but anxiety and frustration costs can also be significant. Police files are also full of reported crimes waiting to be solved (with some never being solved), so many victims bear the full costs of the crimes committed against them and of reporting the crimes—costs that can be considerable (Benson 1998, 50–71)—with no hope of restitution or retribution. Similarly, public prisons are so crowded that most prisoners never serve their full sentences, and convicted criminals queue up in local jails as they wait for a place in state prisons, thus raising costs to local taxpayers, to past victims who do not see satisfactory punishment, and to future victims because of the reduced incapacitation and deterrent effects (Benson and Wollan 1989).

Other rationing mechanisms also are likely to arise. For instance, in the face of excess demands and the high costs of waiting, interest groups may demand that government do something to reduce such costs. As a result, quotas (e.g., rationing coupons, fishing and hunting licenses, sentencing guidelines to ration prison space, etc.) are often implemented, and in many cases they are allocated according to the relative political influence of various groups. In law enforcement, for instance, more police may be allocated to affluent neighborhoods than to poor neighborhoods, at least relative to the threat of crime in the two areas, so that the affluent neighborhood has a large quota of arrests per crime.

Alternatively, because of the lack of monitoring, bureaucrats are likely to be in a position to discriminate among potential buyers, refusing to sell to those who, for some reason, are "less desirable." A police officer may give a traffic ticket to someone who does not show sufficient "respect" (or who is black or Hispanic or female or unattractive), for instance, but not to someone who is polite (or white or male or attractive). Similarly, a judge has considerable discretion to discriminate among cases, and courts typically dismiss or terminate a large number of cases without trial. In order to build up conviction records, prosecutors also have incentives to pursue the easiest cases and to ration through plea bargaining.

Consider the allocation of prison space. Judges (and prosecutors) determine how many criminals to sentence to prison rather than to alternatives such as treatment programs, supervised work release, probation, and so on. If there is no quota system in place that forces a judge to limit the flow of criminals into the state prison (e.g., sentencing guidelines determined by the availability of prison capacity rather than legislators' political goals to appear tough without paying for it), then crowding is inevitable because there is no effective coordination of the sentencing decisions of the dispersed local judges who have "free access" to state prison space. (Federal judges have similar free access to the federal prison system.) Because prosecutors and judges have incentives to demonstrate to their local constituencies that they are "tough on crime," imprisonment is a relatively attractive punishment. Even if these officials recognize that their actions add to prison crowding, the political support they get from their tough image should exceed their personal costs (possibly the anxiety associated with the recognition that they are crowding prisons and raising costs to society at large).[4] Perhaps more importantly, however, their job is not to avoid crowding state prisons, but to protect local citizens and to punish criminals who attack them.

Judges' and prosecutors' sentencing decisions also are not coordinated with decisions about prison release (parole or other early-release programs) made by parole boards and corrections officials. Therefore, it may well be that someone released from prison poses a much more significant threat to society than the entrant who forced him out. On 28 November 1988, for example, only ten days after being released from a Florida prison, Charlie H. Street murdered two Metro-Dade (Miami) police officers. Street had been sentenced to a fifteen-year term for attempted murder but served only half that sentence before he was released because of an early-release program instituted to relieve prison crowding. (This program is discussed below.) One week before Street's release, fourteen people were admitted to the Florida prison system for writing worthless checks. Regrettably, this story is far from unique.

Rationing of resources in the public-sector criminal justice system is obviously much more complicated than what is suggested here, of course. After all, because public officials—including judges, prosecutors, police, and corrections officials—have tremendous amounts of discretion, a wide variety of factors can influence their decisions (Rasmussen and Benson 1994, 18–32), but the primary point is that public provision clearly does not guarantee either technological or allocative efficiency (or justice) or anything close to either one, so even imperfect private alternatives may actually be superior to government production, at least on some dimensions.

Markets and Efficiency. The implications of government rationing processes are discussed in more detail below in the context of the politics of crime and punishment, but in order to see the potential technological and allocative efficiency implications of contracting out, we must first consider the implications of rationing through markets.

When a consumer "casts a vote" (spends a dollar) in the marketplace, he or she knows that the vote will be decisive, in contrast to votes cast in the political arena. No one else shares in the decision (certainly a partner or spouse may have some say before the vote is cast, but once the vote is cast, the result is a "done deal") or in its consequences. The consumer will own the product (or service contract) that is purchased and therefore can decide how he or she will use it (as long as the use is legal and consistent with the contract). That means that the consumer can get as much benefit from consumption of the product as is legally and subjectively possible. Furthermore, although the consumer does obtain a large bundle of goods and services, the expenditure for each component of the bundle is recognized because each is purchased individually, unlike in the political arena, where taxpayer-voters are forced to buy a large bundle of products (or more accurately, a bundle of uncertain promises) with a single decision.[5]

These circumstances imply that consumers buying in markets have very strong incentives to gather information relative to taxpayers-voters in the political arena. After all, the individual consumer captures the benefits from a "good" decision (i.e., the purchase of a product that truly provides more satisfaction than any alternative purchase, given the consumer's money income, or number of votes, and the money prices of alternatives) and bears the costs of a "bad" decision (e.g., the purchase of a product when some alternative would have provided more satisfaction, given money income and prices). Therefore, consumers *benefit directly* from any time, effort, and expenses invested in information gathering and evaluation that increase the likelihood of a good decision. Furthermore, they have access to much better information than voters have.

Consumers making purchases in a market buy individual units of products and pay prices per unit, so they can compare the per unit prices of competitive substitutes in order to help determine value. They can also compare the characteristics of the various products and the reputation of their producers (i.e., past performance records) in order to determine relative quality. Consumer information is clearly not perfect, and information is sometimes costly to gather, so mistakes can be made, but substitutes actually *exist* that can be compared on the bases of price and quality (either by direct measurement or by producer reputation) rather than on the basis of promises about future policy efforts. (Reputations can also indicate the credibility of political promises, of course, but the fact that most people do not effectively monitor the performance of their elected officials means that reputations can also be manipulated by selective distortion.)

Prices inform consumers about the value of the resources being used to produce the specific goods and services they are considering buying. High market prices imply that some of the input resources are scarce relative to their alternative valuable uses. Low prices imply relative abundance, so the search for substitute goods leads to the substitution of abundant resources for relatively scarce resources. Consumers do not have to actually know what resources are being used or how rare and valuable they may be because the prices they pay embody the relevant information. Without such product-specific prices as measures of value, those who consume government-produced goods cannot compare value, so they are much less likely to recognize lower-cost substitutes and to shift their demands in order to conserve the most scarce and valuable resources.

Producers also have better information about what consumers want in markets than they do in the political arena. The prices of different goods and services in the marketplace inform producers of relative consumer evaluations and act to coordinate society's decisions about resource allocation by influencing relative profits. If consumers are willing to pay high prices relative to the current cost of the resources being used, the resulting profits attract investments and entrepreneurial entry, whereas low prices relative to costs of production mean losses, followed by disinvestment and exit. In other words, prices also transmit information to producers that allows them to allocate resources and to specialize in order to meet individual consumers' desires more accurately (and profitably). In fact, whereas legislators and public bureaus cannot take advantage of price signals in deciding how to allocate the scarce resources that they control, private producers in competitive markets *are forced* to pay attention to price signals.

Because so much information is embodied in prices, they serve to *coordinate* the decisions of diverse independent decision makers acting as both consumers and producers. For instance, when consumers want more of some good or service, they bid the price up, and producers who see the higher prices relative to costs move resources into that market in order to earn profits. Of course, the resulting increase in competitive supply pushes price back down, although generally not to its original level. If consumers want more of something, they generally should pay more for it, of course, because the scarce resources used to produce it have alternative uses that must be sacrificed. On the other hand, if consumers do not like what a producer is providing or the price the producer is charging, they turn to alternatives. Entrepreneurs must respond with new products or with lower prices or with both, otherwise they go out of business.

Private entrepreneurs are residual claimants. That is, they are able to retain any profit (sales revenues minus costs) while also bearing any losses if production costs exceed revenues. The resulting profit motive provides strong incentives to produce at low costs. But because consumers are free to choose how they will spend their money, the only way that a private entrepreneur can legally obtain customers and profits is by *persuading* people that a quality product or service is being offered at a reasonable price, relative to the options available. Private producers cannot simply cut costs by cutting quality and continue to count on an undiminished flow of revenues because consumers will turn to substitutes that are of higher quality for the price or to lower-price substitutes of comparable quality. Thus, competition forces private firms to offer relatively high-quality services at relatively low prices. Technological efficiency results from competitive pressures and from the profit motive. Furthermore, because consumers are free to shift their allegiance if someone offers them a better product or a lower price or both, entrepreneurs have incentives to invest in research and development in order to find lower-cost production techniques or ways to improve the quality of their products and to attract consumers and their dollars away from other potential purchases. Public bureaucrats cannot capture the profits that might result from a new innovation, so their incentives to discover new and better ways to serve their customers are much weaker.

Entrepreneurs who want to be in business for a long time have incentives to invest in building a good reputation. By providing a good value for the money and standing behind their product (e.g., with guarantees or cost-effective maintenance services), a producer can attract repeat business, and as consumer loyalty increases, other potential customers see their satisfaction and try the product. The resulting reputation becomes increasingly valuable, and the loss of such a reputation can be very costly. If a reputable firm suddenly starts reducing quality relative to price, for instance, consumer complaints will mount, word will spread, and the firm will quickly begin to lose customers and revenues. Once a firm has a reputation for quality, the incentives to maintain it are very strong. Furthermore, other entrepreneurs trying to compete with the reputable firm will have to compete against both the firm's price and its quality. Significantly, the relevant definition of *quality* is the consumer's definition, not the seller's. In other words, to survive in a competitive environment, firms must be responsive to consumer desires.

Contracting Out and Efficiency. Private entrepreneurs competing in markets are constrained by two factors: (1) they must compete for the attention of customers of other firms, so they strive to offer either products similar to their competitors' at lower costs or superior products at similar costs; and (2) they must produce something consumers will *voluntarily choose* to buy at a certain price. The first point (the competition test) implies that technological efficiency is likely under competition. The second point (the voluntary test) implies that free markets promote allocative efficiency.

When governments contract with private firms, then, if the contracting process is appropriately structured, the cost-reducing and quality-enhancing incentives associated with the competition test can be instilled. The contracting process can be appropriately structured

(Benson 1998, 26–40; Logan 1990), and considerable empirical evidence suggests that the firms who compete successfully for contracts and build reputations that help them attract future contracts do so by finding ways to reduce costs and to enhance quality on a number of dimensions (Archambeault and Deis 1996; Benson 1998, 26–40; Brakel 1992; Logan 1990). However, if political factors prevent competition in contracting—that is, circumvent the competition test—then technological efficiency need not be achieved (this issue is considered in section 5). Perhaps more importantly, political factors in contracting for government services can also circumvent the voluntary test, raising concerns about allocative efficiency.

When the provision of services is through government or political channels—whether it involves direct bureaucratic production or contracting out—rather than through markets, individual "buyers" (taxpayers or voters) have virtually no influence over what they buy. Indeed, as suggested above, political decision makers are concerned with the demands of powerful organized interest groups rather than with the demands of unorganized voters and taxpayers. Thus, resources are allocated to generate benefits for members of powerful political groups even though the aggregate benefits may be smaller than the costs dispersed among general taxpayers. Furthermore, because the consumers of most government services do not pay a unit price, the resulting excess demand leads to crowding or congestion whether the product is provided by private firms or by public bureaus.

Some advocates of contracting out for prisons suggest that such privatization might reduce prison crowding by lowering costs and thereby increase the supply of prisons. However, prison crowding reflects both supply and demand forces (Benson and Wollan 1989). Nonprice rationing inevitably produces excess demand, so crowding is likely to occur even with large increases in supply (Benson and Wollan 1989), in part because demand also grows over time.

The misallocation of resources owing to interest-group demands and nonprice rationing may be far more significant than misallocation owing to bureaucratic production inefficiencies (i.e., allocative efficiency is more important than technological efficiency). Of course, if contracting out does not make the misallocation of resource more likely, then it could still be desirable because of the likely improvements in technological efficiency. In order to determine whether this case applies to prisons, the politics of crime and prison use must be considered in more detail. First, however, one other normative perspective deserves attention.

Liberty. Concerns about contracting out can also arise under a liberty norm. The term *liberty,* as used here, does not mean freedom from responsibility, or freedom from worry (perhaps because the government has promised to take care of everyone), or freedom to do as one pleases regardless of the impact on others. It means being unhindered in the pursuit of one's own interests, so long as that pursuit does not impinge on someone else's liberty. An individual's freedom to act in his or her "domain" must be coupled with a responsibility to respect other people's freedom to do the same thing. Without a wedding between freedom and responsibility, liberty has no real meaning, as the fruits of one person's alleged freedom can be destroyed by another person. This is why the rights to "life, liberty, and the pursuit of happiness" as envisioned by the American Founders include a recognition of the sanctity of private-property rights.

Property rights as conceived here include both *economic rights* and *civil rights.* All people should have property rights to the full privileges of citizenship, just as they should have property rights to their "person", including the fruits of their labor, as well as to their land, capital equipment, and other economic resources. Private-property rights involve an individual's right to use the things he or she owns (the person's body, mind, economic resources, privileges of citizenship, and so on) for whatever purpose he or she wants as long as that use does not infringe on someone else's property rights.

From the normative perspective of liberty, all individuals should be treated as free and responsible beings as long as they respect other people's rights. Someone who intentionally violates another person's property rights through theft or violence should have to forfeit his own property rights (economic and civil) until and up to the point where justice is done. This principle provides a justification for some sort of restitution or retribution, of course, but the point to be made here is a different one.[6] When state institutions with coercive power respond to political demands, prison can be misused to "punish" people who have not violated another person's property rights through theft or violence. In other words, people can be imprisoned for committing political crimes, and to the degree that contracting out lowers the costs of imprisonment, it might make the use of prisons for such political crimes even more attractive. Therefore, in order to determine whether or not contracting out for prison services is problematic from the perspective of either allocative efficiency or liberty (or both), it must be considered in the context of the politics of crime and punishment.

3. The Politics of Crime and Punishment

In many areas of government production, gains in technological efficiency through contracting out may be better than no gains at all, but whether this is the case or not depends on what the relatively efficient private producers are supplying. Private firms under contract to the government produce what interest groups want, not what individual consumer-buyers (taxpayers) want. This maxim is as true in criminal law and its enforcement as it is in any other area of government. As Quinney (1970) states, "criminal definitions describe behaviors that conflict with the interests of the segments of society that have the power to shape public policy," and "since interests cannot be effectively protected by merely formulating criminal law, enforcement and administration of the law are required. The interests of the powerful, therefore, operate in applying criminal definitions" (15–18). Similarly, Chambliss and Seidman (1971) observe:

> Deviancy is not a moral issue, it is a political question. No act, nor any set of acts, can be defined as inherently "beyond the pale" of community tolerance. Rather, there are in effect an infinite number and variety of acts occurring in any society which may or may not be defined and treated as criminal. Which acts are so designated depends on the interest of the persons with sufficient political power and influence to manage to have their views prevail. Once it has been established that certain acts are to be designated as deviant, then how

the laws are implemented will likewise reflect the political power of the various affected groups. (67)

Judge Richard Neely's view (1982) is not quite so all-encompassing; he pointed out that Anglo-American common law has always made a distinction between customary-law crimes (such as murder, robbery, and rape) and positive-law crimes, which "have become crimes exclusively because some group lost a political battle" (29). (Also see Benson 1992, 1994a, 1998, 195–205.) Nonetheless, developments in criminal law are just as political today as they were when the breaking of basic customary law was declared a crime against the king—so that the king could collect fines and confiscate property—rather than a tort with restitution owed to the victim (see Benson 1992, 1994a, 1998, 195–226).

Today the objectives of criminalization are somewhat less clear because of multiple demands of special interest groups, but "criminal law is in every regard political" (Neely 1982, 162).[7] Rhodes (1977) emphasizes that "as far as crime policy and legislation are concerned, public opinion and attitudes are generally irrelevant. The same is not true, however, of specifically interested criminal justice publics" (13). More recent research implies similar conclusions but also makes it clear that one of the most important "specifically interested criminal justice publics" consists of law enforcement bureaucrats (e.g., Benson and Rasmussen 1996; Benson, Rasmussen, and Sollars 1995; Berk, Brackman, and Lesser 1977; Rasmussen and Benson 1994, 119–73).

Consider, for example, the empirical study by Berk, Brackman, and Lesser (1977) of changes in the California Penal Code. These researchers found that during the 1950s the making of criminal law in California could be characterized as an "agreed-bill" process that involved only a few major criminal justice lobbies, generally the California Peace Officers Association (CPOA)—made up of district attorneys, sheriffs, and police chiefs—the American Civil Liberties Union (ACLU), and the State Bar of California (SBC). The agreed-bill process is one wherein lobbyists and a few members of relevant legislative committees negotiate directly in making important decisions (Berk, Brackman, and Lesser 1977, 11; also see Heinz,

Gettleman, and Seeskin 1969). The important part of the legislative process takes place behind closed doors, and most open legislative debate is simply rhetoric for public consumption. Thus, legislators do not initiate or shape criminal law policy; they simply react to the demands of lobbies (Berk, Brackman, and Lesser 1977, 85–86).

During the 1960s, criminal law in California began to involve a wider range of groups than were active in the 1950s, but the process did not change (Berk, Brackman, and Lesser 1977, 86). The most active groups continued to be the ACLU (and its frequent ally, the Friends Committee on Legislation or FCL), the CPOA, and the SBC, but small vocal groups of citizens also initiated attempts to alter the Penal Code. Often they allied themselves with the CPOA or the ACLU. Several established interest groups whose original purpose was not directed at criminal justice also often supported an established criminal justice lobby. For example, the ACLU often enjoyed support from the state NAACP, the Mexican-American Political Association, the Northern and Southern California Council of Churches, the Association of California Consumers, and the Federation of the Poor (Berk, Brackman, and Lesser 1977, 62).

Berk and his colleagues (1977) went beyond other studies of interest groups' impact on changes in criminal justice to provide statistical support for the contention that this influence is extremely important. They looked at the influence of the law enforcement lobby, primarily the CPOA, and the civil liberties lobby, primarily the ACLU and FCL, recognizing that these principle groups often worked with others. They identify *effective influence* in a number of ways. Using newsletters and journals published by the interest groups and information from journalists, politicians, and criminal justice professionals, the researchers made independent evaluations of how effective lobbyists were in shaping the Penal Code. Their statistical analysis uses both zero-order correlations and multivariate analysis. They found that year by year the law enforcement lobby achieved significant changes leading to more resources and powers for police. In regard to the issue of contracting for prison services, law enforcement lobbies' demands also led to increasing criminalization (thereby expanding the scope and power of the law enforcement bureaucracies) and to more severe penalties.[8] That is, these demands tended to increase the demand for prison space. They also had a significant negative impact on rights for defendants, on judicial discretion, and, to a lesser degree, on the rights and resources going to corrections officials. The civil liberties lobbies' efforts were positively correlated with substantial gains in defendants' and corrections officials' rights and in judicial discretion. These lobbies had a negative impact on criminalization, penalty severity, and police powers. The law enforcement lobbies and the civil liberties lobbies were not in direct and constant opposition in all instances, however, and their agendas and impacts were somewhat different. The law enforcement lobbies apparently emphasized criminalization and penalties, whereas the civil liberties lobbies were more interested in limiting police powers and expanding judicial discretion (Berk, Brackman, and Lesser 1977, 201–3).

Berk and colleagues (1977) also found that "public opinion" played no identifiable role in Penal Code revision. Moreover, legislators did not develop and seek support for their own criminal justice agendas; they simply responded to the interest groups that were concerned with such legislation. The authors conclude that criminal law was unquestionably enacted for the benefit of interest groups rather than for the "public good."

As suggested above, enforcement requirements arising from the quantity of laws demanded and instituted through legislation can be expected to exceed the limited supply of enforcement resources (Benson 1990, 97–101). Indeed, as Cole (1973) reports, an important "factor in the crisis of criminal justice is the 'law explosion'—the increasingly complex and demanding pressures placed on law and legal institutions . . . [reflects] the tendency to utilize the criminal law to perform a number of functions for society outside the traditional concerns for the protection of persons and property" (23–24). These "functions" are typically associated with enforcement of so-called victimless crimes, but they appear to be putting ever-increasing pressure on the resources of the criminal justice system, including prisons. A victimless crime is defined as one in which there is no readily identifiable party who has been directly injured.

Thus, the plaintiff must be the state or a governmental agency because no individual has strong incentives to pursue prosecution. Almost without exception, victimless crimes involve prohibitions of voluntary-exchange relations. They include drug use, gambling, and prostitution, for example, all of which are marketed by entrepreneurs and voluntarily purchased by consumers. True victimless crimes clearly violate the liberty norm, so perhaps a better label would be *political crimes.*

The most significant increases in criminalization and in law enforcement effort throughout this century have been with regard to such victimless or political crimes. For dramatic examples, we can look to the experiment with liquor prohibition in the 1920s (e.g., see Thornton 1991), the prohibition of various narcotics beginning with the Harrison Act of 1914, and the prohibition of marijuana after the Marijuana Tax Act in 1937, but state and federal governments have also increased the severity of punishment mandated for drug crimes since their initial illegality and have allocated larger and larger amounts of law enforcement resources to the control of such activities.

Two escalations in the "drug war" have occurred since the mid-1960s, for example (Rasmussen and Benson 1994, 6–10). Prior to the first, between 1965 and 1970, police resources in the United States were allocated so that one drug arrest was being made for every twenty Index I arrests. (Index I crimes are reported crimes against persons and property, including murder, manslaughter, sex crimes, assault, robbery, burglary, larceny, and auto theft.) During the 1965–70 escalation in the war on drugs, arrests for drug crimes rose more than five times. In fact, criminal justice system resources were *reallocated* so that one drug arrest was being made for every four Index I arrests. Drug enforcement relative to efforts against Index I offenses remained fairly constant from 1970 to around 1984–85, but then a new escalation started. By 1989, criminal justice resources were being allocated to make only 2.2 Index I arrests for each drug arrest. Indeed, the most dramatic changes in criminal law emphasis in the last two decades have been in the area of illicit-drug enforcement.

The war on drugs has been a primary factor in producing record increases in the prisoner population and in budgets, which have in turn forced local, state, and federal administrators to consider contracting with private firms (Krajick 1984b, 20–21) in order to continue meeting the political demands for increased uses of imprisonment. Federal court rulings declaring that jails and prisons are "overcrowded" are extremely widespread (Poole 1983, 4; Rasmussen and Benson 1994, 21–22). As prison costs rose in an effort to alleviate crowding, interest groups that were focused on other issues (e.g., groups seeking increased funding for education) began to see prisons as a major competitor for a large share of state and local budgets. Recognizing the threat, politicians and law enforcement interest groups have reacted by looking for some sort of technological innovation in corrections (e.g., alternatives to imprisonment, boot camp programs, sentencing guidelines, and determinant sentencing). But as Peter Greenwood concludes in his study of the correctional system, "when you're looking for innovators you don't look to government; you look to business" (qtd. in Poole 1983, 2). Thus, contracting out is also seen as a potential source of innovation.

When contracts are narrowly focused on imprisonment, however, then so is the resulting innovation. Because private firms have been successful at lowering costs, managers of public prisons are forced to pay more attention to costs as well. Indeed, one benefit of contracting out can be that competition forces the public bureaucracies to improve their technological efficiency (Benson 1998, 261). As costs are reduced, the use of prisons for purposes beyond the control and punishment of property and violent criminals becomes more acceptable (i.e., less of a threat) to other interest groups, and the incentives for innovations in the alternative forms of treatment or punishment are reduced (see Rasmussen and Benson 1994, 191–98, in this regard). Furthermore, the incentives to consider fundamental changes in criminal law are reduced. Those who benefit from existing laws (and, in fact, from increasingly harsh prison sentences and from the expansion of the scope of criminal law) are less likely to be opposed if costs are lowered or the system becomes technologically more efficient (i.e., less of a threat to other uses of tax revenues) or both occur.

4. The Politics of Drug Enforcement and Prison Crowding: Is Contracting Out the Appropriate Solution?

The criminality of drug use is a relatively recent phenomenon, and numerous self-interested political motivations for original legislation on drug criminalization have been identified. Some studies (e.g., Thornton 1991) have noted the incentives of professional organizations such as the American Pharmaceutical Association to create legal limits on the distribution of drugs (there was significant competition between pharmacists and physicians for the legal right to dispense drugs, for example), but others have focused on the strong racial impacts of illicit drug laws and on some groups' desire to control racial minorities through the enforcement of such laws (Helmer 1975; Musto 1973, 1987). Still others have noted that the policing bureaucracies have been a major source of demand for the initial criminalization legislation (H. Becker 1963; Dickson 1968; Hill 1971; Himmelstein 1983; Lindesmith 1965; Oteri and Silvergate 1967). The Marijuana Tax Act was passed in 1937, for example, because of pressure from the Narcotics Bureau of the Treasury Department (H. Becker 1963; Dickson 1968; Hill 1971; Lindesmith 1965; Oteri and Silvergate 1969). In fact, as Thornton (1991) indicates, all of these various self-interests interacted to produce the laws against drug use. But even if this were not the case, the primary sources of the "information" (much of which is inaccurate and unsubstantiated [Michaels 1987, 311–324]) used to justify the war on drugs have been politicians and the police.

Federal, state, and local criminal justice officials joined forces to escalate the war on drugs in late 1984. Some researchers believe that this escalation at the state and local levels occurred because police officials faced an exogenous change in bureaucratic incentives (Benson and Rasmussen 1996; Benson, Rasmussen, and Sollars 1995; Rasmussen and Benson 1994, 119–39). In particular, one section of the Comprehensive Crime Act of 1984 established a system whereby any local police bureau that cooperated with federal drug enforcement authorities in a drug investigation would share in the money or property confiscated as part of that investigation. As a result, in many states whose laws or constitutions limited confiscation possibilities, police began to circumvent these state laws. Moreover, the Department of Justice (DOJ) went beyond that legislation, "adopting" seizures even when no federal agency was directly involved in the investigation and passing the proceeds (minus a processing charge) back to the local agency. Thus, under the 1984 federal statute, a substantial percentage of seized properties were returned to the agency that made seizures, even if the state's laws mandated that confiscations go someplace other than to law enforcement.

Federal, state, and local law enforcement bureaucrats demanded this legislation and its enforcement procedures, such as adoptions (Benson and Rasmussen 1996; Benson, Rasmussen, and Sollars 1995; Rasmussen and Benson 1994, 132–39). An obvious hypothesis is that when Congress and the DOJ told state and local police departments that they would get paid more by focusing their efforts on drug enforcement, they responded with a dramatic increase in drug enforcement effort, and it has paid very well. Unfortunately, the hypothesis that the escalation of the drug war occurred because of the 1984 federal asset-seizure provisions cannot be directly supported with hard statistics because it was a one-time change in incentives. However, if the change in the federal asset-seizure law motivated the increase in drug enforcement that we saw during the 1984–89 period, the same hypothesis also should explain much of the variation in drug enforcement across states (Mast, Benson, and Rasmussen 2000).

To test the hypothesis that police focus more effort on drugs when they can retain asset seizures, Mast, Benson, and Rasmussen (2000) produced an empirical analysis that controlled for other factors affecting the level of drug enforcement. The findings for the impact of asset-seizure laws were robust: police focus relatively more effort on drug control when they can enhance their budgets by retaining seized assets. State legislation permitting police to keep a portion of seized assets raises drug arrests as a portion of total arrests by approximately 20 percent and drug arrest rates by approximately 18 percent—providing direct evidence that local police respond to incentives created by state laws and indirect support for the hypothesis that the upsurge in drug enforcement that started in 1984 is a result of the federal asset-seizure law.

In order to see the consequences for the nation's prisons of the increased effort against drug markets, consider what happened in Florida. In 1980, 7.4 percent of all arrests in Florida were for drug offenses, whereas 31.8 percent were for Index I crimes (murder, forcible rape, aggravated assault, robbery, burglary, larceny, and motor vehicle theft). The remaining 60.8 percent of arrests were for nondrug Index II crimes (which include a variety of crimes, such as simple assault, arson, narcotics, vandalism, vice, fraud, and major traffic violations). In fact, almost 60 percent of Florida's Index II crimes are simply categorized as "miscellaneous." Index I property crime arrests (burglary, robbery, larceny, and auto theft) made up 26.5 percent of the total arrests in 1980. The asset-seizure law changed in 1984, and drug arrests increased to 7.6 percent of total arrests for that year. (In fact, drug arrests as a portion of total arrests had actually fallen to 6.9 percent in 1982 and was 7.1 percent in 1983.) By 1989, drug arrests accounted for 12.5 percent of total arrests, whereas Index I arrests had fallen to 28.7 percent, and Index I property crimes made up only 23 percent of the total. Put another way, police resources were allocated so that 0.28 drug arrests were made for each property arrest in 1980, but by 1989 0.54 drug arrests were being made for each property arrest. Certainly, police resources were substantially increased over this period as Florida's population grew, but the arrest figures indicate that these resources also were reallocated in order to focus increasingly on drug crimes. Drug arrests increased 167 percent (from 32,029 in 1980 to 85,525 in 1989), but property arrests increased by only 36.7 percent (from 115,240 to 157,512), and Index I arrests as a whole increased by just 41.4 percent (138,548 to 195,888).

As a direct consequence of the increase in drug arrests and convictions, the demand for scarce prison space has grown dramatically. A substantial portion of the increased pressure on the prison system traces directly to the war on drugs. For example, there were 1,620 prison admissions in Florida for drug offenses during the 1983–84 fiscal year (FY), accounting for 12.9 percent of total admissions. By

FY 1986–87, this figure had risen to 5,274, or 22.9 percent of total admissions. This latter figure compares to 15,802 drug admissions for FY 1989–90, or 36.4 percent of total admissions (Florida Department of Corrections, various years). Thus, prison admission for drugs rose by 875.4 percent between FY 1983–84 and FY 1989–90, whereas admissions not related to drugs rose by only 158.2 percent (from 10,896 to 27,585).

As the war on drugs heated up, new prison admissions went up substantially more quickly than new prison spaces were built. The historic norm, prior to the war on drugs in the 1980s, was that prisoners served 50 percent or more of their sentences on average. Indeed, this norm continued to hold during the early years of the drug war, so, for example, inmates released during January 1987 had served an average of 52.8 percent of their sentences. However, the increased flow into the prison system forced implementation of a program to "facilitate the transition from prison to civilian life" for fiscal year 1986–87, which lowered sentences to be served in FY 1987–88 by 37 days for eligible inmates. Furthermore, continued overcrowding led to an Administrative Gain Time Program in February 1987, resulting in a 122-day reduction in sentence for almost all prisoners scheduled for release in FY 1987–88.

By January 1988, the average portion of sentences served in Florida had fallen to 40.6 percent, and it reached 33 percent in December 1989. In fact, approximately 37 percent of the prisoners released in December 1989 had served less than 25 percent of their sentences, and some served less than 15 percent. The Florida legislature was forced to hold a special session in 1993 in order to allocate more funds to prison construction and avoid the "gridlock" that was anticipated late in 1993 when no criminals eligible for early release would remain in the system. (Many prisoners cannot be released early under statutes regarding habitual offenders and mandated minimums for various specific crimes, many of which are drug related.) The 1994 Florida legislature allocated funds to expand the state's prison system by an additional 27 percent. Advocates of contracting out pointed to this situation and suggested that crowding might be alleviated by reducing costs and therefore by increasing the supply of prison space. Thus, one option that the Florida legislature pursued was contracting out for private prisons. (The state also built a large number of new state-run facilities.)

Whether the expansion in supply (through contracting out or through bureaucratic production) is desirable or not depends on whether the use of prisons for drug enforcement is appropriate. Given that drug enforcement policy is a major determinant of recent trends in prison crowding, should crowding be alleviated by increasing supply, or would it be more appropriate to reduce demand by reducing the flow of drug criminals into prison? To answer this question from the perspective of allocative efficiency, the costs and benefits of illicit-drug enforcement must be considered.

Primarily as a result of police-promulgated information (Barnett 1984, 53), it is now widely believed that drug crime is the root cause of much of what is wrong with society.[9] That is, even though drug use is a victimless crime, it is claimed that large negative spillovers arise as a direct consequence of drug-market activity. In particular, drug use is claimed to be a primary cause of crime not related to drugs because, it is contended, property crime is a major source of income for drug users. This belief has translated into political demands for the criminal justice system to do something about the drug/crime problem (demands that largely emanate from the police lobbies or from opinions promulgated by the police), and, in turn, it has led to an increasing emphasis on the control of illicit drug traffic as a means of general crime prevention. Such a reallocation of resources may be justified from an allocative efficiency perspective if drugs truly are the root cause of most other crime. Thus, more efficiently providing prisons in a technological sense and increasing their supply through contracting would also be justified from this perspective. But as a larger share of law enforcement resources have been allocated to the drug war, it has become increasingly apparent that society's other ills are not being solved. In particular, efforts at controlling the drug market are not producing the anticipated reductions in other types of crime.

A substantial amount of research[10] casts considerable doubt on the argument that drugs cause Index I (in particular property) crimes.[11] First, note that the drugs-cause-crime argument generally involves an explicit statement to the effect that *drug addicts* are driven to commit crimes in order to finance their habits.[12] But not all drug users are addicts. Longitudinal analysis of drug users suggest that cocaine and heroin users are more likely to cease consumption than alcohol users and much more likely than tobacco users. Furthermore, many drug users report only occasional consumption. Among persons reporting cocaine use in the last year, for example, almost 80 percent said that they used the drug once a month or less. An alternative measure of the frequency of addiction is to compare the lifetime prevalence rate for drug use to the prevalence rate for the last month. Addiction requires current consumption, so the ratio of the last month and lifetime prevalence rates provides an index of how many individuals have been able to use drugs without becoming addicted (or have been successfully treated for addiction). Data from the 1988 National Household Survey of Drug Abuse (National Institute on Drug Abuse, 1989) provides such ratios. For cocaine, the ratios vary from .324 for the twelve to seventeen age group to .228 for the eighteen to twenty-five age group and .091 for the older than age twenty-five group. Thus, even if the drugs-cause-crime argument is true for addicts, it does not follow that an indiscriminate war on drug use by addicts and nonaddicts is an appropriate crime-control policy, let alone a policy that should be made more efficient by contracting out prison service in order to support it. But it also appears that property crime is not the sole source of income for drug users, including drug addicts.

Heavy drug users can have several sources of income other than property crime. In fact, users apparently earn almost as much income through nonvictim Index II crimes such as drug sales, prostitution, and pimping as they do through Index I property crimes (Kaplan 1983, 54; Reuter, MacCoun, and Murphy 1990). Indeed, Gould and colleagues (1974) suggest that half or more of the money spent on heroin in the early 1970s was probably generated through the sale of the drug. But, in addition, drug users also often have legitimate sources of income (Kaplan 1983), such as wages, welfare payments, and money from parents. For example, Reuter, MacCoun, and Murphy (1990) conducted a study of drug sellers in Washington, D.C., and found that drug sellers were also drug users but that they generated income both by selling drugs *and* by holding legitimate jobs. The majority of drug sellers held jobs that earned, on average, approximately twice the minimum wage. These facts are important because they illustrate how estimates of the level of property crime committed by drug users are often misleading (see Kaplan 1983; Michaels 1987). As Kaplan (1983) explains, these estimates often involve an assumption that all drugs are purchased with income obtained through property crime, so the estimated amount of drugs consumed is multiplied times the estimated price of drugs to determine the predicted value of the property stolen to finance drug purchases. Through such a procedure, it was estimated that addicts supposedly stole ten times as much as was reported to police in all property thefts in New York City (Kaplan 1983, 52). Victims' underreporting of crimes certainly cannot explain such a large discrepancy. Indeed, if the estimate of expenditures on drugs is anywhere close to being accurate, it would suggest that at most only approximately 20 percent of those expenditures could be generated through property crime because annual victimization surveys suggest that victims apparently fail to report the majority of the property crimes they suffer, and this figure still assumes that all property crimes are committed by drug users.[13] In other words, perhaps 80 percent (or more) of the drug-using population is not involved in property crime. Such a suggestion is little more than a tenuous conjecture at this point, of course, but several other pieces of information support this conclusion.

Trager and Clark (1989) examined the arrest history of persons in Florida having at least one misdemeanor or felony drug arrest during 1987. Of the 45,906 people arrested for possession, more than 80 percent had never been arrested for burglary, and more than 90 percent had never been arrested for other property crimes. Of those arrested for sales, only slightly more that 25 percent had prior burglary arrests, and again more than 90 percent had no previous arrest for other property crimes. Of course, if police are emphasizing drug crime rather than property crime, such arrest statistics may be quite misleading. Nonetheless, these data suggest that two distinct types of drug offenders may actually exist: (1) a substantial portion of drug offenders do not appear to be committing property crimes (or violent crimes; see Trager and Clark 1989); and (2) many criminals who commit Index I crimes also use drugs.

This characterization of the drug population is reinforced by a recidivism study of Florida prisoners convicted for drug crimes (Kim et al. 1993). The study identified 4,394 persons who had been imprisoned for a drug offense in Florida after 1985 and released prior to 2 April 1990. By April 2, 1990, 49.6 percent (2,180) of these 4,394 had returned to the custody of the Florida Department of Corrections via probation or reincarceration. Approximately 69 percent (1,504) of the returnees were convicted of another drug offense, but approximately only 31 percent were convicted of a non-drug offense (theft, burglary, and robbery accounted for 20.2 percent of the 2,180 returnees). Again, it appears that the majority of drug users may not be involved in nondrug crime, although such a conclusion is not necessarily warranted if the criminal justice system is overlooking nondrug crime in order to obtain more drug convictions. In this regard, however, Kim and colleagues (1993) found that the tendency to recidivate was significantly lower for those individuals who had convictions only for drug offenses than for those who had convictions for both drug and nondrug crimes, reinforcing the perception that there may be two distinguishable groups of drug offenders: those who also commit Index I crimes and those who do not.

Kim and colleagues (1993) also found that drug offenders respond to incentives created by the law enforcement sector. Both increased policing efforts and imprisonment rather than probation do appear to deter unlawful behavior for drug criminals, implying that drugs do not dominate individuals to the degree that the drugs-cause-crime argument often claims.[14] Of course, the fact that drug activity can be deterred by criminal justice resources does not prove that it should be. After all, the criminal justice resources also have alternative uses (e.g., the control of property and violent crimes). Indeed, one finding by Kim and colleagues (1993) bears directly on prison crowding: the length of time served in prison did not affect the probability of recidivating. The war on drugs has involved increasingly long sentences for drug offenders, thereby adding to the prison-crowding problem that contracting out is expected to alleviate, but these longer sentences apparently do not affect the future behavior of the drug offenders in a significant way. Thus, even assuming that deterrence of drug use is an appropriate function of the criminal justice system, prison crowding might be reduced by giving shorter sentences to drug offenders without reducing the deterrent effect that imprisonment itself has. Furthermore, a Rand Corporation study suggests that a dollar spent on drug treatment is seven times more effective at reducing cocaine use than a dollar spent of criminal justice drug-control activities (Rydell and Everingham 1994). These researchers suggest that reducing criminal justice expenditures on drug control by 25 percent and doubling treatment offered to users would reduce cocaine use and save $2 billion. Thus, even if controlling drug use is the goal (perhaps in a vain attempt to control drug-induced nondrug crime), the current level of criminal justice investment in drug control is excessive.

The evidence discussed here suggests that a substantial portion of the drug-consuming population is not heavily involved in property crime. None of this evidence proves, of course, that drugs do not cause crime for a subset of the drug-consuming population (see Benson et al. 1992). There is another issue that deserves attention, however: What happens to drug demand as illegally obtained income rises? In other words, instead of asking, "Does drug use lead to crime?" we might ask, "Does crime lead to drug use?" If the expected return to illegal activities rises (e.g., because the probability of being arrested falls), then under most circumstances we should see an increase in the illegal activity. The resulting increase in income can be spent on goods, including illicit drugs, and if a drug is a normal good, the increase in income will produce an increase in demand for the good. Of course, if the drug is an inferior good, demand will fall.

Few researchers seem to have considered the potential causal relationship running from crime to drug use, a perspective in sharp contrast to the much more frequently claimed causal flow from drug use to crime in order to finance a habit. The recent study of Washington, D.C., drug dealers suggests that there might be an important connection of this type, however (Reuter, MacCoun, and

Murphy 1990). In particular, Rand Corporation researchers found that when juveniles start dealing drugs, they are typically *not* drug users. Thus, they are not committing the crime of drug dealing in order to finance a drug habit.[15] However, the longer someone stays in the drug supply business, the more likely it is that he will become a user and ultimately an addict. In fact, most adult dealers in Washington, D.C., apparently are addicts.

Other studies of the temporal sequencing of drug abuse and nondrug crime also suggest that nondrug criminal activities frequently precede drug use for those who engage in both (Gandossy et al. 1980; Greenberg and Alder 1974). Indeed, Chein et al. (1964) conclude that drug use does not cause delinquency, but rather "the varieties of delinquency tend to change to those most functional for drug use; the total amount of delinquency is independent of drug use" (64–65). Clearly, it could be that once an individual has decided to turn to crime as a source of income, therefore moving into the criminal subculture, he may discover that drugs are more easily obtained within this subculture than they were previously and perhaps that the risks posed by the criminal justice system are not as great as he may have initially anticipated. Furthermore, criminal activity generates the income with which to buy goods that he previously could not afford, including drugs. Thus, crime leads to drug use, rather than drug use leading to crime. Of course, if the individual then becomes addicted, so that his preferences are altered, the drugs-cause-crime relationship might come into play.

Even if drugs are an important determinant of criminal activity for a portion (e.g., 20 percent) of the drug-consuming population, an indiscriminate war on drugs may not be a positive-sum crime policy. First, the benefits of imprisoning drug offenders do not appear to be nearly as substantial as is generally claimed in bureaucratic and political rhetoric (Kim et al. 1993), and, in a relative sense, treatment is a much more cost-effective way to reduce drug use (Rydell and Everingham 1994). But beyond that there are substantial hidden costs.

Using county-level data from Florida, Benson and colleagues (1992) and Benson and Rasmussen (1991) found that reallocating scarce police resources away from the control of property crime toward the control of drug crime significantly reduces the risks that property criminals face. This reduction in deterrence leads to a significant increase in property crime. Indeed, in sharp contrast to the political rhetoric, it seems that *drug enforcement causes property crime.* A one percent increase in drug arrests as a portion of total arrest leads to an estimated .199 percent reduction in the probability of arrest for property crimes. Furthermore, a one percent reduction in the probability of arrest for property crimes leads to an estimated .826 percent increase in property crimes. Therefore, as resources are reallocated to control drug crime, property crime is rising.

The reallocation of policing resources to control drug use explains a substantial portion of the increases in property crime that occurred during the ramp-up of the drug war from 1984 to 1989 (Benson et al. 1992). Eight subsequent studies add support to the conclusion that significant trade-offs can occur as police are shifted into drug-control efforts. Benson and Rasmussen (1992) examined Illinois data and found that as police resources were shifted into drug control, traffic control was significantly reduced and traffic fatalities rose dramatically. Thus, the trade-off need not be in the form of higher property-crime rates; scarcity simply implies that *some* trade-off must occur as drug enforcement is increased by reallocating policing resources. Sollars, Benson, and Rasmussen (1994) used policing jurisdictions data from Florida to replicate the county-level study by Benson and colleagues (1992), and they also conclude that increased drug enforcement led to increases in property crime. Benson, Kim, and Rasmussen (1998) looked at the 1984–87 period and used a fixed-effects model to demonstrate significant increases in total Index I crimes in Florida as a result of increases in drug enforcement, thus reinforcing Benson and colleagues' (1992) findings with what may be a more appropriate empirical model and suggesting that the tradeoff might go beyond property crimes (although property crimes constitute the largest portion of Index I crimes). However, Leburn, Benson, and Rasmussen (forthcoming) noted that the trends in both crime rates and drug control were upward in the 1980s, perhaps suggesting a spurious correlation, so they replicated the Benson, Kim, and Rasmussen (1998) study using Florida county-level data from the 1990s when crime rates were falling, but they found that drug-control efforts continued to rise at a modest rate after a drop off in 1990–91 (i.e., at a slower rate than during the 1984-89 period). By controlling for other factors that cause crime, however, they found that the tradeoff still exists. Index I crime rates would be even lower in Florida if drug enforcement efforts had been reduced.

All of the studies mentioned so far—that have found a tradeoff between drug enforcement and either all Index I crimes or Index I property crimes—have used Florida data, perhaps suggesting that this tradeoff is unique to Florida. (The Illinois study found a different tradeoff, for instance.) However, Mendes (forthcoming) replicated the Sollars, Benson, and Rasmussen (1994) study using data from jurisdictions in Portugal and found the same tradeoff that the Florida studies have emphasized: the probability of arrest for property crime fell with increased drug arrests. Furthermore, Corman and Mocan (2000) employed time-series data from New York City and found that, despite a positive relationship between heavy drug use and property crimes, this relationship was weaker than the effect of drug arrests on property crime. (These results are consistent with Benson et al. 1992.) Consequently, the net effect of using more resources to combat drug offenses in New York City was also an increase in property crime.

Finally, two studies have focused on the impact of drug enforcement on violent crime. Rasmussen, Benson, and Sollars (1993) used Florida jurisdiction-level data to look at the interjurisdictional spillovers in violence that might result from increases in drug-control efforts (i.e., as drug enforcement increases in one jurisdiction, some buyers or sellers or both move to neighboring jurisdictions, and violence increases because of turf wars and the fact that drug buyers and sellers are attractive targets for robbery). They found significant increases in violence as a result of such spillovers.

Resignato (2000) used the DOJ Drug Use Forecasting city data to look at the relationship between drug use, drug arrests, and violent crime, and concluded that drug enforcement leads to violence but drug use does not. Thus, the costs of drug enforcement in terms of forgone control of property, violent, and traffic crimes appears to be quite significant. If the goal is to reduce such crimes, then the best policy appears to be a reduction in enforcement of drug crimes, and therefore in imprisonment of drug criminals.

Drug Crime and Contracting Out for Prisons: Normative Implications

Assuming that control of property crime truly has been a primary motivating force for the war on drugs (an assumption I've already rejected, of course), then the failure of the criminal justice system in this regard and the rising costs in the form of prison crowding, early release, and reductions in the effectiveness of imprisonment as a sanction would seem to imply that the United States should move toward a declaration of peace in the drug war. Deemphasizing drugs and other such "crimes" (perhaps even decriminalizing them) and "the consequent reduction of pressure on police, courts, and correctional services would have a massive impact on the criminal justice system" (Goldstein and Goldstein 1971, 293). Clearly, a reduction in the resources allocated to the control of such crimes would simultaneously reduce prison crowding problems and allow some redirection of criminal justice resources toward the control of violent and property crimes. For instance, in 1971, the Los Angeles district attorney began filing all marijuana possession cases as misdemeanors rather than as felonies. As a direct result, approximately ten thousand fewer felony cases were filed during 1971–72 than during the previous year, cutting the system's felony caseload by 25 percent (Poole 1978, 53).

None of this discussion implies that contracting out itself is undesirable, of course. Rather, it suggests that the use of imprisonment to control drug "crime" appears to be inappropriate. The cost of doing so is obviously very high, and the social benefits are questionable at best. Contracting out for prison services might reduce some of the direct (most obvious) costs, of course, but it may actually allow this allocatively inefficient policy to remain intact longer than it otherwise might because it might reduce the incentives to demand changes in the laws against drug use or to demand increased use of alternatives to imprisonment for the treatment of drug use or both. Thus, although contracting out might improve technological efficiency, it would most likely reduce allocative efficiency.

Furthermore, if we go beyond the efficiency norm and consider a normative standard of liberty, this use of imprisonment becomes even more undesirable. Drugs certainly may harm individuals who choose to consume them (just as tobacco does), but in the absence of significant spillover effects (e.g., the lack of a strong causal relationship between drugs and crime), government-imposed limitations on individual choice are not warranted on liberty grounds either. Similar normative issues come into play whenever prisons are used to imprison people associated with victimless crimes.

It must be emphasized that the arguments presented here are not indictments of contracting out per se. Rather, they are intended to raise concerns about the results of enhancing technological efficiency in the production of law enforcement against victimless crimes in response to the demands of powerful political interests. If Hitler had contracted out some of his law enforcement services, the rounding up and extermination of Jews might have been accomplished at a lower per unit cost, and more Jews could have been exterminated, but the fact that more of these politically defined "criminals" could have been exterminated more "efficiently" in a technological sense does not mean that the contracting out of this process would have been desirable. Indeed, *if* contracting out does enhance technological efficiency, as its advocates argue, then that may encourage even more intensive law enforcement efforts against victimless crimes, thereby reducing both allocative efficiency and liberty. However, when contracting out for prisons is considered in the context of the interest-group process of making decisions about political allocation, it becomes clear that there are forces at work that may actually limit the technological efficiency benefits relative to their potential. That is, it may be that governments will do a poor job of contracting just as they do with most of the other tasks they undertake. In the case of victimless crimes, the fact that government does a bad job of contracting out may turn out to be desirable, of course.

5. Limits on the Potential for Gains in Technological Efficiency through Contracting Out

Given the pervasive influence of politics on allocative efficiency, perhaps the potential gains from technological efficiency might also be tenuous. For instance, because bureaucrats have considerable political influence, they may be able to influence the allocation of expenditures even when contracting out occurs. In this context, local governments are often restricted in their ability to lay off workers by union contracts and by state civil service regulations (Freeman 1992, 136). Thus, employees who lose their jobs to contracting must be transferred to other positions, which "reduces the overall value of the contract because the costs of the contract are reassigned to other departments" (Freeman 1992, 136). Indeed, one frequent criticism of contracting out is that although it may reduce the cost of producing a particular good or service, it does not reduce the cost of government. Rather, costs are shifted into other areas of government.[16] In a study of the gains that chief administrative officers (CAOs, such as mayors and city managers) received from contracting, Martin and Stein (1992) conclude that "to avoid raising taxes, mayors and city managers appear willing to allow their bureaus to retain all of the savings from service contracting" (100). Thus, contracting does not necessarily reduce costs relative to what they have been in the past, but it might limit future tax increases. As Martin and Stein (1992) explain, CAOs face two distinct political constraints:

> The first is a need to promote voter satisfaction by minimizing tax increases. The second is to placate the bureau and agency chiefs and their employees. In this environment, contracting out of services can be a useful stratagem. Contracting can be presented to voter-taxpayers as cost-consciousness evidence by the CAO, and may actually result in a measurable improvement in the quality of services delivered to consumers. . . . In reality, contracting appears to have little effect on either aggregate government spending levels or the budgets of government

agencies charged with the provision of a particular public good. . . . [T]he CAO allows [an agency manager] to increase the average salary of the remaining employees [or transfer-displaced employees]. (100)

Furthermore, bureaucratic behavior in contracting agencies can work to destroy competition in bidding. Some of the agencies are likely to be directly involved with the contracting process, so the bureaucratic attitudes and incentives that influence government production can also affect the contracting process. Consider the belief that "one efficient firm and a knowledgeable government official can reach an agreement to provide services at a cost no higher than it would be if ten suppliers were bidding" (Fisk, Kiesling, and Muller 1978, 5). This attitude might quickly destroy the effectiveness of the contracting out to achieve technological efficiency. It is the threat of competition that forces the private firm to produce efficiently. Furthermore, if an official is so "knowledgeable," why is he or she unable to keep a public bureau producing efficiently? When a single private firm is given a contract with no fear of future competition, it begins acting like a monopolist, not an efficient competitor.

Bureaucratic behavior by contracting agencies can work to destroy competition in bidding even when the bureau claims to seek competition. This elimination of competition occurs because government agencies impose a large number and variety of regulations, standards, and other requirements on the contracting process itself and on postcontract production, which means that:

The high cost of obtaining government contracts, the limitations on salaries and other costs frequently imposed by government regulation, and the problems raised by zealous auditors make government contracting for the typical small firm, and for many large firms[,] a chancy business. The risks impel many firms to limit the amount of government business they seek, and some now go after government contracts only because of ancillary advantages (such as access to information not otherwise available). (Fitch 1974, 518)

In contracting out for prisons, for example, the federal government specifies standards for all aspects of prison life and stations observers in private institutions (Krajick 1984a, 27).

The excuse for heavy monitoring of private firms under contract is supposedly to prevent dishonest private firms from providing poor services. Of course, a sufficiently competitive contracting process would do precisely that, as potential competitors monitor those providing services in hopes of spotting inefficiencies or abuses that will allow them to offer a superior contract. But even with all the regulations, many critics remain "afraid that contract prisons will generate the same kinds of scandals as contract nursing homes, which despite numerous inspectors and standards have still frequently become substandard facilities" (Krajick 1984a, 27). Such concerns may be warranted. After all, as Fitch (1974) notes, many of the regulations "have the effect of putting a greater strain on honest firms than on dishonest firms, which can often find some way of beating the regulation, if only by buying cooperation of government contracting officers" (517).

This issue brings us to another potential barrier to competition in the contracting out process: corruption. As Poole (1978) observes, "instances of corruption have occurred, in cases where the selection process was not an openly competitive situation" (29). But the threat of corruption goes beyond that. Corruption may *prevent* the selection process from being "an openly competitive situation," and, in fact, "contracts are one of the most common and lucrative sources of corruption in government" (Fitch 1974, 517). Political corruption becomes possible when government officials control the allocation of valuable property rights (Benson 1981, 1988). Clearly, the right to act as exclusive supplier of some government service without fear of competition can be extremely valuable, particularly if a public official is willing to turn away when a producer cuts quality to increase profits. Note that critics of contracting out for government services may be absolutely right in such cases when they argue that private firms reduce costs by cutting quality. But they don't reduce costs or cut quality because of market forces; rather, the incorruptible market regulator called competition has been terminated and replaced by the regulation of a corrupt (or perhaps simply inefficient) public official. Incentives for private contractors to engage in bribery, kickbacks, and payoffs obviously exist, and corruption is inevitable if public officials in charge of the contracting process are sufficiently self-interested.

Of course, firms do not have to resort to illegal means in order to "purchase" contracts and other advantages from government. Government decisions reflect the demands of politically active and powerful interest groups, and it is not surprising to find that "private contractors doing business with government are . . . one of the principle sources of campaign funds" (Fitch 1974, 516). In fact,

> In the political community, contractors are expected to make political contributions in order to be eligible for contracts. Contributions may take the form of outright bribes and graft but . . . the more popular form is the campaign contribution—outright grants, subscriptions to fund-raising dinners, and so on. Such potlatch may be expected to take its toll by raising the costs of contract services and loosening the assiduousness of inspection, though the more cautious political operators will insist that work be at least passable, and only the more venal will tolerate [extreme reductions in quality]. (Fitch 1974, 513)

This political pressure has clearly had an impact. Several respondents to the Florestano and Gordon survey on contracting out (1980, 32), for example, admitted that one "criteria" that had been important in awarding large contracts had been "political considerations."

The point is that the potential gains in technological efficiency are themselves at risk because government still controls the demand side of the equation. If corruption and the bureaucratic tendencies for overregulation do not eventually destroy the potential for gains in technological efficiency, then one problem with government—bureaucratic inefficiency—may be in part overcome. But even then contracting can overcome only a few of the problems that arise from government failure. As long as interest groups, including criminal justice bureaucrats, can use the political process to criminalize various victimless voluntary exchanges, any gains in technological efficiency for the criminal justice system through contracting out of prison services, whether modest or substantial, may not be worth the cost in terms of lost liberties and reduced allocative efficiency.

6. Conclusion

Some might suggest that there is a tradeoff between efficiency and liberty, and perhaps under certain circumstances this is true. In the context of interest-group politics, however, the efficiency that is gained through contracting out is a very narrow concept of efficiency: specifically, what interest groups demand may get produced at a lower cost. Although there is apparently a trade-off between this technological efficiency and liberty, it is not necessarily a legitimate tradeoff in terms of either a normative criteria of allocative efficiency or liberty. It must be recognized that the lower costs of prisons that can result from contracting out might make imprisonment even more attractive as an "easy" solution to a wide variety of political problems, but this solution may be undesirable, either in terms of an allocative efficiency or a liberty norm. Substantial reasons for imprisonment of drug users or, to give another example, of undocumented immigrants are apparently that some people get utility from restricting other people's freedom to choose in the first instance and some people collect rents by restricting access to low-cost labor in the second.

Under these circumstances, a tradeoff does arise: the tradeoff involves reducing the cost of doing some things that are desirable while simultaneously reducing the cost of doing other things that are undesirable.[17] Prisons can be used to do desirable things, such as removing violent criminals from society, punishing criminals who do have victims, deterring potential criminals, and rehabilitating existing criminals. Prisons *are* effective at reducing crime (see Avio, this volume, for a review of the evidence). Thus, the question becomes: Is it appropriate to lower the costs of doing undesirable things, thus making it more likely that they will be done, in order to lower the cost of doing some desirable things, thereby perhaps making it more likely that they will also be done? The answer is not obvious and depends not only on the normative weights assigned to liberty and efficiency but also on the size of the actual tradeoffs. The case for private prisons on technological efficiency grounds would be much stronger if the politicized criminal justice system was not today imprisoning large numbers of people for involvement in victimless crimes.

Notes

1. This is an edited and updated version of the original paper with this title that was prepared several years ago for inclusion in an Independent Institute book project on private corrections, penal reform, justice, and society (which was later dropped). An adaptation of the earlier version of the paper was published as Benson 1994b, with permission of the Independent Institute, and parts of it also appear in Benson 1998, in particular chapters 2 and 3. Parts of this new draft are also drawn from Benson 1998. I wish to thank David Theroux, Gary Becker, Murray Rothbard, and Kevin Reffett for helpful comments and suggestions on the earlier manuscripts.

2. Logan (1990) questions a different assumption in this argument, in part by asking "by what right does the state imprison?" (49). He points out, à la Locke, that authority does not originate with the state; rather, authority is granted to the state by individuals. Thus, government's right to imprison is itself a power that private citizens have delegated to the state, and "any *legitimate* governmental authority may be further delegated, through government, to private agents" (53, emphasis added).

3. In fact, bureaucratic employees and managers offer many of the same normative views expressed by opponents of contracting out, and self-interest motives appear to at least color these normative views, if they do not dominate them (Benson 1990, 332–41).

4. Legislators can also make decisions that crowd prisons because, like judges and prosecutors, they have weak incentives to conserve scarce prison resources. When passing laws that increase penalties, such as mandatory minimum sentences, the legislature's actions mandate more crowding of prisons. Of course, the legislature also has the power to offset the resulting overcrowding because it can increase the budgetary allocation for prisons in order to expand the number of prison beds, or it can pass sentencing

guidelines tied to prison capacity that severely constrain judicial discretion. Minnesota actually established capacity-based sentencing guidelines, but the temptation to create the appearance of being tough on crime without actually paying for it ultimately prevailed and crowding reemerged. This result is not surprising because individual legislators also have a local constituency demanding that they do something about local crime conditions *without* raising taxes. Thus, legislators can reap political benefits by passing longer sentences for crimes, so they appear to be tough on criminals, while downplaying the fact that the law can undermine other aspects of the criminal justice system. Because expanding criminal justice resources involves the politically unpopular task of either cutting other government functions or raising taxes, the politically astute course of action is to crowd the common access prisons.

5. Products sold in private markets are priced and purchased individually unless some bundling of complementary goods is desirable. Complementary goods may be bundled when, for example, this action lowers production or transactions costs or both, resulting in a lower full price for the bundle than if the goods were purchased separately. For example, a consumer presumably can buy a car without a radio or tires, etc., and then purchase these items separately, but it would clearly cost more in time and effort (transactions costs) as well as in dollars.

6. See Benson 1998, 227–69, for a discussion of the restitution and retribution alternative from a liberty perspective and 260–318 for the efficiency implications of these alternatives.

7. Also see Barnett 1984; Bent 1974; Quinney 1974; Chambliss 1975; Manning 1975; Allen 1974; Hill 1971; Turk 1966; Cole 1973; Berk, Brackman, and Lesser 1977; Peltason 1955; Eisenstein 1973; Nimmer 1978; Murphy and Pritchett 1961; Heustis 1958; Roby 1969; Heinz, Gettleman, and Seeskin 1969; Benson 1990; Logan 1990; Thornton 1991; Rasmussen and Benson 1994; Benson, Rasmussen, and Sollars 1995; Benson and Rasmussen 1996; and Benson 1998.

8. Police are traditionally very active in the political arena (Rasmussen and Benson 1994, 119–50; Benson, Rasmussen, and Sollars 1995; Benson and Rasmussen 1996), acting as lobbyists and frequently employing tactics more common to labor unions, such as strikes, demonstrations, and protests. Police strikes are often illegal, but "blue flue" has a long history and is increasingly giving way to outright strikes. In addition, as Glaser (1978) observes:

"the leaders of a law enforcement bureaucracy have special advantages for promulgating their views because of their ready access to the heads of the executive and legislative branches of government, their ability to issue official reports and call news conferences, and their consequent control over public information on the effectiveness of the law and need for it" (22).

The term *interest group* is used here to refer to all organizations that apply political pressure in an effort to generate legislation. This definition does not mean that all interest-group members or their representatives are motivated solely by selfish interests. In fact, although potential self-interest motives can often be identified for groups such as the police seeking changes in law, many firmly believe that the changes they demand are in the "public interest." As Wilson (1980) notes, "a complete theory of regulation politics—indeed, a complete theory of politics generally—requires that attention be paid to beliefs as well as interests" (372). Of course, the "public interest" is a normative concept. It is what each individual believes it to be, and an individual's perception is often affected by his or her own self-interests.

9. Former director of the Office of National Drug Control, "Drug Czar" William Bennett, for example, in detailing the effects of drugs and drug use, claimed that "we can cite violent crime, the broken home, the bad schools that are closely associated with—and often mistaken for—the country's drug problem; we can speak of poverty, of disease, of racism" (Office of National Drug Control Strategy 1990, 2). Note in this regard that police bureaucrats obtain significant benefits from the war on drugs, including increased general revenue budgets and discretionary funds from drug-related confiscations (Benson, Rasmussen, and Sollars 1995; Mast, Benson, and Rasmussen 2000).

10. See Rasmussen and Benson 1994, 39–66, for an overview of the abundant literature that addresses the issue of a drug-crime causal connection. The drugs-cause-crime argument is often based on the contention that drugs affect the mental and emotional states of users, making them aggressive or impulsive. Another view, consistent with the arguments presented here, is that some of the same factors that influence the decision to commit crimes also influence the decision to consume illicit drugs—that is, drug use and criminal activity are simply coincident symptoms of other problems such as the lack of economic opportunity. Yet another characterization of the drug-crime relationship is that it is the illegality of drugs that pro-

duces the correlation between drug use and nondrug crime. Kaplan (1983), for example, concludes that because drugs are illegal: (1) the price of drugs is forced up, requiring users to acquire greater resources; (2) steady employment is difficult because of the time and effort required to find a safe source of supply; (3) holding any job becomes difficult because of arrests and general harassment by police; and (4) drug users are forced into the criminal subculture by being forced to deal with criminals. These kinds of arguments are predicated on the assumption that drug use and crime are highly correlated, of course. Evidence discussed later in the essay indicates that this correlation may not exist. See also note 11.

11. It is clear that a large portion of the people arrested and convicted for nondrug crimes are drug users. During the second quarter of 1989, for instance, approximately 84 percent of the male arrestees and 88 percent of the female arrestees in U.S. metropolitan cities tested positive for one or more drugs (O'Neil and Wish 1989). Similarly, in a Bureau of Justice survey of 12,000 prison inmates, more than 75 percent admitted that they had used drugs, 56 percent acknowledged using drugs in the month prior to their incarceration, and one-third claimed to be under the influence of drugs at the time of their offense. So it appears that some of the same factors that influence the propensity to commit nondrug crimes also influence the propensity to use drugs, but these facts do not imply that there is a causal connection running from drugs to crime. In particular, the fact that many criminals use drugs does not prove that most drug users commit nondrug crime.

12. A story that has received a great deal of attention in the literature on heroin runs as follows. The market demand for drugs is typically assumed to have a very low price elasticity because drug addicts with highly inelastic demand dominate the market (e.g., Eatherly 1974; Erickson 1969; Holahan 1973; Koch and Grupp 1971). Therefore, presumably because there is relatively little that can be done to influence demand decisions, law enforcement policy has focused on suppliers. Direct interdiction efforts are made, punishment of suppliers is much more severe than punishment of users, and so on. As long as there is some elasticity to the demand curve, supply-side efforts that raise the risk to suppliers and therefore raise the price also reduce the size of the drug market. But when demand is inelastic, expenditures rise as price rises. If the typical drug addict is at subsistence levels of income, then she will have little in the way of substitution possibilities (e.g., eating less) in

order to pay the higher price, so her only option would be to commit more predatory crimes (Clague 1973; Eatherly 1974; Erickson 1969; Holahan 1973; Koch and Grupp 1971; White and Luksetich 1983). Drug consumption might fall, but predatory crime may not.

Although this scenario is theoretically valid (Rasmussen and Benson 1994, 43–49), it does imply that drug users' labor-supply decisions are different than most other people's decisions. The rising price of drugs causes a change in the "real wage from predatory crime"—that is, the purchasing power of a dollar obtained through illegal actions declines significantly. But this change implies that the drug user's "supply of illegal labor" (that is, the amount of effort he or she exerts in illegal activities to generate income) is negatively sloped. As the real income per offense from such activity falls, more offenses are committed. This conclusion is inconsistent with most evidence on labor supply, and it certainly suggests that drugs significantly distort the behavior of drug users in ways other than are often made explicit. So why do these addict criminals not commit more crime when the real return is higher as well? The traditional justification for the back-bending supply of labor is that as income becomes very high, there is an incentive to work less in order to enjoy more leisure. But working less does not appear to be a relevant option for low-income addicts. What then are addicts substituting for illegal work effort when the real return to such effort is relatively high?

Even if this scenario is correct (and there is some weak empirical support for it; see Brown and Silverman 1974; Silverman and Spruill 1977), it does not appear to explain the aggregate changes that have occurred in Florida property crime rates. The fact is that despite increased law enforcement effort against drugs, the price of the most important drug in Florida appears to have fallen dramatically over the last few years. Estimates indicate that the wholesale price of cocaine in Miami fell within a range of $28,000 to $37,000 per kilogram in 1985, but the range was down to $12,000 to $15,000 by 1987 (*Narcotics Control Digest,* 12 April 1989, 5–6). This general trend has apparently continued. Florida Department of Law Enforcement estimates are that wholesale cocaine prices fell by 69.4 percent between 1987 and 1989, from $32,000 to $9,800 per pound (internal memo). Falling wholesale prices do not prove that retail prices are falling, of course, but when this trend is added to the fact that demand for drugs also appears to be declining (see the 1988 National Household Survey on Drug Abuse), the implication seems to be that falling retail prices are likely. Beyond that, a substantial portion of the drug arrests in Florida are for possession rather than for sales, distribution, production, and so on (Trager and Clark 1989), which implies that Florida law enforcement is not exclusively focused on a supply-side policy.

13. Actual estimates of the portion of property crimes committed by addicts range from approximately 25 percent to more than 66 percent (e.g., Eatherly 1974, 212; Erickson 1969, 485; Wilson, Moore, and Wheat 1972, 12), although these estimates are dated.

14. For example, Fernandez (1969) contends that direct efforts against predatory crimes are likely to be ineffective because "for heroin users, jail sentences cease to be a deterrent" (487; also see Blair and Vogel 1973)— a claim that appears to be incorrect, given results in Kim et al. 1993.

15. The explanations for this behavior include the apparent fact that these juveniles perceive drug dealing to provide an attractive economic opportunity relative to their legal opportunities. These juveniles tend to underestimate the risks associated with law enforcement activities as well, although they also tend to overestimate the risks of violence and injury.

16. For instance, Russell Clemens, representing the American Federation of State, County, and Municipal Employees, made this point at a conference called "Privatizing Criminal Justice: Public and Private Partnerships," sponsored by the Office of International Criminal Justice and held at the University of Illinois at Chicago in March 1995.

17. In fact, many of these things are desirable only in the context of the existing institutional setting. An alternative that emphasizes restitution for victims rather than physical punishment for offenders would lead to a very different system in which prisons would play a much more attenuated role (Benson 1998). In such a system, where, in effect, both the demand and the supply sides of the legal system are privatized, "privatization" can be very desirable, in part because if demand is also privatized, victimless crimes are much less likely to be relevant. See Benson 1998, 227–318, for further proposed changes that might make private prisons desirable under both a liberty and an allocative efficiency norm.

References

Allen, Francis. 1974. *The Crimes of Politics: Political Dimensions of Crime.* Cambridge, Mass.: Harvard University Press.

Archambeault, William G., and Donald R. Deis Jr. 1996. *Executive Summary: Cost Effectiveness Comparisons of Private versus Public Prisons in Louisiana: A Comprehensive Analysis of Allen, Avoyelles, and Winn Correctional Centers.* Baton Rouge: Louisiana State University, 10 December.

Barnett, Randy E. 1984. Public Decisions and Private Rights. *Criminal Justice Ethics* (summer/fall): 50–62.

Becker, Howard. 1963. *Outsiders: Studies in Sociological Deviance.* New York: Free Press.

Benson, Bruce L. 1981. A Note on Corruption of Public Officials: The Black Market for Property Rights. *Journal of Libertarian Studies* 5 (summer): 305–11.

———. 1988. Corruption in Law Enforcement: One Consequence of "The Tragedy of the Commons" Arising with Public Allocation Processes. *International Review of Law and Economics* 8 (June): 73–84.

———. 1990. *The Enterprise of Law: Justice without the State.* San Francisco: Pacific Research Institute.

———. 1992. The Development of Criminal Law and Its Enforcement: Public Interest or Political Transfers. *Journal des Economistes et des Etudes Humaines* 3 (March): 79–108.

———. 1994a. Are Public Goods Really Common Pools?: Considerations of the Evolution of Policing and Highways in England. *Economic Inquiry* 32 (April): 249–71.

———. 1994b. Third Thoughts on Contracting Out. *Journal of Libertarian Studies* 11 (fall): 44–78.

———. 1995. Understanding Bureaucratic Behavior: Implications from the Public Choice Literature. *Journal of Public Finance and Public Choice* 8 (December): 89–117.

———. 1998. *To Serve and Protect: Privatization and Community in Criminal Justice.* New York: New York University Press for The Independent Institute.

Benson, Bruce L., Iljoong Kim, and David W. Rasmussen. 1998. Deterrence and Public Policy: Tradeoffs in the Allocation of Police Resources. *International Review of Law and Economics* 18, no. 1 (March): 77–100.

Benson, Bruce L., Iljoong Kim, David W. Rasmussen, and Thomas W. Zuehlke. 1992. Is Property Crime Caused by Drug Use or Drug Enforcement Policy? *Applied Economics* 24 (July): 679–92.

Benson, Bruce L., and David W. Rasmussen. 1991. The Relationship between Illicit Drug Enforcement Policy and Property Crimes. *Contemporary Policy Issues* 9 (October): 106–15.

————. 1992. Illinois' War on Drugs: Some Unintended Consequences. *Heartland Policy Study* 48 (April): 1–36.

————. 1996. Predatory Public Finance and the Origins of the War on Drugs: 1984–1989. *The Independent Review* 1 (fall): 163–89.

Benson, Bruce L., David W. Rasmussen, and David L. Sollars. 1995. Police Bureaucrats, Their Incentives, and the War on Drugs. *Public Choice* 83 (April): 21–45.

Benson, Bruce L., and Laurin Wollan. 1989. Prison Crowding and Judicial Incentives. *Madison Paper Series* 3 (February): 1–22.

Bent, Alen. 1974. *The Politics of Law Enforcement: Conflict and Power in Urban Communities.* Lexington, Mass.: Lexington.

Berk, Richard, Harold Brackman, and Selma Lesser. 1977. *A Measure of Justice: An Empirical Study of Changes in the California Penal Code, 1955–1971.* New York: Academic.

Blair, Roger D., and Ronald J. Vogel. 1973. Heroin Addiction and Urban Crime. *Public Finance Quarterly* 1 (October): 457–66.

Brakel, Samuel J. 1992. Private Corrections. In *Privatizing the United States Justice System: Police Adjudication, and Corrections Services From the Private Sector,* edited by Gary W. Bowman, Simon Hakim, and Paul Seidenstat. Jefferson, N.C.: McFarland.

Breton, Albert, and Ronald Wintrobe. 1982. *The Logic of Bureaucratic Control.* Cambridge, England: Cambridge University Press.

Brown, G. F., and L. P. Silverman. 1974. The Retail Price of Heroin: Estimation and Application. *Journal of the American Statistical Association* 69: 595–96.

Chambliss, William. 1975. Toward a Political Economy of Crime. *Theory and Society* 2 (summer): 149–170.

Chambliss, William, and Robert Seidman. 1971. *Law, Order, and Power.* Reading, Mass.: Addison-Wesley.

Chein, I., D. L. Gerard, R. S. Lee, and E. Rosenfeld. 1964. *The Road to H: Narcotics, Delinquency, and Social Policy.* New York: Basic.

Clague, Christopher. 1973. Legal Strategies for Dealing with Heroin Addiction. *American Economic Review* (May): 263–68.

Cole, George. 1973. *Politics and the Administration of Justice.* Beverly Hills: Sage.

Corman, Hope, and H. Naci Mocan. 2000. A Time-Series Analysis of Crime, Deterrence, and Drug Abuse in New York City. *American Economic Review* 90: 584–604.

Dickson, Donald. 1968. Bureaucracy and Morality: An Organizational Perspective on a Moral Crusade. *Social Problems* 16 (fall): 142–56.

Eatherly, Billy J. 1974. Drug-Law Enforcement: Should We Arrest Pushers or Users? *Journal of Political Economy* 82 (January–February): 210–14.

Eisenstein, James. 1973. *Politics and the Legal Process.* New York: Harper and Row.

Erickson, Edward. 1969. The Social Costs of the Discovery and Suppression of the Clandestine Distribution of Heroin. *Journal of Political Economy* 77 (July–August): 484–86.

Fernandez, Raul A. 1969. The Clandestine Distribution of Heroin, Its Discovery and Suppression: A Comment. *Journal of Political Economy* 77 (July–August): 487–88.

Fisk, Donald, Herbert Kiesling, and Thomas Muller. 1978. *Private Provision of Public Services: An Overview.* Washington, D.C.: Urban Institute.

Fitch, Lyle C. 1974. Increasing the Role of the Private Sector in Providing Public Services. In *Improving the Quality of Urban Management,* edited by Willis D. Hawley and David Rogers, vol. 8 of *Urban Affairs Annual Review.* Beverly Hills, Calif.: Sage.

Florestano, Patricia S., and Stephen B. Gordon. 1980. Public vs. Private: Small Government Contracting with the Private Sector. *Public Administration Review* 40 (January–February): 29–34.

Freeman, Mike. 1992. Contracting Out: The Most Viable Solution. In *Privatizing the United States Justice System: Police Adjudication, and Corrections Services From the Private Sector,* edited by Gary W.

Bowman, Simon Hakim, and Paul Seidenstat. Jefferson, N.C.: McFarland.

Gandossy, R. P., J. R. Williams, J. Cohen, and H. J. Harwood. 1980. *Drugs and Crime: A Survey and Analysis of the Literature.* Washington, D.C.: National Institute of Justice.

Glaser, Daniel. 1978. *Crime in Our Changing Society.* New York: Holt, Rinehart and Winston.

Goldstein, Abraham, and Joseph Goldstein. 1971. *Crime, Law, and Society.* New York: Free Press.

Gould, Leroy C., Andrew L. Walker, Lansing E. Crane, and Charles W. Lidz. 1974. *Connections: Notes from the Heroin World.* New Haven, Conn.: Yale University Press.

Greenberg, S. W., and F. Alder. 1974. Crime and Addiction: An Empirical Analysis of the Literature, 1920–1973. *Contemporary Drug Problems* 3: 221–270.

Heinz, John, Robert Gettleman, and Morris Seeskin. 1969. Legislative Politics and the Criminal Law. *Northwestern University Law Review* 64 (July): 277–356.

Helmer, John. 1975. *Drugs and Minority Oppression.* New York: Seabury.

Heustis, Carl. 1958. Police Unions. *Journal of Criminal Law, Criminology, and Police Science* 48 (March/April): 643–6.

Hill, Stuart. 1971. *Crime, Power, and Morality: The Criminal Law Process in the United States.* Scranton, Pa.: Chandler.

Himmelstein, Jerome L. 1983. *The Strange Career of Marijuana: Politics and Ideology of Drug Control in America.* Westport, Conn.: Greenwood.

Holahan, John. 1973. The Economics of Control of the Illegal Supply of Heroin. *Public Finance Quarterly* 1: 467–77.

Kaplan, John. 1983. *The Hardest Drug: Heroin and Public Policy.* Chicago: University of Chicago Press.

Kim, Iljoong, Bruce L. Benson, David W. Rasmussen, and Thomas W. Zuehlke. 1993. An Economic Analysis of Recidivism among Drug Offenders. *Southern Economic Journal* 60 (July): 169–83.

Koch, James V., and Stanley E. Grupp. 1971. The Economics of Drug Control. *The International Journal of the Addictions* (December): 571–84.

Krajick, Kevin. 1984a. Private, For-Profit Prisons Take Hold in Some States. *Christian Science Monitor,* 11 April 27.

————. 1984b. Punishment for Profit. *Across the Board* 21 (March): 20–27.

Leburn, Sebastian, Bruce L. Benson, and David W. Rasmussen. Forthcoming. The Impact of Drug Enforcement on Crime. *Journal of Drug Issues.*

Lindesmith, Alfred. 1965. *The Addict and the Law.* New York: Vintage.

Logan, Charles H. 1990. *Private Prisons: Cons and Pros.* New York: Oxford University Press.

Manning, Peter. 1975. Deviance and Dogma. *British Journal of Criminology* 15 (January): 1–20.

Martin, Delores T., and Robert M. Stein. 1992. An Empirical Analysis of Contracting Out Local Government Services. In *Privatizing the United States Justice System: Police Adjudication and Corrections Services From the Private Sector,* edited by Gary W. Bowman, Simon Hakim, and Paul Seidenstat. Jefferson, N.C.: McFarland.

Mast, Brent D., Bruce L. Benson, and David W. Rasmussen. 2000. Entrepreneurial Police and Drug Enforcement Policy. *Public Choice* 104 (September): 285–308.

Mendes, Sylvia. Forthcoming. Property Crime and Drug Law Enforcement in Portugal. *Criminal Justice Policy Review.*

Michaels, Robert J. 1987. The Market for Heroin before and after Legalization. In *Dealing with Drugs,* edited by Robert Hamowy. Lexington, Mass: Lexington.

Murphy, Walter, and C. Herman Pritchett. 1961. *Courts, Judges, and Politics.* New York: Random House.

Musto, David F. 1973. *The American Disease: Origins of Narcotic Control.* New Haven, Conn.: Yale University Press.

————. 1987. The History of Legislative Control over Opium, Cocaine, and Their Derivatives. In *Dealing with Drugs,* edited by Ronald Hamowy. Lexington, Mass.: Lexington.

National Institute on Drug Abuse. 1989. *National Household Survey on Drug Abuse, 1988.* Washington, D.C.: U.S. Department of Health and Human Services.

Neely, Richard. 1982. *Why Courts Don't Work.* New York: McGraw-Hill.

Nimmer, Raymond. 1978. *The Nature of System Change: Reform Impact in the Criminal Court.* Chicago: American Bar Foundation.

Office of National Drug Control Strategy. 1990. *National Drug Control Strategy*. Washington, D.C.: Government Printing Office.

O'Neil, J., and E. Wish. 1989. Drug Use Forecasting (DUF) Research Update. In *Research in Action*. Washington, D.C.: National Institutof Justice (December).

Oteri, Joseph, and Harvey Silvergate. 1967. In the Marketplace of Free Ideas: A Look at the Passage of the Marihuana Tax Act. In *Marihuana: Myths and Realities,* edited by J. L. Simmons. North Hollywood: Brandon House.

Peltason, Jack. 1955. *Federal Courts in the Political Process*. New York: Random House.

Poole, Robert W., Jr. 1978. *Cutting Back City Hall*. New York: Universe.

———. 1983. Rehabilitating the Correctional System. *Fiscal Watchdog* 81 (July): 1–4.

Quinney, Richard. 1970. *The Social Reality of Crime*. Boston: Little, Brown.

———. 1974. *Critique of Legal Order*. Boston: Little, Brown.

Rasmussen, David W., and Bruce L. Benson. 1994. *The Economic Anatomy of a Drug War: Criminal Justice in the Commons*. Lanham, Md.: Rowman and Littlefield.

Rasmussen, David W., Bruce L. Benson, and David L. Sollars. 1993. Spatial Competition in Illicit Drug Markets: The Consequences of Increased Drug Enforcement. *Review of Regional Studies* 23 (winter): 219–36.

Resignato, Andrew J. 2000. Violent Crime: A Function of Drug Use or Drug Enforcement? *Applied Economics* 32 (May): 681–88.

Reuter, Peter, Robert MacCoun, and Patrick Murphy. 1990. *Money from Crime: A Study of the Economics of Drug Dealing in Washington, D.C.* Santa Monica, Calif.: Rand Corporation.

Rhodes, Robert. 1977. *The Insoluble Problems of Crime*. New York: John Wiley and Sons.

Roby, Pamela. 1969. Politics and Criminal Law: Revision of the New York State Penal Law on Prostitution. *Social Problems* 17 (summer): 83–109.

Rydell, C. Peter, and Susan S. Everingham. 1994. *Modeling the Demand for Cocaine*. Santa Monica, Calif.: Rand Corporation.

Silverman, Lester, and Nancy L. Spruill. 1977. "Urban Crime and the Price of Heroin." *Journal of Urban Economics* (January): 80–103.

Sollars, David, Bruce L. Benson, and David W. Rasmussen. 1994. Drug Enforcement and Deterrence of Property Crime among Local Jurisdictions. *Public Finance Quarterly* (January): 22–45.

Thornton, Mark. 1991. *The Economics of Prohibition*. Salt Lake: University of Utah Press.

Trager, Kenneth, and Michael Clark. 1989. *Florida Drug Offender Profile*. Tallahassee: Florida Department of Law Enforcement, Statistical Analysis Center, February.

Turk, Austin. 1966. Conflict and Criminality. *American Sociological Review* 31 (June): 338–352.

White, Michael D., and William A. Luksetich. 1983. Heroin: Price Elasticity and Enforcement Strategies. *Economic Inquiry* 21 (October): 557–64.

Wilson, James Q. 1980. *The Politics of Regulation*. New York: Basic.

Wilson, James Q., Mark H. Moore, and I. D. Wheat. 1972. The Problem of Heroin. *Public Interest* 29 (fall): 3–28.

Index

About the Authors

Editor

ALEXANDER TABARROK is research director for The Independent Institute and associate professor of economics at George Mason University. Dr. Tabarrok has published papers in *The Journal of Law and Economics, Public Choice, Economic Inquiry, The Journal of Health Economics, The Journal of Theoretical Politics* and many other journals. He is editor of The Independent Institute books *Entrepreneurial Economics: Bright Ideas from the Dismal Science* and *The Voluntary City: Choice, Community and Civil Society* (with D. Beito and P. Gordon).

Contributors

KENNETH L. AVIO is professor of economics and former department chair at the University of Victoria in Canada. He received his Ph.D. in economics from Purdue University, and has taught at the University of Western Ontario. He has published in outlets addressed to economists, legal scholars, philosophers, criminologists, political scientists, and policy makers. His contributions include work on capital punishment, property crime, prisons, and the philosophical foundations of the criminal law. He wrote (with C. Scott Clark) *Property Crime in Canada*. His recent work includes applications of discourse theory to criminal law and to other areas of law.

BRUCE L. BENSON is DeVoe Moore Distinguished Research Professor of Economics at Florida State University and Senior Fellow at The Independent Institute. Professor Benson's research interests focus on law and economics with an emphasis on private alternatives to publicly provided law and legal services, the evolution of legal institutions, and the economics of crime. He has published over 100 articles in scholarly journals, contributed more than 30 book chapters, and authored four books: *The Enterprise of Law, The Economic Anatomy of a Drug War: Criminal Justice in the Commons* (with D. Rasmussen), *American Antitrust Law in Theory and in Practice* (with Melvin L. Greenhut), and The Independent Institute book *To Serve and Protect: Privatization and Community in Criminal Justice*.

SAMUEL JAN BRAKEL is vice president of administration, legal affairs development, at the Isaac Ray Center in Chicago. He is also director of research of the Health Law Institute and adjunct professor of law at DePaul University College of Law. Professor Brakel has published widely on issues of civil and criminal law, law and psychiatry, prison privatization, and many other areas. His most recent book is *Law and Psychiatry in the Criminal Justice System* (with Alexander D. Brooks). Professor Brakel is a recipient of the Manfred S. Guttmacher Award from the American Psychiatric Association. He has a B.A. from Davidson College (1965) and a J.D. from the University of Chicago Law School (1968).

CHARLES H. LOGAN received his Ph.D. from Indiana University and is a professor and associate head of sociology at the University of Connecticut, where he has taught since 1970. He has published widely on many criminal justice issues and is an early and major contributor to the empirical literature on privatization in corrections. He has been a visiting fellow at several agencies within the U.S. Department of Justice, and has received support for his research from the National Institute of Justice, the Bureau of Justice Statistics, the Federal Bureau of Prisons, and the National Institute of Corrections. He is the author of *Private Prisons: Cons and Pros* and many other publications on private prisons.

KIMBERLY INGERSOLL GAYLORD is a freelance researcher and legal writer. She has a B.S. from Cornell University (1990), a J.D. from Northern Illinois University College of Law (1995), and an L.L.M. from the Health Law Institute at DePaul University College of Law (1998).

CHARLES W. THOMAS is vice president for quality assurance at the Homeland Security Corporation and has been Director of the Private Corrections Project in the Center for Studies in Criminology and Law at the University of Florida. He received his Ph.D. in sociology from the University of Kentucky in 1971 and has served on the faculty of Virginia Commonwealth University (1969–73), the College of William and Mary (1973–75), Bowling Green State University (1975–80), and the University of Florida (1980–99). Dr. Thomas also has served as a member of the Board of Directors of Prison Realty Trust and the Corrections Corporation of America, and is now a board member at Avalon Correctional Services, Inc. Examples of his more than 100 scholarly publications have appeared in the *Journal of Criminal Law & Criminology, Crime & Delinquency, Social Problems, Criminology, Vanderbilt Law Review, Louisiana Law Review,* and *Florida State Law Review.*

INDEPENDENT STUDIES IN POLITICAL ECONOMY

THE ACADEMY IN CRISIS
The Political Economy of Higher Education
Edited by John W. Sommer
Foreword by Nathan Glazer

AGRICULTURE AND THE STATE
Market Processes and Bureaucracy
E. C. Pasour, Jr., Foreword by Bruce L. Gardner

ALIENATION AND THE SOVIET ECONOMY
The Collapse of the Socialist Era
Paul Craig Roberts
Foreword by Aaron Wildavsky

AMERICAN HEALTH CARE
Government, Market Processes
   and the Public Interest
Edited by Roger D. Feldman
Foreword by Mark V. Pauly

ANTITRUST AND MONOPOLY
Anatomy of a Policy Failure
D. T. Armentano, Foreword by Yale Brozen

ARMS, POLITICS, AND THE ECONOMY
Historical and Contemporary Perspectives
Edited by Robert Higgs
Foreword by William A. Niskanen

BEYOND POLITICS
Markets, Welfare and the Failure of Bureaucracy
William C. Mitchell and Randy T. Simmons
Foreword by Gordon Tullock

**THE CAPITALIST REVOLUTION
IN LATIN AMERICA**
Paul Craig Roberts and Karen LaFollette Araujo
Foreword by Peter T. Bauer

CHANGING THE GUARD
Private Prisons and the Control of Crime
Edited by Alexander Tabarrok
Foreword by Charles H. Logan

CUTTING GREEN TAPE
Toxic Pollutants, Environmental Regulation
   and the Law
Edited by Richard Stroup and Roger E. Meiners
Foreword by W. Kip Viscusi

THE DIVERSITY MYTH
Multiculturalism and Political Intolerance on Campus
David O. Sacks and Peter A. Thiel
Foreword by Elizabeth Fox-Genovese

Entrepreneurial Economics
Bright Ideas from the Dismal Science
Edited by Alexander Tabarrok
Foreword by Steven E. Landsburg

FREEDOM, FEMINISM, AND THE STATE
An Overview of Individualist Feminism
Edited by Wendy McElroy
Foreword by Lewis Perry

HAZARDOUS TO OUR HEALTH?
FDA Regulation of Health Care Products
Edited by Robert Higgs
Foreword by Joel J. Nobel

HOT TALK, COLD SCIENCE
Global Warming's Unfinished Debate
S. Fred Singer, Foreword by Frederick Seitz

LIBERTY FOR WOMEN
Freedom and Feminism in the Twenty-First Century
Edited by Wendy McElroy
Foreword by Wendy Kaminer

MONEY AND THE NATION STATE
The Financial Revolution, Government
   and the World Monetary System
Edited by Kevin Dowd and Richard H. Timberlake, Jr.
Foreword by Merton H. Miller

OUT OF WORK
Unemployment and Government
   in Twentieth-Century America
Richard K. Vedder and Lowell E. Gallaway
Foreword by Martin Bronfenbrenner

A POVERTY OF REASON
Sustainable Development and Economic Growth
Wilfred Beckerman

PRIVATE RIGHTS & PUBLIC ILLUSIONS
Tibor R. Machan, Foreword by Nicholas Rescher

REGULATION AND THE REAGAN ERA
Politics, Bureaucracy and the Public Interest
Edited by Roger Meiners and Bruce Yandl
Foreword by Robert W. Crandall

SCHOOL CHOICES: True and False
John D. Merrifield

TAXING CHOICE
The Predatory Politics of Fiscal Discrimination
Edited by William F. Shughart II
Foreword by Paul W. McCracken

TAXING ENERGY
Oil Severance Taxation and the Economy
Robert Deacon, Stephen DeCanio,
H. E. Frech, III, and M. Bruce Johnson
Foreword by Joseph P. Kalt

THAT EVERY MAN BE ARMED
The Evolution of a Constitutional Right
Stephen P. Halbrook

TO SERVE AND PROTECT
Privatization and Community in Criminal Justice
Bruce L. Benson, Foreword by Marvin E. Wolfgang

THE VOLUNTARY CITY
Choice, Community and Civil Society
Edited by David T. Beito, Peter Gordon
   and Alexander Tabarrok
Foreword by Paul Johnson

WINNERS, LOSERS & MICROSOFT
Competition and Antitrust in High Technology
Stan J. Liebowitz and Stephen E. Margolis
Foreword by Jack Hirshleifer

WRITING OFF IDEAS
Taxation, Foundations, and Philanthropy in America
Randall G. Holcombe

For further information and a catalog of publications, please contact:
THE INDEPENDENT INSTITUTE
100 Swan Way, Oakland, California 94621-1428, U.S.A.
510-632-1366 • Fax 510-568-6040 • info@independent.org • www.independent.org